Vision Critical Studies

General Editor: Anne Smith

The Homosexual as Hero in Contemporary Fiction

THE HOMOSEXUAL AS HERO
IN CONTEMPORARY FICTION

Stephen Adams

VISION

Vision Press Limited
11–14 Stanhope Mews West
London SW7 5RD

ISBN 0 85478 204 4

**In memory of
Michael Turner-Holden**

Printed in Great Britain
by Clarke, Doble & Brendon Ltd
Plymouth and London
MCMLXXX

Contents

Acknowledgements

Grateful thanks are due to the following for permission to reprint copyright material: excerpts from *The City and the Pillar* and the Author's Afterword (E. P. Dutton & Co., Inc., 1965), copyright © 1965 by Gore Vidal, reprinted by permission of William Morris Agency, Inc.; excerpts from *Myra Breckinridge*, copyright © 1968 by Gore Vidal, reprinted by permission of Little, Brown & Co.; excerpts from *Nobody Knows My Name*, copyright © 1954, 1956, 1959, 1960, 1961 by James Baldwin, excerpts from *Notes of a Native Son*, copyright © 1949, 1950, 1951, 1953, 1955, 1964 by James Baldwin, excerpts from *Giovanni's Room*, copyright © 1956 by James Baldwin: reprinted by permission of Michael Joseph Ltd.; excerpts from *Eustace Chisholm and the Works* (Farrar, Straus & Giroux, Inc., 1967), copyright © 1967 by James Purdy, reprinted by permission of Curtis Brown Ltd.; excerpts from *Narrow Rooms*, copyright © 1978 by James Purdy, reprinted by permission of Arbor House Publishing Co.; excerpts from *City of Night*, copyright © 1963 by John Rechy, excerpts from *Numbers*, copyright © 1967 by John Rechy, excerpts from *The Sexual Outlaw*, copyright © 1977 by John Rechy: reprinted by permission of Grove Press, Inc.; excerpts from *The Wild Boys*, copyright © 1969, 1970, 1971 by William S. Burroughs, reprinted by permission of Grove Press, Inc.; excerpts from *Maurice* by E. M. Forster, excerpts from *The Life to Come* by E. M. Forster: reprinted by permission of Edward Arnold Ltd.; excerpts from *The World in the Evening*, copyright © 1954 by Christopher Isherwood, reprinted by permission of Curtis Brown Ltd.; excerpts from *Down There on a Visit*, copyright © 1962 by Christopher Isherwood, excerpts from *A Single Man*, copyright © 1964 by Christopher Isherwood: reprinted by permission of Methuen & Co. Ltd.; excerpts from *Hemlock and After*, copyright © 1952 by Angus Wilson, excerpts from *Anglo-Saxon Attitudes*, copyright © 1956 by Angus Wilson, excerpts from *As If By Magic*, copyright © 1973 by Angus Wilson: reprinted by permission of Martin Secker and Warburg Ltd.; excerpts from *The Bell*, copyright © 1958 by Iris Murdoch, excerpts from *A Fairly Honourable Defeat*, copyright © 1970 by Iris Murdoch: reprinted by permission of Chatto & Windus Ltd.; excerpts from *Our Lady of the Flowers* by Jean Genet, translated by Bernard Frechtman, copyright © 1963 by Grove Press, Inc.; excerpts from *Querelle of Brest* by Jean Genet, translated by Gregory Streatham, copyright © 1966 by Anthony Blond Ltd.

A portion of Chapter 3 has already appeared in somewhat different form in my book *James Purdy*.

Here I wish to acknowledge a particular debt to the writings and approach to homosexual literature of Rictor Norton and Roger Austen, and the critical forum provided by journals such as *Gay News*, *Gay Left*, *Gay Sunshine* and *The Body Politic*.

I should also like to thank my friends Tony Silcox and Elizabeth Cook for their practical assistance; Felicity Smith for giving generously of her time to help with my final corrections; and Michael Goodwin for his patient criticism and support.

Introduction

In recent years a number of pioneering studies have begun to rescue homosexual literature from the obscurity to which it had been relegated in the past.[1] That larger task of reclaiming and interpreting a literary tradition is outside the scope of this book which seeks, instead, to consider the work of certain contemporary novelists. Whilst it is illuminating to uncover the subtexts of earlier writers and necessary to break down the scholarly embarrassment that has denied, sometimes wilfully, our understanding of literature from past centuries, there is also a need to examine the body of work that has emerged in the comparative freedom of our own time.

It is only in the increasingly liberal climate of opinion of the last thirty years or so that the right to depict the full sexual dimension of relations between men and women has been won—a struggle that has extended similarly to the open exploration of homosexual themes. Before the turning point of the Second World War, homosexuality was almost a proscribed subject and so, for the most part, its literary history is a story of indirection, subterfuge, disguise, or outright suppression. Writers wishing to deal with such themes were under an obligation to censor their materials and camouflage their concerns if they were to run the gauntlet of publishers, watchful courts, reviewers, and the conventional expectations of readers, without offending any party along the way.[2]

Indeed, as cultural taboos have broken down, the literature of the period betrays an obsessive concern with sexual matters and because homosexual themes have become commonplace, this study limits itself to certain areas of interest, the selection of which requires some explanation. I do not subscribe to the notion that homosexuality is synonymous with male homosexuality yet, because of the proliferation of relevant literature and in order to allow for a detailed evaluation of certain writers, I omit any proper consideration of the treatment of homosexual women. It is also a fact—albeit regrettable—that writers themselves tend to deal exclusively either with homosexual men or women, rarely with both, and a comprehensive comparison would yield more than enough material for a separate book. Furthermore, the radical feminist movement has prompted numerous studies of women in literature and the portrayal of female homosexuality, in particular, has already attracted the attention of critics.[3]

Rather than embark on any exhaustive survey of homosexual themes in contemporary fiction then, I prefer to focus on a selection of writers whose work marks the emergence of the male homosexual's quest for selfhood from the literary landscape of compulsory villainy and tortured ambiguity. Although the facile equation of homosexuality with evil can no longer be made with the confidence of the past—as Norman Mailer concedes in his essay 'The Homosexual Villain' (1954)[4]—by regarding the homosexual as a potential hero, my aim is not to suggest that there has been an effusion of liberal sentiments in the novel whereby homosexuality is now equated as unthinkingly with goodness, but to explore, in a broader sense, a range of works in which the artistic vision of serious writers endows with heroic qualities the homosexual's need to create his own values. To view the homosexual in these terms is part of a larger re-evaluation of the heroic ideal seen in the variety of outsiders, rebels and victims with whom in the modern novel we are invited to sympathise or identify. If the post-war period can be characterised in one way by a preoccupation with redefining traditional sexual roles and identities, then an important strand in this dialectic of 'sexual politics' has been the questioning of rigid concepts of manhood from the standpoint of the homosexual experience.

The writers are chosen not only because of their readiness to deal explicitly with homosexual themes but also for the diversity and individuality of their approach. The analysis is structured in two main sections, dealing respectively with American and British writers; by way of contrast, and because he has set such a distinctive stamp upon our images of the homosexual, the final chapter turns to the work of a writer outside these two cultures—Jean Genet. The selection does not present a sample of 'gay writers' or 'gay novels' as such, for whilst these positive terms are useful in a polemical context, their built-in assumptions are elsewhere misleading. They suggest a category of writers and novels with a restricted outlook, and the notion of a minority literature written by, for and about homosexuals, carries the danger of its trivialisation or dismissal by those outside that grouping. This is not to deny the therapeutic charge of these concepts and their ability to foster a new sense of identity and community. Nevertheless, the relegation of such literature to a specialised genre can obscure its complexities and its contribution to our more general cultural debate on sexuality and the definitions of the self. Another of my aims, then, is to consider wherever relevant the relationship between homosexual and other themes in a novel. The inclusion of specific writers does not imply (for in some cases this would be quite wrong) that they are representative *homosexual* artists—if indeed such artists exist. Their sexual preferences and private lives are none of my concern, except where their published views and statements seem relevant.

Critical appreciation of homosexual themes in literature must take account of the wider social and cultural context in which it is produced. The process of judgment is peculiarly complicated by conditioned responses to this subject, so that the quality of a relationship or work of art is frequently overshadowed by its categorisation. The word 'homosexual' has itself accrued many built-in associations and currently has its place in an ideological battleground. As an adjective, its use as a clinical term to distinguish a phenomenon in sexual pathology is hardly an instance of moral neutrality. In the public mind, its descriptive functions have multiplied, promoting it to use as a noun that pretends to encompass anything about an individual from his or her life-style and personality down to details of dress and manner. On a more ironic level, the militant liberation movements in Britain and America have, of course, short-circuited these ingrained assumptions by adopting the colloquialism 'gay', with the result that nowadays the correspondence columns endlessly bewail the corruption of a self-respecting word—by a bunch of (self-respecting) 'queers'.

Although public attitudes have changed in the post-war period the goals of complete equality and unthinking acceptance are, despite legislative concessions and a degree of tolerance, still a long way off. Our liberalism is only skin deep in some areas and, quite apart from continuing instances of persecution, it is salutary to remember that the American Psychiatrists' Association 'declassified' homosexuality as a mental illness only as recently as 1974, whilst in 1977 came the (admittedly ludicrous) spectacle of the British newspaper, *Gay News*, being convicted of blasphemy after the publication of a poem using homosexual imagery to *praise* Christ.

In some respects, the recognition of homosexuality as a social fact and the accompanying appetite for information has succeeded only in substituting new categories for old. The outright condemnation of the past has given way to a prurient inquisitiveness. Recent years have seen the proliferation of well-meaning psychological and sociological studies which have sought to explain the homosexual spectre in our midst. Unfortunately, many of these have also tended to preserve the notion of homosexuals as social curiosities, as case histories brought to dance to the tune of the latest theory.[5] Too frequently, homosexuals are cast in one image, reduced to purely sexual dimensions, and stripped of their individual dignity and uniqueness. Kate Millett makes this point incisively when she describes the homosexual as 'our current "nigger" of love.'[6] In literature as well as in everyday life the idea of the homosexual comes to efface the person. My own title might seem to reflect this labelling process, yet I wish neither to be coy in the declaration of the subject matter nor to indicate anything other than a sexual preference liable to infinite individual variation as well as to common constraints.

As might be expected, the judgment of homosexual themes in literature has for the most part reflected the degree of hostility in the surrounding society, with heterosexual bias masquerading as 'objectivity'. In the past, critics conspired to ignore or denigrate such themes; when writers undertook a degree of self-censorship in the interests of acceptability, their calculated ambiguities would be overlooked; where homosexual concerns were too blatant to avoid comment, they would often be dismissed as regrettable lapses of taste. (Rictor Norton and Louie Crew provide an excellent account of this tradition of academic dishonesty in their editorial to the special issue of *College English*, 'The Homosexual Imagination'.[7]) Criticism of contemporary writers has been conducted along subtler lines as prejudice loses some of its former strength and authority. Although condemnation on grounds of subject matter alone continues in some quarters, in general there has been a new willingness and even enthusiasm to examine the homosexual theme. But freer discussion of the subject has not always disentangled it from the myths and abstractions of the past, as can be seen in some recent approaches to 'homosexual art'.

Jeffrey Meyers, in *Homosexuality and Literature 1890–1930* (1977), puts forward the view that the emancipation of the homosexual has led paradoxically to the decline of his art. Aside from the fact that few homosexuals would agree that legal modifications have brought 'emancipation', the author bases this view on a narrow range of writers, citing Burroughs, Genet, Rechy and Selby as examples of those who content themselves with defiant disclosure of homosexual acts. He argues a connection between the need for dissimulation and the skilful use of symbolism and ambiguity that confer greatness on earlier works. However, it seems unreasonable to suppose that these qualities are the only recipe for significant art, and unlikely that the writers with whom he deals (Wilde, Gide, Mann, Musil, Proust, Conrad, Forster, T. E. Lawrence and D. H. Lawrence) achieve the ideal or the definitive rendering of the homosexual theme. His aversion to explicit treatments seems to betray a distaste for the subject itself, as if its acceptability and artistic merit depended upon the resourcefulness of its codification in 'polite' terms. In his opinion, once the creative process is unencumbered by that necessity for restraint which both 'elevates' and acts as a 'safety-valve' for homosexual sentiment, it degenerates to the gross depiction of the sexual act. Such rigid criteria would soon be dismissed if they were applied to the portrayal of heterosexual acts. Meyers places homosexuals in a special category of individuals whose 'gross' impulses must be subject to control and constraint.

If, in the past, the fact of a writer's homosexuality was studiously ignored, nowadays, its acknowledgement can produce other kinds of distortion. We seem to have moved from an age of innuendo to one of frantic confession, judging by the current spate of revelatory memoirs of literary and public figures. Certainly, such candour in biography and autobiography is welcome and in some cases long overdue, but the result has occasionally been to trivialise or sensationalise those concerned. The fact of a writer's homosexuality assumes undue proportions and is often seized upon as the ultimate interpretative key, as if sexual preference rendered artistic integrity suspect. The unique qualities of a writer's work are also diminished by the eagerness to generalise about a special

11

class. Susan Sontag's essay, 'Notes on Camp',[8] has popularised the notion of a recognisable homosexual style which is incompatible with moral seriousness and arises out of the perception of the world as little more than an amusing aesthetic phenomenon. At the other extreme, there are those who emphasise content at the expense of form and, borrowing techniques from psychoanalytic theory, treat a text as a casebook of neurotic symptoms. For example, a French critic, G. M. Sarotte, in his study *Comme un Frère, Comme un Amant* (1976), takes his cue from Fiedler's approach to American literature and is careful not to look foolish by condemning homosexuality on old-fashioned moral grounds. Instead, he systematically developes the thesis that homosexual writers cannot be 'free', and that their works cannot help but testify to their own neuroses and self-hatreds, thereby confirming the view of homosexuality as a pathological failure to achieve maturity, as an impaired form of masculinity.

Regardless of a writer's own sexuality, homosexual characters—however skilfully they are presented—tend to be judged by criteria which would not normally be applied to their more conventional counterparts. We take it for granted that the relationship between a man and a women, one of the novel's staple ingredients, can be rendered and felt in an infinite variety of ways, and that the given elements in a character's situation—their gender, class, or heredity—are always tempered by personal experience. But this assumption of uniqueness is not always extended to those individuals who happen to be homosexual, and writers as well as critics are often guilty of this failing.

It is time that this ubiquitous urge to generalise and to stereotype was discredited; it continues a form of oppression experienced by homosexuals in everyday life. The whole subject of homosexuality has long been overburdened by monolithic theorising and literature, at its most imaginative, can act as an antidote. If we accord literature a special ability to take us into 'another country' and allow the novel, in particular, to speak to us intimately of the private worlds of other individuals, then we recognise its power to counteract the stereotyping and failures of understanding we engage in and encounter elsewhere.

NOTES

1. Some general works on the homosexual literary tradition are: J. Z. Eglinton, *Greek Love* (New York, 1964); Timothy d'Arch Smith, *Love in Earnest: Some Notes on the Lives and Writings of English "Uranian" Poets from 1889–1930* (London, 1970); Rictor Norton, *The Homosexual Literary Tradition: An Interpretation* (New York, 1974); Roger Austen, *Playing the Game* (Indianapolis/New York, 1977); Jeffrey Meyers, *Homosexuality and Literature 1890–1930* (London, 1977). See also Note 3.

2. Such tactics of accommodation are wittily summarised by Rictor Norton and Louie Crew in 'The Homophobic Imagination: An Editorial' from the special issue of *College English*, 'The Homosexual Imagination' (Vol. 36, No. 3, November 1974) pp. 274–76.

3. See, for example, Jeanette Foster, *Sex Variant Women in Literature* (New York, 1956); and Jane Rule, *Lesbian Images* (New York, 1975).

4. Norman Mailer, 'The Homosexual Villain', *One* (3, 1955) pp. 8–12, reprinted in *Advertisements for Myself* (New York, 1959).

5. See, for example, Jeremy Seabrook's *A Lasting Relationship: Homosexuals and Society* (London, 1976). Purporting to be a serious social document, his edited conversations with homosexual men and women are wrought into a vaporous theory which moralises about their new found status as victims in a consumer-orientated economic system.

6. Kate Millett, *Sexual Politics* (Garden City, N.Y., 1970), p. 336.

7. See Note 2; see also Rictor Norton's essay 'Ganymede Raped: Gay Literature—The Critic as Censor' in Ian Young, *The Male Homosexual in Literature: A Bibliography* (Metuchen, N.J., 1975), pp. 193–205.

8. Susan Sontag, 'Notes on Camp', *Partisan Review* (No. 31, 1964), pp. 515–30.

1

Gore Vidal

In an afterword to the revised edition of *The City and the Pillar*, Gore Vidal remarks that in 1946 when his novel was written, 'it was part of American folklore that homosexuality was a form of mental disease, confined for the most part to interior decorators and ballet dancers'.[1] But the age-old bias against homosexuality was not confied to folklore alone and in the United States it had long been found expedient to implement ferocious laws and penalties where homosexual acts were concerned. Despite a relaxation of sexual mores and the advent of radical liberation movements, many of these laws and the attitudes they embody are still in existence. In fact, to such an extent does male homosexuality continue to be seen as a threat to cherished definitions of masculinity that the American psychologist, Dr Serge Weinberg, has argued that nowadays 'homophobia'—the fear of intimacy between males—is more properly to be regarded as a national neurosis in need of treatment.[2]

Published in 1948, *The City and the Pillar* was received with shock and disbelief. No doubt the critics' sense of a betrayal was exacerbated by its departure from the masculine ethos and wartime atmosphere of *Williwaw* (1946) and *In a Yellow Wood* (1947), the two novels which had established their author's reputation. As Vidal recalls: '*The New York Times* refused to take advertising for the book, and most of the reviews were hostile. The press lectured me firmly on the delights of heterosexual love, while chiding the publishers for distributing such a lurid "memoir" ' (p. 158). His fall from grace was complete when *The City and the Pillar*'s 'lurid' reputation assured it the status of a best-seller, thus making it one of the first homosexual novels to reach a vast audience. The complacent, condemnatory attitudes of previous decades had been challenged and, more especially with the publication

15

shortly afterwards of Kinsey's *Sexual Behaviour in the Human Male*, homosexuality became a subject of fierce controversy.

In this same afterword, Vidal discusses his motives for tackling such a topic and explains, 'I was bored with playing it safe. I wanted to take risks, to try something no American had done before' (p. 157). Nonetheless, his claim to a pioneering role needs to be understood in a special sense, for although *The City and the Pillar* was thought a shocking aberration in the career of a young war novelist, it does exploit established literary traditions. Nowadays in fact, homosexuality tends to be seen as *the* unconscious theme of classic American literature. That idealisation of male friendship noted by D. H. Lawrence[3] is further explored in Leslie Fiedler's *Love and Death in the American Novel* (1960), which has popularised the view that such literature deals typically in homoerotic romances between runaway males who escape the 'civilising' influence of woman and the adult sexual relation she symbolises, by retreating to some primordial wilderness. Furthermore, as Roger Austen reveals in his history of the homosexual novel in America, *Playing the Game* (1977), prior to Vidal there had been conscious attempts to deal with this theme, especially in popular fiction, although earlier writers were timid by comparison and adopted the strategy of discretion summed up in the title of his study. Scenes of sexual explicitness had indeed become common in novels published during and just after the Second World War. A number of these portrayed homosexuals in a bolder light. In particular, John Horne Burns's *The Gallery* (1947) and Truman Capote's *Other Voices, Other Rooms* (1947) acquired a certain notoriety. Yet the portrait of homosexuals in *The Gallery* is confined to one section and UnAmerican Activities in the form of sexual tourism are rendered less threatening by being placed in an exotic, foreign locale—at the safe distance of a war-time Naples gay bar. Discretion also plays its part in *Other Voices, Other Rooms* where the central character is just thirteen years old and the full implications of his homosexuality are avoided or only obliquely glimpsed in the gothic twilight world which represents his future. Homosexuality does not come under complete scrutiny in either of these two novels and moreover is presented in terms of bizarre excursions outside the mainstream of human experience.

The City and the Pillar heralded a new type of homosexual fiction, frank and unapologetic. For the first time an established

16

male novelist put his reputation at risk by tackling single-mindedly and explicitly a subject which had long been taboo. The reading public had been willing to have its prejudices pandered to by fiction which presented homosexuals as villains or as tragic misfits, as effete foils to that variety of manly hero perfected by the Hemingway school or as local colour in sagas of war and foreign lands, but Vidal committed the heresy of choosing a clean-cut all-American boy as his protagonist. As in the case of Kinsey, the public were shocked by the projection of the sheer ordinariness of homosexuality. Not only is the despised faggot of American folklore promoted to the status of hero, but the character of Jim Willard is at first sight one which promises development towards that same manly heroism sacred to a more conventional American novel. He is also the archetypal 'boy next door', the homespun hero of the pulp romance 'kidnapped' by Vidal and caused to represent the naturalness of homosexual relations.

There is little in Jim Willard or Bob Ford to suggest the conventional 'sissy' stereotype: neither is unmanned by an adoring, overbearing mother, though, to their 'credit', both evince a certain contempt for their father. Their virile good looks and athletic skills establish their masculinity in glamorous terms; Jim is a tennis champion and Bob is a favourite with the girls. Individual traits temper these contrasting 'butch' stereotypes, however, and account for their friendship. Bob's popularity with the opposite sex wins him few male friends and his isolation is increased by his father's reputation as the town drunkard. Another version of Huck Finn, he determines to 'light out for the territory'—in his case, the sea. Jim dreams of escape, too, unhappy that his best friend is graduating ahead of him and so preventing their shipping out together. Like Tom Sawyer before him, he rebels against the dull conformity of the small town, here personified by his petty-minded father. As with Twain's pair, the rejection of 'civilising' influences takes the shape of escapes to the woods. Bob opts to spend his last weekend with Jim in an old slave cabin they frequent, down on the banks of the Potomac where the river, complementing their passion, is running high. The return to nature proceeds with the discarding of clothes, the ritual of bathing, and a wrestling match that leads imperceptibly to love-making. In this Edenic setting the old myth is reversed and it is the taboos of society that fall before the expression of a love which is innocent and guileless: 'Now they

17

were complete, each become the other, as their bodies collided with primal violence, like to like, metal to magnet, half to half and the whole restored' (p. 24).

In this episode, Vidal invokes that nostalgic dream for the companionship of two men on the run from domesticity, but makes his own comment on this tradition by placing the love-making of the two youths in the hallowed locale where manhood was forged. The underlying homoerotic romance that Fiedler perceives in so many American novels—and always interprets negatively as evidence of immaturity and failed heterosexuality—is here developed as a possible fulfilment of a friendship. In *The Apostate Angel* (1974), Bernard Dick goes so far as to suggest, '*The City and the Pillar* is the American wilderness novel demythologised; or rather it exposes the awesome truth the myth concealed' (p. 39). But Vidal's sly satire on the conventional chastity of male comradeship scarcely amounts to 'awesome truth' and Bernard Dick loses sight of the novel's more central concerns when he insists on its importance 'as a mythic novel, not a homosexual one' (p. 38). Vidal's homosexual pastoral with its Platonic references recalls not so much the frontier novel as that past age of the Greek warriors when masculinity was not held to ransom by heterosexuality. Indeed, the bathing idyll and the wrestling match are staple ingredients in literary treatments of homosexuality. Similar scenes occur in D. H. Lawrence's *The White Peacock* and *Women in Love*, or in E. M. Forster's *A Room with a View*, and Rictor Norton cites many other examples in *The Homosexual Literary Tradition* (1974), where he traces the evolution of these archetypes from the 'Hylas ritual' of Greek mythology. The episode in the woods functions as a prologue to the main action, presenting Vidal's thesis on the naturalness of the bisexual impulse and serving to measure the distortions of this ideal in the society in which the two youths must subsequently make their way.

There can be no return to nature, of course, and the greater part of *The City and the Pillar* dramatises the petrification of this innocent sexual love and the 'romantic fallacy'—ironically imaged in Vidal's title—of always looking back. The momentary feeling of wholeness and completion will never be recaptured and the narrative's circular form is an empty reminder of that lost union. The account of Jim's progress from the fulfilment of a dream to its disintegration is encapsulated by his drunken reminiscing in a bleak,

18

anonymous New York bar. In a sense, Vidal is depicting the impossibility of his own dream too, for despite his belief in a universal bisexual potential which is dramatised in this scene in the woods, by the end of the novel Jim clearly is homosexual, whereas Bob, emphatically, is not. The separation of their individual destinies from this point marks their gravitation towards the rigid sexual categorisation society inculcates. In the woods, Bob's sheepish remark that 'guys aren't supposed to do that with one another' (p. 25) is given the lie when they fall to love-making once more, but it prefigures the masculine 'ideology' which will dictate their future.

Accordingly, when Jim is able to set out in pursuit of his friend, life at sea, instead of re-uniting him with Bob, merely introduces him to the forces that will keep them apart. The swaggering virility of Collins, the seaman who befriends him, is by default a reminder of Bob's superiority and at the same time an ironic anticipation of what the latter will become. Guessing Jim to be a virgin, Collins delights in procuring his first woman. Predictably the youth fails the ritual test: the seduction takes place in sordid circumstances with a view of Collins labouring brutishly over his partner. Jim abandons the drunken, pathetic girl provided for him, since 'her eyes were bright, shiny, bestial. He had seen the same look in Collins's eyes, in Emily's eyes, yet not in Bob's eyes' (p. 41). His flight boosts Collins's sense of his own masculinity and he cries out scornfully, 'Let the queer go! I got enough for two' (p. 42).

If such an assertion of 'manhood' appears unnatural by the standard of his experience with Bob, the homosexual milieu into which Jim subsequently drifts is presented as equally crude and loveless. A tennis coach at a fashionable Hollywood hotel, he learns that most of the bellboys arc homosexual and allows them to introduce him to their world:

> If only out of a morbid desire to discover how what had been so natural and complete for him could be so perfectly corrupted by these strange womanish creatures.
>
> (p. 52)

But it is from this point that Vidal's attempt to show the 'naturalness' of his protagonist's homosexuality fails to be convincing. The 'strange womanish creatures' presented as foils to Jim's superior self constitute a sneer at effeminacy and associate it somewhat gratuitously with corruption. Increasingly, Jim's exemplary ordinariness depends on displays of a studied masculinity—a saleable asset in this community as he is quick to realise. Assiduously cultivating his reputation for being 'straight', he enters into an affair with a film star, Robert Shaw, for reasons which do little to endear to us his contrasting 'naturalness'. His vanity is flattered by Shaw's attentions and, what is more, he can make a quick profit by giving tennis lessons to his patron's wealthier friends.

In his eagerness to counter the equation of homosexuality with effeminacy and in order to assert his hero's manliness, Vidal tends to draw upon the crude stereotypes he reproves elsewhere. Those who belong to the homosexual coteries in Hollywood can supposedly be identified by their common desire to 'move in narcissistic splendour through the lives of others, to live forever grandly, and not to die' (p. 46). Jim rationalises his subsequent attraction to a writer, Paul Sullivan, in equally dismissive terms. Contrasting him with the usual guests at Shaw's parties, he decides: 'Sexually they were obvious, unlike Sullivan, who appeared perfectly normal' (p. 62). 'Normal' in this context can be taken as an approving acknowledgement of manliness. The positive, propagandist assertion of Jim's 'naturalness' is further undermined as it comes to be indistinguishable from his ignorance and naïvety. The withdrawal from emotional involvements and the refusal to identify with the homosexual subculture which preserve his illusions of masculinity, spring simultaneously from the ingenuous belief that he will eventually meet up with his boyhood friend and carry on the relationship from where it left off.

Nonetheless, Jim has traits in common with the Hollywood cliques from which he would proudly dissociate himself. The film star, Robert Shaw, incarnates all the presumed aspirations of the gay community. He has wealth, fame, a circle of knowing sycophantic friends, and the adulation of a vast audience of women who regard him as a love object, 'unattainable, but useful as a companion in dreams' (p. 48). Like them, and like Jim, Shaw lives in a world of illusion. He acquires in the tennis coach a status symbol and a means of creating envy, imagining how they will be worshipped 'as a dazzling couple, two perfect youths, re-enacting boyhood dreams' (p. 52). But Jim exhibits similar characteristics: he is highly susceptible to flattery; he too cultivates a profitable image by 'passing for straight'; and his emotional life is arrested in worship of a dream lover—in his case, Bob.

The attempt to demonstrate the 'naturalness' of homosexual relations is also in conflict with the form Vidal gives to his novel. The circularity of the narrative is dictated by the image of its hero as someone whose chances of happiness in the present are destroyed by his obsession with the past. What had been the natural, spontaneous expression of sexual affection in the woods atrophies with its fixation in memory until, in the city life Jim adopts, it ironically engenders in him its opposite: the pillar of salt. Nature suggests flux, change and growth, but Jim loses this capacity to respond freely and flexibly to experience and enters into relationships with calculation and a degree of dishonesty. It is as if Vidal must compromise his sympathetic portrayal of homosexuality so as to preserve this conception of the novel and thus Jim can be brought into contact only with those individuals who will not disturb the set pattern of his experience. What begins as a 'commonsense redefinition of the homosexual-ist in American life' (p. 159), transforms itself into a study of self-deception. Jim's inability to enter deeply into any relationship is rendered credible by the fact that the principal contenders for his affections—Shaw, Sullivan, and Maria Verlaine—are equally self-absorbed and incapable of giving themselves up to love. Their similarities lend a psychological interest and unity to the narrative of Jim's rootless, wandering existence and present his deficiencies of character in terms of more widespread failings in life and not as a necessary consequence of his homosexuality.

Sullivan reverses all Shaw's characteristics so exactly that the two men are seen to be fundamentally alike. Both manufacture a compensatory version of life: the actor fabricates a technicolour dream world to exclude the possibilities of pain; the writer turns experience into an artificial nightmare to inflict masochistic tortures upon himself. The latter avoids the real pain and the possible joy of loving someone by taking refuge in a contrived and comfortable despair. He tells himself that the affair with Jim 'looked to be most promising, with endless possibilities of disaster' (p. 70). Sullivan's preconceived notions about life are especially evident in his theories of homosexuality. But Jim's views on the subject are equally rigid and he chooses to ignore the fact that his own relationship with Bob fits neatly into one of Sullivan's categories.

21

To Jim's mind, homosexuality is synonymous with disaster, what-ever the pattern: 'If he was really like the others, then what sort of future could he have? Endless drifting, promiscuity, defeat?' (p. 65). These words conjure up the very consequences of his re-fusal to identify with and to enter into relationships with others 'like' himself. His conviction that he and Bob are unique leads Jim to withhold his innermost self from Sullivan and, given the writer's secretiveness and self-hatred, they lose the opportunity of revising their set outlooks on life and conspire to bring about their own defeat. They drift aimlessly, each refusing to make the commitment that might shape a future until, in New Orleans, Sullivan takes a morbid pleasure in destroying his own chances of happiness by in-volving Jim with a woman friend who would be likely to appeal to him.

Maria Verlaine has a penchant for 'lost causes' and for 'doomed' relationships with 'artists': 'Her imagination could transform the most ordinary of men into dream lovers' (p. 78). Jim's imagina-tion has long performed an identical feat, but the circle his life describes is endlessly repeated in Maria Verlaine's short-lived ro-mances. In the glow of her adoration, he can summon up affection but physical love proves impossible. But although deprived of any remaining doubts as to his sexual preferences, there is only a sem-blance of motion and progress in Jim's life. The advent of war re-leases him from the tangle of dishonesty in his relationships with Maria and Sullivan, but it does not bring the hoped-for resolution of his destiny in action. Training camp merely introduces him to a new form of limbo and his observation of the sexual hypocrisies of army life makes no dent in his innocent belief that Bob will always be able to respond to him as he did in the past. Self-deception is rife: the ugliest of men are apparently forever being propositioned by 'fairies'; the gay Sergeant whispers that 'it's a lot cheaper to buy milk than to keep a cow' (p. 92); Jim himself is reduced to plotting and planning to seduce a young Corporal he lusts after and, when his clumsy scheme misfires, is merely baffled that the same Corporal should subsequently be won over by the Sergeant's surreptitious flattery. Jim makes his most determined effort to come to terms with himself after an illness brings about his discharge from the army and he becomes a partner in a New York tennis business. The period of convalescence had allowed him ample time to reflect on his experiences and to try to gather together the threads of the past by writing to friends and family. He cultivates the few acquaintances he has, and Shaw, Sullivan and Maria Verlaine drift in and out of his life again, but there can be no more than a superficial companionship with them since their lives, like his, describe circles and admit only surface changes.

As always, Jim's emotional growth is blocked by his holding himself in abeyance for that dreamed of reunion with Bob. Consequently, the novelty of presenting an 'ordinary' homosexual is endangered by the imaginative restrictions of the hero's fixed obsession and the plot mechanics it dictates. Jim is predictable, even dull. The outcome of his quest is long foreseen and only his mode of revenge carries any surprise. Because he 'lives' in the past, his partial acceptance of his homosexuality is never made the driving force of his quest for personal fulfilment, and so his long flirtation with the gay underworld in New York which occupies the latter part of the novel is void of the need and anguish that might carry him beyond its stylised masks. Instead of progressing to a sympathetic understanding of other individuals or allowing them insights into himself, Jim merely poses. When Shaw provides him with an entrée into the chic upper echelons of this world, Jim is apt to grind out in his deepest voice that he is a tennis player, observing the 'queens' who squeak with delight and are roused to unlikely conversations about the relationship between virility, homosexuality and neurosis. Although such acquaintances provide flattering reassurance to his ego, he finds a more congenial world of make-believe in the bars around Times Square where purely sexual contacts are negotiated behind a smokescreen of manly behaviour. His favourites are those who wake up next morning with amnesia, to exclaim, 'Gee, I sure was drunk last night!' (p. 135).

This ploy of satisfying desire without disturbing the *status quo* of masculinity is Jim's final means of reconciling himself to his homosexuality. Yet, as the strategy by which he hopes to win Bob again, it is also the cause of his defeat. Because he has gained no real insight into the workings of the masculine code in himself, he miscalculates its hold on his friend. Bob has carefully 'forgotten' what Jim has never ceased to remember, with the result that neither is capable of physical spontaneity when the acquaintance is renewed and the naturalness that once transfigured it has gone. Having capitulated to convention, domesticity and a future in insurance, Bob can only conceive of his last 'fling' in New York in the

23

traditional terms of alcohol and easy women. Jim pays lip service to this code whilst carefully manœuvring towards the seduction scene to which he believes Bob will tacitly consent. Appropriately, it turns into a savage parody of the past: two drunks sprawled on a hotel bed, one reaches for the other's sex and dream turns to nightmare at the words, 'Let go of me, you queer' (p. 150). The playful wrestling of old is transformed into a murderous combat, each having suffered a deadly blow to his manly pride. Bob is killed, somewhat melodramatically, in the original, and raped in the revised version—considered here the definitive text. In this way, Jim's life has its long awaited resolution in action, rape being a more suitably ironic image of love's inversion to brutal vengeance.

The incident in Norman Mailer's *Why Are We in Vietnam?* (1967) where a rape almost forms the climax of a friendship between another two youths makes a revealing comparison. Mailer's adolescent pair never know the natural affection Jim and Bob once tasted, even in the wilds of Alaska when they escape from the adults in their hunting party. Instead, homosexual desire is the quarry each must hunt down if they are to win through to 'manhood'. Love can only be contemplated in the form of aggression, with rape as the secret weapon in the arsenal of *machismo*. Both are hopelessly corrupted by that masculine ideology which despises affection, gentleness and passivity as feminine. D.J. 'had never put a hand on Tex for secret fear that Tex was strong enough to turn round and brand him up his ass' whilst Tex 'was finally afraid to prong D.J. because D.J. once become a bitch would kill him'.[4] Too scared to be lovers, D.J. and Tex become killer brothers, turning aggression outwards to fulfil their destinies as 'men' in Vietnam.

Jim takes his revenge on such 'manhood' in its own unnatural terms, but, by doing so, confirms that he himself is trapped within that same system of values. In some ways, then, he is a new type of hero in homosexual fiction, but, given the circularity of his experience, he fails ever to become *heroic*. His anger is not transformed into an awareness that he must revise the values by which he lives or into a compassionate sense of fellowship with others in his situation. Indeed, he wallows in drunken self-pity and we are left with the image of him amusing himself by scorning the advances of some 'little fag'. 'Endless drifting, promiscuity, defeat' —such was the future he conjured up for himself as an 'ordinary' homosexual, as if this were the only alternative to Bob. It is appropriate, therefore, that he should reappear in one of Vidal's subsequent novels, *The Judgment of Paris* (1958), hustling in Paris, a poseur to the last.

How can the naturalness of the homosexual drive be incorporated into a satisfying individual identity in a society where people are imprisoned by myths of masculinity and femininity, and rigid gender roles? This question, framed in the character of Jim Willard, is taken up again in several of the stories from the collection *A Thirsty Evil* (1956), and, most notably, in the novel *Myra Breckinridge* (1968).

Three of the stories from *A Thirsty Evil* develop aspects of Jim's situation. 'Three Stratagems', with its account of a male hustler cruising the beach at Key West, points to his most likely future. Jim's mentality finds its extreme form in the figure of the hustler —someone who panders to, and is trapped by, dreams of a traditional masculinity uncompromised by homosexual activity. In this instance, the young prostitute, 'Michael', has a despairing awareness of the cycle of degradation that plays itself out beneath the codified surface of behaviour and token pose of heterosexuality. The story takes on elegiac tones as 'Michael' contrasts his innocent childhood perceptions of such a beach with the worldly knowledge of his practised eye. His sense of loss links him to the aging clients, who 'sat watchfully beneath umbrellas, admiring the cold and radiant angels who could, they believed, exorcise the graceless shadows of the years and with firm flesh recreate youth and a sense of permanency, or its illusion'. He tells us that 'sometimes I am frightened when I watch their sad courtship of the treacherous angels, for I see in them my own eventual fall from beloved angel to deluded monster'.[5] His understanding of their stratagems allows him to perfect his own, knowing exactly how and when to assume the character appropriate to their fantasy. Yet, ironically, at the moment when his present client has been brought within grasp of the desired illusion, the youth suffers an epileptic fit, and the virile, athletic image he calculated is thereby destroyed. The 'seizure' suggests that although he can manipulate the surfaces of life, he is like a beautiful but hollow shell, subject to collapse from within, as his own 'treacherous angel' stirs.

'Pages from an Abandoned Journal' gives a comic rendering of another form of love's corruption. The narrator, a conventional young American with his eyes fixed on marriage and a doctorate, recounts his introduction to a bohemian homosexual coterie in Paris, in 1948. Despite his prissy heterosexuality, he is attracted to the central figure of Elliot Magren, an aging high society 'courtesan', and led to reflect on the dullness of his own existence. That dullness is a measure of his contrived conventionality, for when he witnesses Magren's unselfconscious romp with a French youth at Deauville, memories he had carefully interred flood back and he confesses to his own sexual experiences with a school friend, Jimmy. The journal is resumed in 1953 to detail his social life over Christmas and we soon gather that the narrator is now established in a homosexual identity which is as predictable and as pretentious as his heterosexual self had been. His affected gabble shows him to be a mere social climber who has exchanged one form of artifice for another and continued to betray the naturalness of those adolescent experiences by the adoption of a stylised mask.

'The Zenner Trophy' strikes a more positive note. When two eighteen-year-olds, Sawyer and Flynn, are expelled from school because of their love affair, they cause further consternation by their contempt for the establishment's smug values. Once more, Vidal portrays a homosexual relationship between two outwardly conventional males (their names are calculated to recall Twain's celebrated pair of adolescent rebels), developing happily and spontaneously—until the wrath of popular prejudice makes itself felt. With his freckled face and crew-cut, Flynn is the epitome of American manhood; universally popular, he is the school's 'chief ornament' and 'finest athlete', the only possible choice for the Carl F. Zenner trophy (for *clean* sportsmanship)—which must now be denied him. As the school's best sprinter, Sawyer completes the picture of healthy masculinity. The spirit and vitality of these two is set against the sanctimonious posturing of the Principal, a 'rock' of solidified opinion, and the timid conformity of one of his subordinates, Beckmann, whose job it is to inform Flynn of his expulsion. Flynn's refusal to show shame and his determination to stand by his relationship with Sawyer causes Beckmann to reflect sadly on his own subservience.

Unlike Jim and Bob of *The City and the Pillar*, the masculinity of these two youths is not contingent upon the appearance of sexual conformity. However, their ability to transform their rebellious stance into a long term strategy for survival raises questions which are unanswerable within the scope of the short story.

Unfortunately, a writer with none of Vidal's talent has taken up the challenge of imagining the future of someone like Flynn. Patricia Nell Warren's novel, *The Front Runner* (1974), deals with a champion athlete, Billy Sive, who, along with two friends, is suspended from university for being gay. Although the subsequent 'love story' of Billy and his coach at a small New York college dramatises the sexual politics of being openly and proudly homosexual in that bastion of virility, the sporting world, its radical message is trivialised by mawkish sentimentality, a clichéd, inept style, and a preposterous plot.

Whereas Vidal creates moral fables by manipulating sexual stereotypes to satiric purpose, in the hands of lesser artists, the device of presenting homosexuality in impeccable masculine 'packages' can seem not only contrived but an evasion of more fundamental problems of how society values 'masculine' and 'feminine' qualities. For example, a novel by James Barr, *Quatrefoil* (1950), sets out to elicit our sympathy for a love affair between two naval officers by showering them with 'redeeming' virtues; not only are they paragons of virility, but they also enjoy great wealth, looks, intellect, and the exquisite refinement of manners that is in keeping with their high social position. Pillars of society, Commander Danelaw and Phillip Froelich would refute the notion that sexual aberration necessarily spells social disaster. Barr makes an agonised, intelligent, but ultimately embarrassing attempt to present them as a special case; modern avatars of the Spartan ideal of warrior and youthful initiate, their love is transfigured by cultural exchange to distinguish them from the 'degeneracy' of those ordinary mortals condemned to mere sexual passion. This is homosexuality on its best behaviour, promising infinite discretion and an allegiance to the *status quo*.

It is in *Myra Breckinridge* that Vidal returns to give shape to Jim Willard's blind anger and to transform Flynn's gesture of defiance into a full-scale assault upon society's rigid sexual categories. The earnest moralising of *The City and the Pillar* is translated into outrageous comedy; its prosaic realism is exchanged for a high camp travesty of artistic forms. Myra Breckinridge is the loveless (but loveable) monster born of Jim's anger, and vengeance is the shaping force of her existence. The 'rape' of the conventional male provides the starting point as well as the narrative climax of this novel. With a comic logic reminiscent of James Purdy's lunatic

27

rapist hero in *Cabot Wright Begins* (1964), the victim of society's assaults upon individual identity retaliates in appropriately symbolic terms. Myra is no pillar of salt, paralysed by nostalgia, but more of a 'well groomed human lance' (which is how one commentator has described Vidal's television personality[6]) who stalks her prey with the double perversity of a Lovelace disguised as Clarissa.

Vidal satirises Hollywood's cultural stranglehold on sexual identity by presenting Myra as its spiritual child. Through her, he mocks the myths of masculinity and femininity it has imprinted upon the nation's subconscious, as well as the phoney intellectualism that now pays homage to the Golden Age of Forties films. According to Myra,

> In the decade between 1935 and 1945, no irrelevant film was made in the United States. During those years, the entire range of human (which is to say, American) legend was put on film, and any profound study of those extraordinary works is bound to make crystal-clear the human condition.[7]

Myra has engaged in such a study or, rather, she hopes to complete her 'husband', Myron's, work, on Parker Tyler and the films of the Forties. Parker Tyler's *Magic and Myth in the Movies*[8] has been a source of inspiration to them both; in fact, Myron and Myra take it upon themselves to live out consciously the myths that work subliminally upon their contemporaries.

We learn that Myron was 'ravished', if not destroyed, by the values those myths inculcated. Although he too had yearned to be a film star, as a homosexual there was no room for him in the pantheon of virile heroes. While those like Buck Loner, his cowboy filmstar uncle, have the monopoly on self-respecting manhood, Myron is dismissed as a 'fag' and a 'sissy'. He had made fervent studies of the source of this oppression, producing amongst other things a scholarly treatise on the rear ends of all the major cowboy stars, a feat his uncle grimly recalls. Rather than accept his inferiority in this hierarchy of power, Myron had pursued a curious revenge, 'purchasing' the most obviously heterosexual men to penetrate him, thus subverting their self-image and imposing his will on a forbidden deity. His masochistic pose served sadistic ends and he delighted in using such men as they used women. He inverted the outward image of manly aggression in himself (withholding his own splendid penis from those who might desire it), only to revel in a more covert manner of domination. His metamorphosis to Myra, thanks to surgery and silicone, is the ultimate development of this strategy, the perfect weapon. Steeped in the lore of Hollywood's Golden Age, he knows that calculated femininity can be the guise of an aggression that matches that of any man. Little wonder, then, that Myra should liken herself to the beauteous Fay Wray who could reduce King Kong to a 'mere simian whimper' (p. 1). As a man, Myron cultivated the deceitful passivity of a woman, despite his virile strength; as a woman, Myra aspires to the brutality of the superstud, despite her demure exterior. Denying her wondrous attributes to those who might desire them, she forces herself unnaturally, with the aid of a massive dildo, upon the very person who does not. The outrageous comedy and crazy logic of these double negatives present a calculated travesty of traditional notions of sexual role and gender.

It is appropriate that Vidal should cast his novel in a form which invites the description of 'high camp' for, similarly, in everyday life the affectation of a camp style can be a way of mocking oppressive masculine stereotypes and of converting a despised effeminacy into a subtle form of attack. Traditionally, homosexuals have had to practise skills of impersonation and this has undoubtedly fostered an acute awareness of image-making in others. In literary terms, a camp style might be described as one which eschews the 'masculine' qualities of sober, unadorned, unemotional prose, in favour of surface brilliance, mannerisms, emotional posturing—all conceived in a playful spirit of exaggeration. Susan Sontag has gone so far as to describe camp as a largely homosexual sensibility, in essence a love of the unnatural, arising from a perception of the theatricalisation of experience.[9] But *Myra Breckinridge* contradicts her argument that camp is antithetical to moral seriousness. Whilst the novel is 'high camp' in so far as it is constructed from a pastiche of what are held to be meretricious art forms, reproducing on a larger scale its heroine's own delicious artificiality, this should not obscure the earnestness of the underlying moral fable which holds society's artifices up to ridicule. Myra's person and her narrative are a wicked combination of the *avant-garde* and the old-fashioned, the sophisticated and the utterly vulgar. Myra tells us bossily that since the novel is dead, there is no point to writing made-up stories, yet proceeds to document her own story of triumphant self-invention. She culls her literary pretensions from the French theorists of the *nouveau roman*, making knowing references to Robbe-Grillet: 'Nothing is *like* anything else. Things are themselves entirely and do not need interpretation, only a minimal respect for their precise integrity' (p. 6). But Myra's journal is a parody of such theorists' solemn desire for scientific objectivity in their writings. The actual materials upon which she exercises her up-to-date literary genius are farcically incongruous; academic precision is lavished on the staple ingredients of the pornographic novel as Myra takes a pedantic delight in itemising her violations of a young stud's 'precise integrity', or ponders philosophically upon the *exact* meaning of her upsurge of lesbian feelings for Mary-Ann. Her borrowings from avant-garde literature, coupled with the comic scale of her sexual experimentation, make a mockery of the *nouveau roman* and the conventions of the sexual fantasy.

Nowadays, the films of Hollywood's Golden Age may seem decidedly camp. That is to say, their larger-than-life projections of personality are often thought to be comic, exaggerated and stylised. It is as if Parker Tyler's analysis of the discrepancy between intended and unintended effect, surface script and subconscious framework of myth, anticipated the more sophisticated perceptions of future audiences. To appreciate the camp qualities of such films is to demystify their gods and goddesses, to perceive the structuring of their images, and to view the stars almost as 'drag artists' and 'impersonators' of the sexual roles they portray. As well as satirising literary models, Vidal actually shapes his plot and characterisation along the epic lines of a Forties film. Its surface story is suitably banal: the newly-widowed mysterious beauty, Myra Breckinridge, arrives in Hollywood to secure her share of the family inheritance, an orange grove, now the site of her uncle's Academy of Modelling and Drama; the scheming uncle resists her claim and the heroine must enter into a battle of wits to assert her rights. But this scenario is soon overtaken by a subplot the mythical dimensions of which read like something out of Parker Tyler: Myra is the avenging spirit of the past and the New Woman, an Amazonian in the borrowed clothes of a screen goddess, penetrating to the heart of the image-making world in order to overthrow its male deity. From her hotel room on Sunset Boulevard, she plots 'the destruction of the last vestigial traces of traditional manhood in the race in order to realign the sexes, thus reducing population while increasing human happiness and preparing humanity for its next stage' (p. 42).

To appreciate Myra as a camp creation is to relish the sheer scale of her artificiality. She is both an old-fashioned screen goddess and a modern revolutionary, yet formerly she was a man. Her combination of pseudo-intellectual sophistication, megalomania and tasteless vulgarity is irresistible. At one extreme she indulges in esoteric name-dropping (Lévi-Strauss, etc.) and outbids the avant-garde with her view of the televison commercial as the New Art, yet at the other extreme she drools shamelessly over her own miraculous breasts or entertains herself by sadistic explorations of male genitalia. Nonetheless, the qualities that make Myra camp are simultaneously the vehicle for Vidal's scathing satire: she is a monstrous symbol of American culture and an exaggerated version of all around her. Buck Loner's Academy provides an image of this larger culture where everyone is learning a part. Myra proves to be a 'natural' teacher; self-taught in the school of Hollywood's greats, she can upstage anyone. Even the arch con-man Buck is no match for her; when he launches 'huskily' and hypocritically into praise for his late sister, not to be outdone in the huskiness department by a mere man, Myra 'rasped through a Niagara of tears unshed' (p. 14). Her impersonations are so studied that she can even identify the film, reel and particular shot of whatever attitude she is striking.

Although Myra is the grotesque product of the society Vidal satirises, she is brought to attack those same values. Self-conceived in the spirit of revenge, she rises phoenix-like from Myron's despair and torment. Equipped with many of the ideas Vidal has developed in his essays, she engages in diatribes against the television generation for its ignorance of literary culture, its debasement of language, its passivity and obeisance to 'norms' of behaviour and, properly roused, her topics extend from the dangers of overpopulation to the fraudulence of psychiatrists and even to laments for the vanishing foreskin. But the central 'thrust' of her narrative is in its attack on patriarchal attitudes. In her analysis, the aggressive image of traditional manhood has reduced human relations to a power struggle and bred a retaliatory lust for domination in others. The homosexual male, the woman, and eventually the lesbian, join forces within the person of Myra Breckinridge to

31

overthrow this tyranny. Buck Loner presents her with one version of male dominance and Rusty Godowsky, one of his students, with another. Myra sets out to topple them both.

Buck Loner is a joking caricature of the rugged hero. Cowboy screen idol turned entrepreneur, his rapaciousness and thirst for wealth conceal themselves beneath a show of love for his students who are fed on artificial hopes and fleeced of their money. He is comically arrogant about his sexual potency and believes Myra to be hungering for a taste of the old 'Buck Loner Special', little realising that his castration is more what she has in mind. As Myra's schemes drive him to distraction his hard exterior fractures, revealing the mentality of a little boy whose dwindling energies must be catered to by his numerous masseuses and his wife's culinary expertise. Outwardly though, he remains the oppressive patriarch that Myra, as widow of his 'fag nephew', sets out to destroy.

Rusty Godowsky is the target of Myra's deeper mission, which is no less than to shatter the image of traditional manhood and to rearrange it along her own more meaningful lines. Rusty, as his name implies, symbolises a manly type which to Myra's mind is now obsolete. He is the 'inarticulate hero', the dumb stud whose breeding potential and 'serene and as yet uncompromised old-fashioned virility' (p. 47) bring a gleam to Myra's eye. Ironically he too is an 'impersonator', calculating the effect of his boots and faded jeans, another imitation of the brawny cowboys of a bygone era. Myra sees his outfit as the typical costume for 'young men, acting out their simple-minded roles, hopefully, constructing a fantasy world in order to avoid confronting the fact that to be a man in a society of machines is to be an expendable, soft auxiliary to what is useful and hard' (p. 69). Male and female 'impersonators' are brought into comic conflict, then, as Myra launches her offensive. Rusty, who would never dream of selling his body to a 'fag', is ready nevertheless to suffer every indignity to achieve the 'blessing' of celluloid. Under the pretext of 'correcting his posture' and carrying out a required medical examination, Myra abuses her authority and acts out her wildest fantasies. She systematically humiliates Rusty, and with infinite cunning reduces him to the status of a whimpering little boy. Stripped of his manly arrogance and, treacherously, of his jockey shorts, his sexual equipment (over which she secretly rejoices) is exposed to her scathing, tasteless criticisms. The campaign to 'unman' him includes sadistically squeezing his testicles

and forcing them back into the 'ancient cavity' and, finally, with
the aid of a massive dildo, she 'deflowers' the seat of masculine
honour—as Norman Mailer is apt to think of it.[10]

Their reversal of roles is complete: Myra, the superstud, ravishes
her quivering victim and so avenges Myron's life of torment. From
this climactic point, sexual categories swap and change in a dizzying pattern of inversion. Myra had dreamed of a time when all the
shaping contours of sex—the world's 'pots'—would be broken
to 'allow the stuff of desire to flow and intermingle in one great
viscous sea' (p. 233). But what ensues is a comic parody of this,
as characters leap from one 'pot' to the next. Ironically, we learn
from Rusty's girlfriend, Mary-Ann, that his aggressive pose had
concealed a gentle, loving nature. Myra, however, transforms him
temporarily into a sadistic brute whose excesses go far beyond what
she might have attributed to him. Letitia Van Allen, a famous
agent, is the willing vehicle through which he can work out his
hatreds. Like Myra, she uses men as they have used women but,
like Myron, her triumphs are perversely achieved by means of
masochistic submission. Myra, on the other hand, goes from the
mentality of a lunatic rapist to that of a courtly lover, the object
of her unrequited passions now being Mary-Ann. Whilst Rusty
graduates from Letitia to homosexuality, Myra's career as a lesbian
is brought to an abrupt halt by a road accident which causes her
own celebrated 'pots' to be broken and removed, reconverting her
to Myron and a future of neutered heterosexual bliss with her
adored and adoring wife, Mary-Ann. But the outflow of sexuality
from within society's containers is not stopped here, for as the
sequel to this novel, *Myron* (1976), reveals, Myra Breckinridge is
ready to smash through any screen that stands in the way of her
fanatical mission.

Gore Vidal touches upon homosexual themes in many of his
writings, but *The City and the Pillar* and *Myra Breckinridge* reveal
the inevitable development of the theme towards a concentrated
satire upon traditional concepts of manhood. He views homosexuality not as a cause meriting special pleading but quite simply
as a normal, healthy, human response that has been distorted by
society's narrow prescription of the *right* sexual equation. If Jim
Willard looks backwards, trapped by the naïve belief that two men
might love one another 'naturally' without disturbing their self-
images or their place in society, then Myra Breckinridge suggests,

in her own perverse manner, that the way forward is to strike down those rigid concepts of masculinity and femininity and so to liberate the minority in each of us.

NOTES

1. The revised edition, published in 1965, with an afterword by the author, is taken as the definitive text (London: Panther, 1972), p. 158. Subsequent page references are to this edition.
2. This is the major thesis of *Society and the Healthy Homosexual* (New York, 1972).
3. Themes of male friendship are touched upon throughout D. H. Lawrence's *Studies in Classic American Literature* (1923).
4. Norman Mailer, *Why Are We in Vietnam?* (1967). (London: Panther, 1970), pp. 139–40.
5. Gore Vidal, *A Thirsty Evil* (1956). (London: Panther, 1974), p. 11.
6. Krim Seymour, 'Reflections on a Ship That's Not Sinking at All', *Londone Magazine*, (10, May 1970) p. 26.
7. Gore Vidal, *Myra Breckinridge* (1968). (New York: Bantam, 1968), p. 13. Subsequent page references are to this edition.
8. Parker Tyler, *Magic and Myth in the Movies* (1947).
9. See Notes to Introduction, No. 8.
10. See Mailer's comments on homosexuality in prisons, *The Prisoner of Sex* (New York: Signet, 1971), pp. 116–24. It is also interesting to note that whilst the female anatomy is 'fair game' for literary description, excisions which obscure the significant details of this assault upon 'masculine honour' were imposed on the British edition of *Myra Breckinridge*.

2

James Baldwin

'I think that I know something about the American masculinity which most men of my generation do not know because they have not been menaced by it in the way that I have been', declares James Baldwin in 'The Black Boy looks at the White Boy'.[1] The male homosexual is also menaced by definitions of manhood that are used to denigrate his existence and individual dignity. Baldwin is passionately involved with the problems of both racism and homosexuality, so that his portrayal of racial conflict within a society often lends special authority to his analysis of that society's sexual stereotypes, and vice versa. He testifies to the difficulties of achieving a satisfying personal identity in a society which superimposes its conceptions of *the* negro or *the* homosexual upon individuals and which creates false images of people only to persecute them with those same images.

Baldwin's identification with these minorities has sometimes brought his status as an artist into question; to regard him as a 'black writer' or as a 'homosexual writer' is to suggest limits on his individuality and on his treatment of his chosen subject matter. Such labelling underlines the tenacity of the very stereotypes Baldwin fights. A racial or a sexual identity which does not coincide with that of the majority is frequently presumed to disqualify a writer from entering into territories beyond that minority experience. In *After the Lost Generation* (1951) John W. Aldridge pontificates on the nature of the 'homosexual talent' and concludes: 'it can develop in only one direction, and it can never take the place of the whole range of human experience' (pp. 101–2). In *The Literary Situation* (1954), Malcolm Cowley amuses himself with references to the arrival of the 'fairy-Freudian' novel and wonders whether the homosexual writer who attempts to portray 'normal passions' can never do so without transposing the sexes or indulging in spiteful malice. *Giovanni's Room*, which deals with the affair between David, a white American, and Giovanni, an Italian, has called forth critical comments which illustrate the reductive implications of the 'black writer' label. In *The Return of the Vanishing American* (1968) Leslie Fiedler remarks that 'one suspects Baldwin's Giovanni of being a Negro disguised as a European, and the book consequently of being a disguised Southern'.[2] On the other hand, G. M. Sarotte would have us believe that David is the Harlem Negro in disguise—the author in a blond wig, in fact, taking a holiday from himself.[3] It is doubtless only a matter of time before these insights are pieced together as proof of the narcissism of the 'homosexual writer'.

When heterosexual prejudice joins forces with racial convictions, as in Eldridge Cleaver's essay 'Notes on a Native Son' (in *Soul on Ice*, 1968), then the complexity of the individual writer's work is lost in a set of emotional generalisations. Cleaver, for whom homosexuality is a 'sickness' on a level with 'baby-rape', attacks Baldwin by likening him to the black homosexual who, deprived of his masculinity by worship of the white man, turns his self-contempt on other blacks, whilst fawning on his white lover. Cleaver colludes in the white man's myth of the Negro's sexual potency, to dismiss the black homosexual as a traitor, a carrier of some white 'disease' Clearly, the knowledge Baldwin claims of American masculinity— as one who has been menaced by it—has an authority which in turn menaces preferred images of manhood, both black and white. He puzzles over his own definitions in ways which explode the notions of narrowness in the experience of a racial or sexual minority. The Negro or the homosexual are, in his analysis, 'inventions' which reveal, ironically, more about the workings of mainstream culture. Just as he portrays the Negro in a manner which challenges White America to take stock of itself, so the heterosexual confronted with his 'blackening' of the outcast homosexual can be brought to greater self-awareness. This is made satirically explicit in his remark:

> People invent categories in order to feel safe. White people invented black people to give white people identity. . . . Straight cats invent faggots so they can sleep with them without becoming faggots themselves.[4]

In their various ways Baldwin's first four novels reflect the difficulties of individuals for whom the question of personal identity—

because of their psychic make-up, colour, or sexuality—bears an urgent relation to that of social survival. *Go Tell It on the Mountain* (1953) and *Giovanni's Room* (1956) explore the extent to which inner drives can be contained within the available, approved models of identity. In the first novel, John Grimes strives to sublimate his adolescent sexual confusion, his rebelliousness, and his fears of the brutal Harlem ghetto with its encircling white world, within the traditional sanctuary of the church. David, the white protagonist of the second novel, seeks a refuge in the conventional, outward trappings of manhood in a vain attempt to exorcise his homosexual longings. Both novels dramatise mechanisms of self-betrayal and the sacrifice of personal fulfilment to the gods of conformity. *Another Country* (1962) and *Tell Me How Long the Train's Been Gone* (1968) deal with characters who rebel against the destiny society would prescribe for them, though not all survive to give that rebellion meaningful form. In *Another Country* failures in love are redeemed through a pattern of atonement whereby the characters commit themselves to personal relationships which defy social prejudice, whilst the tone of the later novel is angrier, in keeping with its wider focus on a rebellion which reaches out from individual lives across the whole social and political plane.

Of all Baldwin's novels, least attention is paid to *Giovanni's Room*. Most frequently it is dismissed as thinly disguised autobiography or condemned for an alleged narrowness of theme and treatment. The first person confessional style naturally encourages the view of David as Baldwin's surrogate, and given the autobiographical nature of *Go Tell It on the Mountain* and that like his protagonist Baldwin had turned to Europe in search of greater personal freedom, it is perhaps inevitable that, like *The City and the Pillar*, this novel should have been misconstrued as a 'lurid memoir'. Undoubtedly it draws heavily upon the author's own experience, but this does not justify its relegation to the category of 'unprocessed raw material of art'—which is how Robert Bone has described it.[5] The confessional style is the necessary expression of David's character and situation and it is unfair to ignore Baldwin's conscious artistic intention and to treat his hero simply as a vehicle for psycho-analytical speculation on his author's own sexual dilemma.

David is successfully presented as a representative white American, one whose experiences dramatise the thesis Baldwin expounds in 'A Question of Identity' (1954), regarding a particular generation of young Americans drawn to the bohemian life in Paris, 'the city where everyone loses his head, and his morals, lives through at least one *histoire d'amour . . .* and thumbs his nose at the Puritans'.[6] But as this surfeit of freedom unnerves the traveller, 'he begins to long for the prison of home—home then becoming the place where questions are not asked' (p. 110). David fits into this pattern, attempting at all costs to preserve his 'innocence', a quality Baldwin associates specifically with white Americans. In the essay 'The Black Boy looks at the White Boy', he argues:

> The things that most white people imagine they can salvage from the storm of life is really, in sum, their innocence. . . . I am afraid that most of the white people I have ever known impressed me as being in the grip of a weird nostalgia, dreaming of a vanished state of security and order.
>
> (p. 172)

In David's case, 'innocence' is a version of himself he wishes to recover as a defence against the guilty secret of his homosexual drives; although he goes to Paris, typically, to 'find' himself, what he hopes to discover are proofs of his innocence. A tourist on a psychological level, he flirts with the gay underworld to persuade himself that his 'home' is not there. However, his sense of his identity is shattered when he falls in love with the Italian barman, Giovanni, and he makes a last desperate bid to secure himself from homosexual guilt by committing himself to his relationship with an American girl, Hella.

Far from constituting a self-indulgent fictionalised memoir, narrow in theme and treatment, *Giovanni's Room* stands in ironic relation to that genre perfected by Henry James, where the American innocent is put to the test of experience in the Old World. Indeed, it is a genre which continues to be redefined in homosexual terms, as is evident in the work of another American writer, Donald Windham. His novel, *Two People* (1965) deals with the love affair between Forrest, a young American business man, temporarily estranged from his wife, and Marcello, a seventeen-year-old Italian youth living in Rome, who is undergoing a crisis in his relations with his family. Their affair is presented as a stage in self-discovery; it offers a refuge from their problems, a basis from which to re-appraise their need for the 'closeness and security' of their respective homes, and (perhaps unrealistically) it allows each to develop or to resume heterosexual relationships with a new confidence.

David and Hella exemplify the process Baldwin discerns in the experience of fellow American expatriates. Both, ostensibly, dedicate themselves to a quest for personal identity through sexual freedom and the bohemian life, but when this raises questions which are too threatening they seek refuge in convention, looking backwards to America to restore some sense of order and security in their lives. Reflecting on the 'peculiar innocence and confidence' of their early nights of 'fun', David admits that 'nothing is more unbearable, once one has it, than freedom. I suppose this was why I asked her to marry me: to give myself something to be moored to'.[7] Hella arrives at a similar conclusion. She is a student of painting until she realises her lack of talent and is ready to throw herself in the Seine, she thinks of herself as a modern, independent woman until the novelty of promiscuity palls and commitment to someone like David seems the only alternative. There is little evidence of passion in their relationship and marriage is a calculated choice. On her return from Spain where she had gone to consider David's proposal, Hella communicates in clichéd terms which betray her apologetic retreat into convention and her lack of genuine feeling. She does not want to 'miss the boat' and, like all good heroines, she confesses, 'I'm not really the emancipated girl I try to be at all. I guess I just want a man to come home to me every night. . . . I want to start having babies. In a way, it's really all I'm good for' (pp. 92–3). Her fears of not being a 'real' woman coincide with David's fears of not being a 'real' man. He feels as if he had fallen out of some 'web of safety' and longs to be on the inside again, 'with my manhood unquestioned, watching my woman putting my children to bed' (p. 79). The 'innocence' the American couple seek to preserve is juxtaposed with the sufferings of Giovanni. His despair underlines the self-indulgence of their fears of 'missing the boat', their 'fun', their fashionable existentialism and their suicidal fancies.

The framework of David's relationships with Hella and with Giovanni is underpinned by religious and metaphysical dimensions which are suggested by the comment Jacques makes when David tells him how he wishes that Giovanni could have stayed happily in Italy and sung his life away. 'Nobody can stay in the garden of Eden . . . I wonder why' (p. 23), Jacques remarks. The question continues to haunt David who reflects that if everyone has their own Eden, 'they have scarcely seen their garden before they see the flaming sword. Then, perhaps, life only offers the choice of remembering the garden or forgetting it. Either, or: it takes strength to remember, it takes another kind of strength to forget, it takes a hero to do both' (p. 23). The passage crystallizes the novel's underlying dialogue of extremes: innocence and guilt, heaven and hell, cleanliness and dirt, ideal love and perfunctory sex.

Both David and Giovanni have their own private memory of an Eden, and the sword which bars their return. David remembers his adolescent love for his best friend, Joey, and the idyllic summer weekend they spent alone together. The morning after a playful wrestling match had turned into ecstatic love-making, David's puritan conscience had struck such fear and remorse into him that the 'beautiful creation' of Joey's body, for which his body still longed, became 'the black opening of a cavern . . . in which I would lose my manhood' (p. 11). From then on, David had been a stranger to himself, his father and to all around him. He willed himself to forget Joey, he buried his sense of guilt and battened down the hatches on his psyche. Where Giovanni is concerned, expulsion from Eden came when the girl he loved in his home village gave birth to his grey, twisted, dead son. As in the case of David, it was as if life had played him a cruel trick to put his manhood in question. He had raged against this treachery, spat on the crucifix, and walked out for good on his girl, his family and his village. Both men had taken refuge in an extreme attitude to life. Giovanni surrendered himself to the 'dirty world', to despair, as if to do penance for his sins; David had run away from what Giovanni later describes as the 'stink of love', in order to safeguard his purity and moral 'cleanliness'. But through their love for each other, they are given the chance to abandon their narrow philosophies, to end their self-imposed exiles, to enter into what Baldwin insists upon as the necessary dialectic of joy and pain in any relationship, and so to make a 'home' for themselves in the world.

For David, the 'dirty world' from which he seeks to dissociate himself is symbolised by the homosexual milieu into which his friend, Jacques, occasionally introduces him. If indeed that world is 'dirty', then David's attitudes and behaviour help to make it so. His efforts to prove to himself and to the company of Guillaume's bar that he does not 'belong' are such that we share Jacques' relish at the moment when David's '*immaculate* manhood' is compromised by his evident attraction to the new barman, Giovanni. Until then, the American has been the picture of unsullied heterosexuality, enjoying the envy he arouses, and bolstering up his sense of his own masculinity by the process Baldwin refers to elsewhere as the 'invention' of 'faggots'. David, who exploits Jacques' loneliness and despises Guillaume, sneers at the inmates of this 'peacock garden' which 'sounded like a barnyard' (p. 24)—a caricature of that lost Eden.

If the gay underworld seems squalid and shameful, this is not depicted as any exclusive concomitant of homosexuality. Hella's account of the pensioned widows in Spain ogling anything in trousers, and David's abuse of the American girl, Sue, to convince himself of his continued ability to 'perform', demonstrate a complementary lovelessness in the heterosexual world. Furthermore, David's contempt for the homosexual milieu indicates his failure to understand and to see beyond the promiscuity to the pain of someone like Jacques. Jacques, like a mentor, seeks to make David face up to his own involvement in meaningless sex and recommends him to think of those encounters when he 'pretended nothing was happening down there in the dark' (p. 45). If Jacques' life is shameful, then it is partly because of those who like David are too ashamed to love.

Giovanni is presented as the living example of Jacques' conviction that homosexuality is not in itself 'dirty'. He is encountered *within* that underworld, his dignity, freshness and vitality framed by the gaudy antics of its inmates and their sordid dramas of prostitution—like a figure in a religious icon, with 'all the light of that gloomy tunnel trapped around his head' (p. 36). Jacques voices Baldwin's positive philosophy of homosexual love when he urges David to seize his opportunity for happiness: 'you can make your time together anything but dirty . . . if you will *not* be ashamed, if you will only *not* play it safe' (p.46). Given the contrast between the customers of Guillaume's bar and the two heroes, one might expect their love affair to be idealised. Indeed, for the

41

author sympathetic to homosexuality, the temptation must be to disprove the death of Romantic literature since any pair of homosexual lovers has an in-built potential for a dramatic, if not tragic, destiny. But with the exception of the bright haloes and starry-eyed fatality of their encounter (Giovanni's eyes actually are 'unbelievably like morning stars'), Baldwin depicts the more complex reality of such a relationship and it is unfair to accuse him, as does Irving Howe, of 'whipped cream sentimentalism'[8] whenever he deals with homosexual love.

The first flush of passion is quickly put to the test of everyday living by the need to give their relationship some framework other than the walls of Giovanni's room. Though David, with his economic security, feels the burden of Giovanni's salvation to be on him, it is clear that Giovanni has the more onerous task of rescuing David from the workings of sexual shame. The Italian's frankness, warmth and uninhibited desires are set against the other's duplicity, reserve and feelings of guilt. These differences form part of a cultural dialectic, the Mediterranean temperament being pitted against the North American in a confrontation between pagan and puritan outlooks on life. Whereas Giovanni is ready to scorn the 'dirty words' that David's countrymen would apply to their situation, the latter is crippled by conventional morality. David tells himself: 'The beast which Giovanni had awakened in me would never go to sleep again; but one day I would not be with Giovanni any more. And would I then, like all the others, find myself turning and following all kinds of boys down God knows what dark avenues, into what dark places?' (p. 64), revealing a fondness for melodrama and self-pity.

Giovanni's room comes to symbolise all the complex facets of their situation, and not, as Colin MacInnes supposes, 'the sterility and self-destruction of homosexual love',[9] At the outset, the room is a sanctuary from prying eyes and life there seems idyllic, out of time, as if it were taking place beneath the sea. But, for David, as Hella's return becomes imminent, the dimensions of the room shrink, it seems claustrophobic, a trap, an interrogation chamber. It has become a waiting room, where time hangs like a sword threatening to fall—anticipating those separate rooms where David and Giovanni will wait under the shadow of the guillotine. In retrospect, David, who attempted to think of it always as *Giovanni's* room, admits that it is like every room in which he has ever been or ever will be. That is to say, he is trapped in his own compartmentalised ways of thinking, in the prison of his own flesh.

David thinks of the dirt and debris in the room as a token of Giovanni's 'regurgitated life', not just a matter of temperament but of 'punishment and grief' (p. 66). Thus the room suggests more than the material shape of Giovanni's poverty, it is a chosen hell, a sign of his refusal to take responsibility for his own life and of his surrender to despair. It is a plea to David to transform his corner of that 'dirty world'. As David remarks, 'I understood why Giovanni had wanted me and had brought me to his last retreat. I was to destroy this room and give to Giovanni a new and better life' (p. 67). The transient feel of the room is contrasted with the idea of 'home' in the novel and with the desire to translate temporary sexual relationships into secure commitments. But David, a tourist to the last, will work only to make his stay more congenial. And though he resents playing 'housewife' to Giovanni the 'bread-winner', in reality David is the one with the means for them to leave the room and transform their situation. He tells himself he is right to abandon Giovanni by projecting his fears of a lasting homosexual commitment upon the room itself: it is a *maid's* room, squalid and dirty, echoing his view of the underworld and the 'black cavern' which seems once more to be closing in on his precious manhood. It even has its own mocking reminder of the realm he has forsaken; on the wall is the image of a lady in a hoop skirt and a man in knee breeches, perpetually walking together in a garden of roses. When his father's letters ('Dear Butch . . .') and finally Hella's return combine in urging him to 'come home', he loses his nerve, repeats his adolescent flight from Joey, from the 'stink of love'—and also from its redeeming possibilities.

The two men regress to their separate spheres: Giovanni to squalor and despair, David to salvage his 'purity' and to 'cleanse' himself. But like Giovanni, David enters into an artificial hell of his own making—as the name of his fiancée intimates. Giovanni once told him, 'You don't have a home until you leave it and then, when you have left it, you can never go back' (p. 88). David is fated to bear witness to this comment for when he is reunited with Hella, it is 'like a familiar darkened room in which I fumbled to find the light' (p. 91), an ironic reversal of his earlier longing to be safe in a lighted room with his manhood unquestioned and his

43

woman putting his children to bed. Furthermore, his sad realisation that Giovanni's room was where he really belonged is framed
by the novel's recurrent image of him in the deserted rooms of the
house in the South of France where, abandoned by Hella, he cleans
away the last traces of his presence.

In his essay 'The Male Prison' (included in *Nobody Knows My
Name*), Baldwin criticises Gide for separating sex and love in his
life, for the irresponsibility of his homosexuality and his attempt
to have his pleasures without 'paying' for them. Similarly, David
contrives to escape the responsibilities of his sexual love, to obtain
for himself temporary pleasures. In the same essay, Baldwin also
states that today's homosexual 'can only save himself by the most
tremendous exertion of all his forces from falling into an underworld in which he never meets either men or women, where it is
impossible to have either a lover or a friend, where the possibility
of genuine human involvement has altogether ceased' (p. 131).
This passage touches upon the dilemma of both his characters.
Giovanni casts himself to this underworld, to be used and defiled
by it until, as once before, a passionate gesture of defiance seals
his fate; in the past he spat on the crucifix, now he murders Guillaume, the symbolic lord of this 'dirty' realm. David reaches his
impasse by a different route: fleeing from love and its suffering
he becomes, in Giovanni's words, 'a lover who is neither man nor
woman, nothing that I can ever know or touch' (p. 104), a prophecy confirmed by Hella when she eventually finds David in a gay
bar. However, Giovanni's death is the ritual sacrifice which saves
David from the 'male prison', the tragic source of his self-knowledge and ultimately the catharsis from which a real spiritual purification can be hoped for. The long night of penance which shapes
the novel, is an agonising endorsement of the love for Giovanni
that he once sought to deny and more especially of Baldwin's own
belief in the paradoxical beauty and dignity of suffering. David
attempts the heroic role of bringing himself both to remember and
to forget his garden of Eden—and so he walks off into the morning with 'a dreadful weight of hope' (p. 127).

As in *The City and the Pillar*, the emphasis in this novel is upon
the unrealised possibilities of homosexual love. In both cases, a
homosexual Eden, briefly glimpsed, is destroyed by the combined
action of a rigid masculine code and a puritan legacy of guilt.
Neither Jim nor David can sustain adult relationships and both are

paralysed by memories of a past innocence. But this backward-looking stance, embodied in the form of these two novels, also has the effect of introducing an element of melodrama and self-pity into the act of remembering. Furthermore, the murder that serves as a climactic event imparts to the preceding action a sense of fatality which sometimes obscures our view of the heroes as victims of their own limitations. The individual's responsibility for his own destiny is also shifted to some extent to the homosexual underground itself, this being portrayed by both Vidal and Baldwin as a destructive, hellish domain—perhaps as facile an oversimplification as those contrasting images of a lost Eden. However, *Giovanni's Room* is far more powerful in its impact than Vidal's novel. It presents a genuinely tragic love affair between two men whose characters are vividly imagined and whose passion and suffering engage our sympathy in a way that Jim Willard, who seems insipid by comparison, never could.

Another Country was received by many critics as further confirmation of the opinion that Baldwin, whilst superb as an essayist, failed in his fiction to match the early promise of *Go Tell It on the Mountain*. There would seem to be some correlation between this decline in critical esteem and the increasing prominence given to the homosexual theme in his novels—a subject only hinted at in that first novel and tackled only rarely in his essays. Baldwin himself recalls publishers advising him that *Giovanni's Room* might 'wreck' his career and his agent telling him to 'burn' the book.[10] Indeed, one reviewer was to urge him to go back to 'American subjects'.[11] In 1962 when *Another Country* was published, racial issues, it could be argued, were an acceptable liberal cause to the literary establishment, whereas homosexuality was not. Eric, the homosexual hero of *Another Country*, is generally singled out as the prime reason for the novel's 'failure' and his crucial, redemptive role has attracted heated criticism.

Homosexuality is just one of the 'countries' to which Baldwin transports us in this novel, and it is the act of journeying that he invests with significance, not the destination. We move away from the familiar world and the utopian vision of America, miniaturised in New York as 'that city which the people from Heaven had made their home',[12] to a Dantesque underworld of poverty, anguish, racial hatred, promiscuity and despair. It is a journey away from everyday classifications of people—'black', 'white',

45

'faggot', 'whore'—towards individual worlds which render this initial geography obsolete and dangerous. It is only by submitting to an inner journeying, the novel suggests, that we are able to enter into our own reality as well as that of others and to glimpse a further country beyond the suffering this process of self-discovery involves—that of love.

Rufus Scott, a young black musician, crushed by the forces of racism, the loneliness of the city and his own angry pride, becomes a savage comment on his country's ideals of freedom and brotherhood when he jumps to his death, from the George Washington Bridge. The city landscape through which he wanders during his last days presents images of a frenzied loneliness and a breakdown of communication which form a resumé of his experiences: the jazzmen unable to reach their audience; the loveless ghetto of prostitution; the crowded subway trains where each traveller transforms his inch of space into an 'isolation cell'. Scenes from the past illuminate his aimless journey through the streets and focus upon his broken relationship with a poor white woman, Leona, which has brought him to despair. Even in Greenwich Village where Rufus had moved to escape the poverty-trap of Harlem and had begun to make a name for himself as a drummer, he found only a semblance of freedom from racial and sexual convention. He and Leona could not walk out together without seeing themselves reflected in the eyes of passers-by as the 'black stud' and his 'fallen woman'. Rufus and his friends have internalised such prejudices too, and the giving or receiving of affection is inextricably bound up with sexual fears and fantasies. Leona, who fled the brutality of her husband and craves gentleness from Rufus is fated nonetheless to be the target for more violence. When they first meet, his 'weapon' shoots 'venom' into the 'milk white bitch' and he wants, initially, to shut his mind to her 'story', for this would involve his entering into her individual complexity and sharing her suffering.

Like the saxophonist he recalls from his last gig, Rufus hurls at the world the question 'Do you love me?' (p. 4). But such is his history of rejection that he can place no trust in any of the answers that he receives. For him to love, is to open himself to all his doubts and fears as to whether he is wanted for himself, whether he is worth loving. Even though they isolate themselves from black and white communities alike, he and Leona become helpless victims caught up in a pattern of self-destruction which duplicates those

forces which they had hoped to shut out. Leona has only platitudes and dumb devotion with which to defend herself against
Rufus's jealous rages and hypersensitivity to insult; if Rufus brings
about her insanity, her weakness and masochistic submission drain
him of his strength and direct him towards suicide. They drag
one another down and, at the same time, are sacrificial victims to
society's ignorance and prejudice.

Rufus's journey into despair precipitates a similar movement
in those who were close to him and the remainder of the novel
focuses upon the efforts of this group of friends, including Rufus's
sister, Ida, to come to terms with his death. In their own lives, Cass,
Vivaldo, and Eric seek to atone for failures of understanding which
Rufus's suicide has so dramatically brought home to them, whilst
Ida, like her brother, is drawn into a conflict between the desire
for love and for revenge. These characters involve one another in
a chain reaction until, within the permutations of their relationships, a kind of rehabilitation takes shape.

For Cass and Vivaldo this inward journey is set in motion as
they travel into Harlem to Rufus's funeral. The bleak streets stir in
them a sombre mood as if Harlem were that other country they
had protected themselves from knowing in the person of Rufus.
Although Vivaldo is no stranger there, his excursions to the black
ghetto were from self-regarding motives; they were contrived attempts to advertise his alienation from his own Brooklyn background. Similarly, his friendship with Rufus was limited by his
desire to identify himself vicariously with another outcast. Cass
is the critic of the shallow thinking he displays in his complaints
that Rufus's family did not really accept him despite his creden-
tials as a slum child and his conviction that he could comfort Ida.
She also feels that Vivaldo romanticises the horrors of his Brooklyn past—as recollected in the account of his part in an attack
on a young homosexual—and denies the darker side of his nature
while seeming to examine his secrets. Vivaldo dreams of rescuing
Ida from her Harlem ghetto and reconciling her to the world in
the warmth of his love, but she also has the power to deliver him
from his childish view of life. Ida, who is like her brother in many
ways, affords Vivaldo the opportunity to recognise and to redeem
some part of his failure with Rufus. His previous relationships
with women have been superficial and he had preferred to travel
up to Harlem to 'pay' for his pleasures with black prostitutes. But

although Ida engages him in an inward journeying which is at once more perilous and more profound, by her prostituting of herself to further her career as a singer she is also to make Vivaldo 'pay' for his pleasures in a deeper sense.

Vivaldo's apprenticeship to life is mirrored by the difficulties he has with his writing. His novel is about Brooklyn and it is to be presumed that for subject matter he is drawing on his own past. Yet his characters seem to resist his efforts to know them—like Rufus and Ida, they do not trust him. On the night Rufus goes to him for help, Vivaldo eventually feels tired of the troubles of real people, 'He wanted to get back to the people he was inventing, whose troubles he could bear' (p. 56). But the artistic block he develops corresponds to his unwillingness to know in himself and others what might disturb him, as when he shies away from knowing what life is really like for Rufus and Ida and from the sexual and racial tensions inherent in the love he offers them. Appropriately, he fantasises that Ida is in league with his characters, that she ordains their silence and refusal to surrender their privacy. Nonetheless, Vivaldo's love matures in the school of suffering to which Ida leads him. At first he strives 'to strike deeper into that incredible country in which, like the princess of fairy tales, sealed in a high tower . . . she paced her secret round of secret days' (pp. 135–36), but the path from romance to reality only reveals those secrets to be the harsh facts of the racial hatreds she nurtures and their expression in his betrayal. As he is finally allowed into her private world to listen to her sorrowful confession, the end of his apprenticeship is signified as a long sought-for detail in his novel falls, miraculously, into place.

Cass is another social rebel, having rejected her upper class New England background to marry Richard who is of Polish immigrant stock and without money. Inspired by her faith in him, he succeeds as a teacher and as a writer, so that in contrast with other characters, Cass would seem to have no cause for dissatisfaction— with her two children, her devoted husband and his literary success, the future looks bright. However, the journey to Harlem casts a chill over her, seeming to confront her with threatening images of a hidden chaos in her own life. She is destined to feel the weight of her advice to Rufus concerning his guilt over Leona: 'I think, that we all commit our crimes. The thing is not to lie about them—to try to understand what you have done, why you have done it' (p. 63). Although Rufus is too far enmeshed in his misery to heed her words, here Cass indicates the path she and her friends must take if they are to atone for their 'crimes' and redeem Rufus's death through their own lives. In her case, she must face her secret realisation that Richard's book is a fraud, but she must also face the fact that she has helped to make him what he now is.

In contrast with this bleak portrait of New York, Baldwin presents the image of two lovers, Eric and Yves, in a warm sunlit Mediterranean garden. But this glimpse of a far off country of love scarcely supports the accusation that the author proselytises in favour of homosexuality. Eric (a braver and wiser version of David in *Giovanni's Room*) has made a commitment which has yet to be tested back in New York where Yves is to join him, and the romanticism and sentimentality of the present moment is qualified as Eric's mind swings from past to future, facing up to the longer journey in which this is only an interlude. Yves shares his conviction that, 'In order not to lose all that he had gained, he had to move forward and risk it all' (p. 176). The idyllic setting does not contrive a positive image of homosexuality, then, but suggests the provisional rewards of a hard-won trust and honesty in a particular relationship which has transformed the lives of the two men concerned. At the same time, it is a symbol of transient, superficial pleasures which must be sacrificed in the struggle towards a more permanent union.

In terms of the novel's symmetrical grouping of relationships, the love between Eric and Yves provides another framework within which the mistakes of the past can possibly be repaired in the present. Yves, with his combination of toughness and vulnerability, reminds Eric of Rufus, his former lover. Although the suffering in which the latter had involved Eric had been the cause of his flight to Paris, it had also given him the necessary strength to deal with Yves. Yet Eric has by no means arrived at some complacent plateau of self-knowledge; instead, he testifies to the author's belief that facing up to oneself is a constant and painful process. It is for this reason and not because of his sexuality that Eric represents the heroic ideal in the novel. Eric's homosexuality gives him a superiority to other characters only in so far as it has involved him in an additional burden of suffering.

Eric's sexual experiences bear comparison with those of Rufus.

Both are weighed down by the role of symbolising a coveted, despised or feared sexuality and their reduction in the eyes of the world to exclusively sexual beings makes their search for love all the more agonising and urgent. Yet the role in which they are cast gives them sharp insights into the hypocrisies of society and a cynical sense of the way its surface divisions and classifications are continually contradicted at a deeper level to create an underworld where sexual contacts proliferate but only add to the sum of loneliness. The realm of bleak physical exchanges seen in Rufus's wanderings through the city streets and in Vivaldo's descriptions of battles where 'the girl wished to be awakened but was terrified of the unknown' (p. 103), is analysed most fully in Eric's examination of past encounters where the sexual act resulted only in the alienation of the parties involved.

Eric's formative years were spent in Alabama where his erotic friendships outraged racial as well as sexual prejudices in the small town in which he grew up. Like Vivaldo, his rebellion took the form of identification with the outcast black community. But after the failure of his relationship with Rufus, Eric recognises that he too has been guilty of relating to a fantasy rather than to the complicated individual his lover is. His homosexuality, like Rufus's colour, takes him into society's chaotic underworld and leads him to an understanding of its hidden secrets. He reflects on the 'army of lonely men' who made him the 'receptacle of an anguish which he could scarcely believe was in the world' (p. 163). Eric is credited with a vision of a universal longing for tenderness and affection between males which has been 'frozen' and placed under taboo by the heterosexual orthodoxy. Such men surrender to him, in darkness, the burdensome role of sexual aggressor, giving themselves up to passivity and the illusion of receiving affection from another man. Yet shame and fear condemn these contacts to the quality of dreams, imitations of love which procure only momentary relief. Finally, Eric rejects the lovelessness and sexual hypocrisy of this double life, seeking to formulate his own existentialist position:

> He knew that he had no honour which the world could recognise. His life, passions, trials, loves, were, at worst, filth, and at best, disease in the eyes of the world, and crimes in the eyes of his countrymen. There were no standards for him except those he could make for himself.
>
> (p. 165)

These values are discovered and given shape in his relationship with Yves, the 'guest' for whom Eric 'established a precarious order in the heart of his chaos' (p. 166). He displays a patient willingness to enter into the reality of the other person, a determination to avoid the 'common, brutal bargain' and to overcome the fear of vulnerability that inhibits love—he embarks upon a courtship, in fact. Yves, a young hustler in flight from a whorish mother, presents almost as great a challenge as did Rufus. His background is scarcely likely to inspire in him faith in love, yet the chaste friendship of the two men is transformed when, after a time of warily testing one another's affections, they visit the cathedral town of Chartres. Baldwin uses the image of the cathedral in a way that recalls D. H. Lawrence's presentation of Lincoln Cathedral in *The Rainbow* to symbolise the transfiguration of ordinary life and the apprehension of some other mysterious realm. The shadow of Chartres Cathedral lies over the town like a warning and like a question mark, but also as a benediction upon the two lovers who meet its challenge to bring meaning into life. When they do finally make love each becomes a gateway to that unknown country where, in a reversal of the Eden myth they experience a sense of innocence regained, and where sex takes on a religious mystery of vows exchanged to affirm homosexual pride in place of shame.

The role Eric subsequently plays in the lives of Cass and Vivaldo is what critics commonly identify as the novel's major weakness. Robert Bone's comments in *The Negro Novel in America* are typical:

> To most, homosexuality will seem rather an evasion than an affirmation of human truth, the novel substitutes for the illusions of white supremacy those of homosexual love.[13]

Bone insists that Eric's redemptive powers cannot be taken seriously since the latter regards heterosexual love merely as 'superior callisthenics' and, while protesting that it is not the business of the literary critic to debate the merits of homosexuality, he proceeds with an alliterative sneer to denounce Eric for offering 'rectal revelation' and 'salvation through sodomy' to unregenerate heterosexuals. Yet this is a sly misrepresentation of Eric's involvements with Cass and Vivaldo; Eric does not proselytise for his sexual preference, but learns as much from his friends as they from him. His return to New York throws him back into the difficulties, the isolation and the remembered shames of the past. 'His only means of navigation' (p. 177) is the light that the experience with Yves causes to shine from him, but this in turn is threatened by the task of learning to live in the city once more. Mutual revelation and confession form the keynote of this last section, as the common bond with Rufus draws his friends together and brings them to face up to the past. Whereas Eric's relationship with Rufus had previously posed unspoken barriers, now it is acknowledged, giving Eric the further confidence to discuss Yves and his impending arrival. The isolation and secrecy that had had such destructive effects in the past is replaced by honesty and a process of mutual rehabilitation. If Rufus perished for the lack of a friend, Cass, Vivaldo and Eric help one another to surmount the various crises in their emotional lives.

The 'light' that seems to emanate from Eric inspires in his friends new confidence in their own weary battles; it makes him attractive to them and commands their respect. At the same time, this confidence is only achieved by a process in which relationships are tested and put at risk. Cass feels as though 'she might be able to help him endure the weight of the boy who had such power over him' (p. 255), but it is not so much her compassion as her desirability that provides Eric with a further challenge to self-knowledge and a trial of his strength. Their affair extends a temptation to opt for safety and to escape the fear inherent in his love for Yves, the fear that at some point in the future the youth will no longer need him and he will drop back into the city's promiscuous underworld. If he emerges with the view of heterosexual love as 'superior callisthenics', this is offered not as a general truth but in the context of a conversation with Vivaldo where Eric reaffirms his personal commitment to the anguish, terror and joy of a sexual relationship with a man. For Cass, the affair secures for her a sympathetic friend and a renewed sense of herself as an individual. At the same time, the act of putting her ailing marriage in jeopardy clarifies her feelings for Richard and makes him face up to the extent of their estrangement. What is at fault in the presentation of the relationship between Eric and Cass is not the conclusion the former draws but the unconvincing speed and the air of fatality with which the affair gets under way.

Against the accusation that Baldwin engages in propaganda for a minority sexuality stands the love of Vivaldo and Ida, corresponding as it does to Eric's conviction that suffering as well as joy is inevitable whenever a relationship involves one's deepest self. Far from converting him to homosexuality, Vivaldo's 'rectal revelation' frees him from his fears of it and from the 'manly' shame that held back any expression of his love for Rufus on an occasion when he knew it might have saved his friend from despair. In a scene which recreates this episode, Vivaldo, now himself in despair over Ida, wakes from a dream about Rufus, one of vengeance and forgiveness, to seek comfort in Eric's 'proud' embrace. Each man proves to the other that he is worthy of love at a time when both, in their respective battles, are in danger of succumbing to sexual fears and guilts. Revelation comes with the act of daring to know another person: Vivaldo goes forth strengthened to meet that challenge in Ida, meanwhile Eric has defeated the shames and anxieties which New York had reawakened in him. From this point onwards, he, Cass and Vivaldo will support and bear witness to one another. At the close of the novel, each is in the position of having put his or her 'house in order', to wait patiently for the 'guest' of love to return. 'Toward Bethlehem', as this last section is entitled, implies a hard-won faith in renewal for 'the city which the people from Heaven had made their home' and, appropriately, the novel concludes with the arrival of Yves—who descends from those skies bringing his message of hope.

It is understandable that by choosing a Southern, white homosexual as his hero, Baldwin should have incurred the wrath of militant black critics such as Eldridge Cleaver. His motives are perhaps expressed in the film in which Eric plays a small but crucial part. Like Baldwin's own novel, it is 'one of those politics, sex and vengeance dramas', but one where endless arguments as to how the world's ills ought to be solved are eclipsed by the director's strategic placing of Eric's face, with its compelling combination of strength and gentleness. Strength and gentleness, toughness and vulnerability, these are the qualities the major characters struggle to balance, and suggest Baldwin's prescription for survival—ideally, the courage to combat society's definitions and one's own internalised shames, while preserving an openness of heart and a willingness to surrender oneself in love. And if, in this instance, the author places more faith in the individual's capacity for growth than in political action, that struggle—given his characters' artistic ambitions—is not without its effects on others. Set against the evasions of a novelist like Richard is the affirmation of intimate communication in the world of jazz musicians and singers, in Vivaldo's writing, and in Eric's acting. This is reiterated in the contrast between the desolate, chaotic canvasses of the Museum of Modern Art and the intense personal style of Bessie Smith, whose songs, with their unique mixture of hope and despair, run as a refrain through the novel and act as a chorus to its action.

The emphasis on individual growth and on the therapeutic role of art gives way, somewhat uneasily, in *Tell Me How Long the Train's Been Gone* (1968) to an endorsement of the revolutionary fervour of black militancy. However, these sentiments are presented unconvincingly within the framework of a homosexual relationship between an aging, famous black actor, Leo Proudhammer, and a young revolutionary, Christopher, who is inspired by love to find his vocation in guns and the preparation for violent struggle. The 'birth' of Black Christopher is supposed to confer a retrospective meaning and purpose to Proudhammer's life, yet nowhere do we see the reality of the relationship between the two men—indeed, much of the novel is concerned with Proudhammer's early hardships and his long road to fame and fortune. When Black Christopher finally appears, the serenity of their love rings false and he seems more a product of Baldwin's wishful thinking than a consistent and believable individual. Black militants and homosexuals make for strange bedfellows and, in a novel where large sections are devoted to the perils of being a 'sissy' in the tough Harlem ghetto, the author stretches our credulity in suggesting there are no deeply-rooted conflicts in the love of these two men. The concept of manhood which the black militants have developed is not noted for revolutionary fervour where sexual roles are concerned, and in so far as homosexuality is looked on as the 'white man's disease', one suspects that for the black homosexual, however famous, their 'train' left long ago.

NOTES

1. Included in *Nobody Knows My Name* (1964). (London: Corgi, 1965), p. 172. Subsequent page references are to this edition.
2. Leslie Fiedler, *The Return of the Vanishing American* (1968; London, 1972), p. 18.

3. G. M. Sarotte, *Comme un Frère, Comme un Amant* (Paris, 1976), p. 117.

4. *James Baldwin Nikki Giovanni, A Dialogue* (1973; London, 1975), pp. 88–9.

5. Robert Bone, *The Negro Novel in America* (New Haven, London: Yale University Press, 1966), p. 226.

6. Included in *Notes of a Native Son* (1964). (London: Corgi, 1965), p. 108. Subsequent page references are to this edition.

7. James Baldwin, *Giovanni's Room* (1957). (London: Corgi, 1963), p. 8. Subsequent page references are to this edition.

8. Irving Howe, 'James Baldwin: At Ease in Apocolypse', *Harper's Magazine*, No. 1420 (September 1968), p. 237.

9. Colin MacInnes, 'The Dark Angel: The Writings of James Baldwin', *Encounter* (August 1963), p. 27.

10. See *The Furious Passage of James Baldwin*, by Fern Marja Eckman (New York, 1966), p. 139.

11. Anthony West, in his review of *Giovanni's Room, The New Yorker* (November 10, 1956).

12. James Baldwin, *Another Country* (1963). (London: Corgi, 1965), p. 338. Subsequent page references are to this edition.

13. Robert Bone, *The Negro Novel in America* (New Haven, London: Yale University Press, 1966), p. 234.

3

Gothic Love: Truman Capote, Carson McCullers and JAMES PURDY

If the codified novel was once the only means of treating the homosexual theme and corresponded to the masks adopted in everyday life, so the image of a journey away from conventional society gives a characteristic form to novels that deal with the passage from self-concealment to self-expression. Nowadays this process is summed up in the gay liberation concept of 'coming out', but in the past 'going away' was the more likely starting point in the homosexual's assertion of his or her identity. Kerouac's Beats could take to the road out of sheer exuberance, but the homosexual breaks away as a result of more urgent motives and a more immediate sense of alienation.

The literary modes which succeeded the codified novel are those which portray extreme situations. In a period when homosexuals must fight for the right to form relationships at all, they are not likely to be accorded the luxury of ordinariness by being represented, say, in the comedy of manners with its scrutiny of domestic life—except perhaps as caricatures. Frequent recourse to the picaresque reflects the form into which homosexual experience is commonly forced. Apart from the fiction of Vidal and Baldwin in which social protest is shaped around the journeys and missions of their heroes, writers as different as Christopher Isherwood and John Rechy illustrate by their use of 'travelogue' frameworks the vagrant and exiled status of the homosexual. If the picaresque is one way of accommodating the *extraordinary* quality of homosexual life and the imperative to set out for 'another country', other novelists less preoccupied with social realism and direct protest involve us in a different kind of journey away from everyday life—to the private worlds of individuals trapped within their compulsions and sexual

56

obsessions. The haunting and sometimes frightening nature of their fictions has earned them the title of 'gothicists'.

Truman Capote, Carson McCullers and James Purdy have been linked in this manner as writers whose supposedly gothic imaginations seek out their material in the grotesque. However, the label of 'gothic writer' often conceals a distaste for the rendering of a homosexual theme. Leslie Fiedler, for example, waxes lyrical over 'innocent' homosexuality in classics of American literature, yet more conscious investigations of the subject elicit his sarcasm. He censures writers such as Truman Capote and Tennessee Williams as 'Effete Dandies' and Homosexual Decadents', and others such as Carson McCullers are identified with a recognisable Southern homosexual style: 'pseudo-magical, pseudo-religious, pseudo gothic'.[1] And even though James Purdy comes from the Mid-West, critics are equally fond of dubbing him with the same 'gothic' label.[2]

To denigrate a novel for its gothicism is to level a charge of irrelevance, to imply a perverse neglect of the common walks of life in favour of some abnormal world of ghosts and demons. Yet, in the public mind, homosexuality itself is essentially 'gothic'—a question of violated taboos, dark secrets, guilts and fears. Certainly, some novelists might pander to this view, creating fictions that permit readers to flirt vicariously with the homosexual spectres of their dreams or nightmares. Such an approach, playing on prejudice and morbid curiosities, would indeed be in line with the original tactics of the gothic novel, and would allow for many a cheap thrill before a peepshow of freakish individuals. Truman Capote, in his first novel, *Other Voices, Other Rooms* (1948), might be accused of such a ploy, but the works of Carson McCullers and James Purdy make quite different appeals to the reader.

It is scarcely surprising that *Other Voices, Other Rooms* should have fostered the notion of a recognisable homosexual style, since the world it creates is animated by characteristics popularly attributed to the homosexual male: freakishness, affectation and effeminacy. The story of a young boy's discovery of his homosexuality is decked out with all the trappings of gothic melodrama. Joel Harrison Knox, with his girlish features and quaint manner, is cast in the cliché of the 'sissy'. He embarks on a journey to a bizarre new life when, after his mother's death, he must search out his father

who is living outside a remote Southern town. The locals drop om-
inous hints about his destination, Skully's Landing (Skull's Landing,
to them), and he has to travel through desolate countryside in the
company of a wizened, pygmy-like Negro to reach the decrepit
mansion which is to become his home. The house boasts every
gothic convenience: said to be sinking into the swampy ground,
it is ramshackle and ghostly, rife with secrets and legends. Joel's
step-mother proves cold and enigmatic; his father is shut away
and apparently ignores him; red tennis balls bounce into rooms
from nowhere; and from the garden, the boy catches sight of a
queer bewigged lady signalling to him from an upper window. But
these mysteries are not so much unravelled as compounded; doors
swing open on to inner 'rooms' and 'voices' that become steadily
more weird.

Despite the heavy-handed symbolism of the boy's quest for
identity, the novel remains very much on the level of a peepshow,
with Cousin Randolph, a homosexual and secret 'drag queen', as
one of its main exhibits. As such, it enlarges upon the game of
spying into strange houses under cover of darkness that Joel recalls playing. On one occasion he had been puzzled by the sight
of two men kissing one another in an ugly room—a phenomenon
he is to understand and move towards through his friendship with
Cousin Randolph. By Joel's identification with Randolph, Capote
implies that homosexuality is a failure of manliness—an 'ugly
room', yet one which fantasy can prettify. There is a mysterious
and somewhat arbitrary absence of the masculine principle in the
novel's world. The traditional models of manhood are either
crippled (Joel's father turns out to be a human vegetable), lost in
the past (like his grandfather, Major Knox, a hero of the Civil War,
and all the proud patriarchs who once brought their wives and
children to the nearby Cloud Hotel), or have vanished into legend
(like Pepe Alvarez, the prize-fighter, who haunts Randolph's memory and inspires him to dispatch letters to poste-restantes all over
the globe). Predictably, Joel fails the ritual test of virility when,
armed with an ancestral sword, he cannot slay the 'dragon'—in the
shape of a deadly snake with the eyes of his father—that blocks
his escape from Skully's Landing, and the task falls to Idabel, his
tomboyish girl companion. Renunciation of the outside world
eclipses any initiation into adulthood when Randolph takes the boy
to the Cloud Hotel, an even more spectacularly gothic ruin complete

with ghosts and gory legends. The journey, cementing the bond between Joel and Randolph, represents a ceremonious farewell not only to childhood innocence but also to dreams of becoming a man.

Randolph, with his talcumed face, yellow ringlets, hairless body, kimonos and artistic tastes, is simply a grown-up version of the 'sissy' stereotype. Pathetic and narcissistic, he is given to dressing up in women's clothes and acting out sentimental fantasies. Joel constructs similar compensations in an inner room of his mind; he conjures up snowy scenes he has never known and invents a strange assortment of characters, among them Mr Mystery, a magician. But instead of life displacing these desperate imaginings, it draws the boy further into an hallucinatory realm until, finally, that inner room and the world around him converge with Randolph's apparition at his upper window, where snow seems miraculously to be falling. Bewigged and beckoning once more, he is like Mr Mystery in one of his magical guises, come to rescue the boy from his loveless plight. In this oblique and coy manner, Joel's forthcoming sexual initiation is suggested and his identity confirmed as he moves off to join Randolph, casting a final glance at the self he is leaving behind.

Initiation is deemed here to be a question of choosing one's own 'voice' and 'room' from the display of peculiarities to which life has been narrowed down. Capote's characters are consistently bizarre and, as at the freak show that comes to town, Joel wanders through a gallery of grotesques. We learn of, or encounter: a giant Negro stevedore; a one-armed barber; a dwarf doctor; the hairy, ape-like proprietress of a bar; the pygmean Negro servant, Jesus Fever, who dies in a fit of giggles; his baby son, 'murdered' by a Persian cat; his daughter, Zoo Fever, who bears gruesome scars from her lunatic husband's attempt to slit her throat on their wedding night; a toothless hermit; a midget, Miss Wisteria, given to fondling young boys; Randolph's mother who grew an amazing beard. . . . With this lurid assortment, one might be forgiven for thinking Capote to be concocting a parody of all the paraphernalia of Southern Gothicism—a *Cold Comfort Farm* version of Faulkner, perhaps. Yet the relationship between Randolph and Joel is such that undoubtedly we are meant to take all of this seriously. Furthermore, the language of the novel reflects Randolph's own way of speaking; it is multi-layered, ornate, weighed down with detail, decoration and gaudy effect.

If homosexuality is one of the available 'rooms', then Capote's characterisation of it is essentially coy and negative. It derives its whimsical charm only from being set in a context of so many grotesques. Randolph's inner 'room' is presented in the teasing manner of Chinese boxes and when we are finally treated to the story of his 'doomed' love for Pepe Alvarez which has condemned Randolph as well as Joel's father to a living death, homosexuality is presented in melodramatic terms: 'But we are alone, darling child, terribly, isolated each from the other; so fierce is the world's ridicule we cannot speak or show our tenderness; for us, death is stronger than life, it pulls like a wind through the dark, all our cries burlesqued in joyless laughter; and with the garbage of loneliness stuffed down us until our guts burst bleeding green, we go screaming round the world, dying in our rented rooms, nightmare hotels, eternal homes of the transient heart'.[3]

For Capote, then, the homosexual's initiation into adult life is more of an act of resignation to a deathly, ghost-ridden existence. *Other Voices, Other Rooms*, with its florid style, aspires to the sophistication and dark poetry of Djuana Barnes's novel of lesbian love, *Nightwood* (1936), and like this earlier work, its gothic mode tends ultimately to reinforce the notion that homosexuality condemns one to a freakish, tormented world. This is not the case with either Carson McCullers or James Purdy, writers for whom the failure of love and not its category is the real gothic nightmare.

Carson McCullers' avowed theme of spiritual isolation is emphasised by her focus on individuals who because of physical defects, chosen modes of sexuality, colour, private obsessions, or even because of their very youthfulness, stand outside the conventional realm. Whereas Capote is fascinated by deformities and bizarre case-histories for their own sake, McCullers, like Purdy, transforms surface characteristics of alienation into more universal symbols. Her first novel, *The Heart is a Lonely Hunter* (1940), gives a positive, compassionate portrayal of one man's love for another. Singer's predicament as a deaf-mute and his yearnings for Antonapoulos, a fellow mute, create a powerful image of homosexual alienation without limiting itself to that meaning. Although the relationship between the two men carries no explicit sexual dimension, it conveys the author's conviction that love pays no heed to the formulas society would prescribe for it, and can be inspired by the most 'outlandish' people. Singer and Antonapoulos also symbolise her view of love as a precarious venture, typically a one-way direction of longing instead of an interplay of mutual response. Singer is never sure whether his friend understands him, and the more impassive and sphinx-like the Greek becomes, the more desperate are the other's attempts at communication. The androgynous, bisexual qualities of McCullers' characters have often been noted—from the boyish adolescent girls like Mick Kelly, to the man, like Biff Brannon with his 'feminine' tenderness and willingness to love 'anybody decent' who might come along. Above all, this author refuses to draw moral distinctions between different types of love; in *Clock Without Hands* (1961), her last novel, Jester Clane's crush on a school hero and afterwards on a Negro youth, Sherman, is treated as sympathetically as the adolescent fixation Mick Kelly has for Singer in that first novel.

If *Reflections in a Golden Eye* (1941) deals with homosexuality in terms of the grotesque, this is only in the sense that it pictures the deformities brought about by the repression of desires. Events take place in a peacetime army camp where 'all is designed according to a certain rigid pattern'[4]—a phrase which conjures up the fixed expectations of manhood in this microcosm of society, as well as the fateful scheme of action that counters with its own 'rigid pattern'. Captain Penderton's obsession for a young soldier is a story of self-mutilation, an extreme rendering of the gulf between lover and beloved. Penderton has used the army to try to impose a conventional shape upon a threateningly protean self, but has succeeded only in effecting a stalemate between the male and female elements within himself. His friend, Major Langdon, is the masculine type he emulates, but the Captain's tics and neuroses contrast markedly with the other's bluff manners and joviality. Whereas the Major's riding skills earn him the nickname of 'The Buffalo', Penderton's stiff, graceless manner causes him to be known as 'Flap-Fanny'. Effeminacy is dishonourable in this world, as we see when the Major insists that even his wife's Filipino servant, Anacleto, could be transformed into a 'man' by a spell in the ranks, instead of 'dancing around to music and messing with watercolours'. Penderton asks, despairingly,

> You mean, that any fulfilment obtained at the expense of normalcy is wrong, and should not be allowed to bring happiness. In short,

it is better, because it is morally honourable, for the square peg
to keep scraping about the round hole rather than to discover
and use the unorthodox square that would fit it?

(p. 112)

Homosexual repression is matched in this novel by heterosexual abandon. There is little that is morally honourable in the
'normal' world that the Major represents. His mistress is Penderton's wife, a vacuous, sensual woman who scorns her husband's
impotence; contrastingly, the Major's own sickly, neurotic wife is
driven to such despair by his infidelity that she slices off her nipples
with a pair of garden shears. Alison's self-mutilation corresponds
to the mean, vindictive acts that give vent to the Captain's pent-up
feelings. He is both sadistic and masochistic, punishing himself
by many secret acts—forcing himself to ride, for example, yet
on one occasion cruelly beating Firebird, his wife's horse, when it
goes out of his control. The claustrophobic social life of the two
couples is a routine of card parties and dinners throughout which
the healthy if irresponsible sensuality of the two lovers is set
against the suppressed aggression of the two onlookers. But the
sense of stalemate which characterises Penderton and is implicit in
this whole situation is broken as his attention comes to focus upon
a young soldier. Private Williams is symbolically linked to the
horse, Firebird; he is responsible for its care and possesses some of
its qualities; both man and beast seem clumsy at first glance, an
impression giving way to one of proud gracefulness as soon as they
move. The soldier is an image of the natural, instinctual world from
which the Captain is excluded; in the depths of the woods, he rides
naked or sunbathes, his lithe movements causing him to be likened
to a 'wild creature'. But despite these polarities, Williams is in his
own way as repressed as the Captain. If the army offers the latter a
bulwark against his homosexual inclinations, it is also seen by the
young soldier as a refuge from more conventional temptations of
the flesh. Williams comes from an all-male household, where his
Calvinist father had taught him to abhor women as though they
were carriers of some deadly disease.

This rigid pattern of inhibitions composes its own ironic design, unfolding with dream-like logic as each man becomes the
other's nemesis. The private goes into a trance-like state after
glimpsing the naked body of the Captain's wife, and begins nightly
pilgrimages to gaze on her sleeping form. Penderton, meanwhile,

in the course of a desperate ride through the woods, struggles to master the horse which, like his wife and the young soldier, seems to represent all the physical world that mocks him, only to be brought face to face with Williams who is sunbathing naked. Whilst Leona has inspired a 'dark slow germination' of desire in the soldier, the latter has awakened voluptuous sensations in her husband. Penderton feels as if 'a great dark bird alighted on his chest, looked at him once with fierce, golden eyes, and stealthily enfolded him in its dark wings' (p. 54). This image, recalling both the stallion's name and the novel's title, suggests the predatory consuming nature of the passions that have been unleashed. Williams has eyes like 'amber buttons', those of the Captain are 'steady, cruel and bright', and it is the lack of a fully human consciousness behind their eyes that makes them horrific; neither is capable of 'reflection' in the sense of a rational effort to shape what is happening, and hence they leave themselves prey to some fierce 'bird' of 'fire'.

In Penderton, McCullers draws a haunting portrait of a man trapped between homosexual desires and shame. He feels an 'aching longing' to break down barriers between Williams and himself. He dreams of sharing with him the warm camaraderie of the barracks, little realising that the soldier is as much of an isolate as himself. But at the same time, these feelings threaten the persona behind which he hides, causing equally delirious fantasies of violence to take shape: 'it was as though he and the young soldier were wrestling together naked, body to body, in a fight to death' (p. 77). Indeed, death is the only 'resolution', for when the Captain finally discovers Williams squatting in reverent contemplation by his wife's bedside, he shoots him. Yet this is less the act of an outraged husband than the reflex of a lover exacting revenge for the beloved's betrayal, thereby confirming the passion it would deny.

Reflections in a Golden Eye is often compared with D. H. Lawrence's story 'The Prussian Officer', since it employs the same contrasts between a wooden, doll-like officer and a soldier whose animal magnetism obsesses his superior. But whereas Lawrence implies homosexuality to be an evil, sadistic force, Carson McCullers' moral judgments are directed against both men for denying life and for shutting themselves off from the possibilities of whatever variety of love fulfils their deepest nature. (There is in fact a long tradition, from *Billy Budd* to *The Naked and the Dead*, of officers serving as homosexual villains, a phenomenon Roger Austen investigates in an interesting essay comparing works by Melville, Lawrence, McCullers, Murphy and Purdy. He argues that only McCullers and Purdy avoid the conventional equation of homosexuality with evil.)[5]

James Purdy, in certain of his works, deals more openly and explicitly with homosexual themes than either Capote or McCullers and, perhaps because of this, reactions to his work have been more hostile. Furthermore, his disregard for the literary conventions of social realism and strict psychological verisimilitude has never earned him the approval of liberal critics interested in topical relevance or the documentation of a subculture. Similarly, his tragic view of life would not endear him to the freedom-fighters of the gay movement. Whilst he is concerned for the individual's liberation, the obstacles to self-fulfilment are, in his analysis, more deeply entrenched in human nature than political or minority pressure groups would care to admit.

Purdy's themes are ambitious—he has described his work as an exploration of the American soul, using a style based on the rhythms and accents of native speech. But if his language draws on the idioms of the Mid-West, it is also replete with erudite literary and biblical references which point to his idiosyncratic re-telling of the age-old story of how a being charged with life's spiritual and divine potential is denied kinship in the social world. Undoubtedly, it is because themes of such scope and seriousness are often embodied in terms of a homosexual metaphysic that his work provokes indignation in some quarters. It is ironic that Purdy should be dubbed with the gothic label and its implications of irrelevant escapism when his work endlessly satirises the compulsion to turn life into a fiction. But there is also a true sense in which his works are both haunting and haunted, 'memorials' to the realities his culture excludes. Indeed, he sees the world around him as essentially gothic and escapist in character, a chamber of horrors which he dramatises in symbolic form.

Eustace Chisholm and the Works (1967), his fourth novel, marks the full emergence of the homosexual theme—and of critical hostility. Martin Seymour-Smith, justifying Purdy's disfavour among American critics, states that this novel disastrously over-indulges the author's hitherto 'delicate penchant' for 'homosexual

Gothic'.[6] Even those critics sympathetic to Purdy's work fall over themselves to be dissociated from the subject matter of *Eustace Chisholm and the Works*. Henry Chupack, for example, merely reads his own prejudices into the novel when he claims it is about the 'condition' of homosexuality with its 'devastating effect' upon the 'afflicted', and concludes:

> Publicity in the last few years has thrown much light on homosexuality and on the attendant circumstances and conditions from which it evolves. And, while more thoughtful citizens may become more understanding and more aware of this sexual phenomenon, we query whether a novel almost totally involved with this subject is not inflating an aspect of human existence that is at best only an abnormal sexual experience. . . .[7]

But Purdy neither proselytises for homosexuality nor depicts it as an 'affliction'. He simply accords it the same power to damn or to save as any other kind of love.

Eustace Chisholm and the Works is set in Chicago during the Depression years, yet as a 'period piece' it stands in ironic relation to the naturalistic novel of social protest associated with that epoch. The details of human waste and deprivation that supply its historical authenticity and local colour become the framework for a more metaphysical enquiry, according to which the 'economic burnout' is the sign of some underlying spiritual collapse. Eustace is an impoverished writer, reduced to labouring with charcoal sticks on old newspapers to transcribe his epic narrative poem on 'original stock'. This hints comically at his author's larger enterprise—Purdy's recourse to the stark dramatic image with which to emblazon upon the prosaic narrative materials of everyday life his own poetic diagnosis of the fate of American 'stock', its utopian ideals and dreams. The contents of Eustace's epic may be gauged from his other 'works': that group of friends who seek his guidance and become his 'characters'. Eustace prides himself on being a realist, seeing life's power to disappoint (recapitulated in the nation's history and currently imaged in the Depression) in terms of the mystery of love. He likens love to a poisoned cup, infused with an ancient fatality, yet urges his friends to follow his example by savouring to the full its potent blend of hope and despair. Carla, his wife, shrinks from his growing obsession with this 'unknown'; she is 'trained in the rationalism and liberalism of the epoch and partisan to its simple-minded definition of human nature', having also, 'the American woman's fixed idea'[8] that love can heal all wounds. Their conflicting views are dramatised in the narrative movement with its dialectic between dreams of an ideal, consolatory love and the grim reality of the material world. Whilst Eustace's bisexual ménage with Carla and Clayton Harms gives a comic illustration of his philosophy, and Maureen O'Dell, one of his most successful 'disciples', provides another, the tragic failure of love between two men, Amos and Daniel, comes to form the central motif.

Daniel Haws is a paragon of American manhood, an embodiment of 'original stock'. Coming from a long line of coal miners, there is something of the pioneer about him, as well as a hint of Indian blood. He has an inbred resilience and a physical perfection which ensure his survival in the midst of the 'industrial whirlwind'. In fact, thanks to hard work and self-discipline he has become the landlord of a small rooming house, which he runs with a strictness in keeping with his army training and ingrained puritanism. But when he falls in love with Amos Ratcliffe, one of his lodgers, he thinks of it as the latest in a long line of disasters that have dogged his life. Though Daniel is the familiar 'tough guy' of American mythology, his inability to express his love for another man strikes more deeply than any internalisation of societal and masculine prejudice. He has never allowed himself to have any faith in life, reducing it to the mere struggle for bodily survival in a harsh environment, clinging to externals to give existence some shape: 'The only things which held him to life after his separation from the service had been his Army clothes, his barracks bag, his shoe brush, and his military routine, until Amos' (p. 82). Amos symbolises the possibility of love in which Daniel refuses to believe. Yet something deep within him does respond to the youth, for though Daniel 'scrubs his flesh as only a man who hates himself can' (p. 61), nothing will subdue his body's rebellious aspiration to give and receive love. At night, he sleepwalks into the boy's room to bestow the tender caresses so puritanically denied in his daily routine, where, 'alone with him in the empty rooms, he felt that they were in the Army together, and that he was Amos's sergeant' (p. 82).

Amos's 'case-history' has none of the 'period' flavour of Daniel's. He seems to be in the 'wrong book', if not the 'wrong world'. In contrast to his landlord's compulsive cleanliness, the youth neglects his appearance and dirt seems only to emphasise his dazzling good looks. Like a visitor from another planet or the avatar of a Greek God, he appears out of place in the filth and misery of the urban ghetto, as if in exile from some heavenly home. His 'earthly' past is sketched in terms of a doting mother who, concealing her real identity, calls herself Cousin Ida, and a father who has cast him off. But at another level, Amos represents a different kind of 'original stock'—life's tantalising promise of love and beauty, the lost spirit or soul of that utopian dream of America.

The type of perfection each man embodies is an abstraction of the dialogue between 'antique dream' and 'material reality' that Eustace recommends. Both Amos and Daniel have been schooled in one side of life only; each needs to enter into relation with the qualities the other possesses. Whereas Daniel has secured a home for himself, Amos's poverty has caused even the refuge of the University (where, significantly, he studied Ancient Greek) to be denied him. If the youth offers a connection with the spiritual realm, then the older man, with his much admired masculinity, offers a model of the skills necessary for survival in the material world. The relationship between officer and private that spells disaster in McCullers or Lawrence might here have fulfilled itself in appropriately Greek terms of 'warrior' and 'novice', again recalling that epoch when homosexual love and initiation into manhood were perfectly compatible.

But although the 'materials' are brought together, nothing happens. Eustace urges his two characters to the brink of action, insisting that they give themselves up to the present moment and accept life's gift of love, yet neither can confess his feelings in the 'daylight' world. Their conversations become tense ventures across a tightrope of ambiguities; as when, in the middle of a lecture on Amos's self-neglect, Daniel blurts out, 'Suppose you want to show the world you're tough in spite of your peachbloom face', and he pauses on the word, 'peachbloom'—'as if it was this quality he would tear from all creation' (p. 50). Daniel wants to annihilate the deceit that life with its 'peachbloom' quality seems to be practising upon him. The subsequent course of their love develops this image of a promise being *torn* from all creation with, by the end of the novel, a horrific literality. Indeed, the ending is often singled out as evidence of Purdy's sensational dealings in 'homosexual Gothic', and yet the careful foreshadowing of those last events persuades us of the logic and moral seriousness of their context.

Purdy's treatment of homosexuality does not isolate the purely sexual element. Physical attraction between Amos and Daniel is only one aspect of a relationship that might have allowed each of them to fulfil himself. It is in this sense that Daniel's self-betrayal is also seen as a failure of parenthood. Instead of presiding over Amos's initiation into the world, he allows an 'abortion' of love to take place. The idea of something precious being torn from creation is given a gruesome rehearsal when the unwanted offspring of one of Daniel's routine, soldierly fornications is ripped from Maureen O'Dell's womb. The battered foetus is described in such a way as to be linked with Amos and to prophesy Daniel's rejection of homosexual parenthood, too. His evasion of responsibility is completed when he refuses to intervene in the 'purchase' of his celestial visitor by Reuben Masterson, another surrogate father, and so drives Amos from his preferred home. And yet Daniel strays into the room Amos has vacated with the trepidation of a parent entering the abode of a dead child. The letters from Cousin Ida that he discovers there form an epitaph on his own tardiness: Ida's pleas for Amos to come home unwittingly anticipate the present moment when she laments, 'if only he had looked after you as a real father should' (p. 101). From this point, Amos and Daniel recede further and further into their separate realms of 'darkness' and 'light'. Instead of being bound together, each enters into a perverse mockery of a marriage; Amos ascends to a 'heavenly' zone, thanks to Reuben Masterson, his god-like benefactor, and Daniel descends to a hellish domain, to embrace what Eustace so aptly describes as his 'dark bridegroom'—the army.

We see another strand in the pattern of national failure and native 'stock' when Reuben Masterson offers himself as guardian to the fragile spirit of love. The scion of a great 'front' family, the avaricious energies that founded his dynasty have atrophied in him to the extent that he is nothing but a name 'mucilaged' together with money. He merely pays 'lip-service' to the ideal of love, before depositing the youth, like an acquired treasure, in the family 'vaults'—that is to say, in the custody of his redoubtable mother. The old matriarch, Mrs Masterson, cannot decide whether to make Amos her heir or whether to expel him from her house, confusedly recognising him both as the principle she has excluded from her life and for which she now yearns, and as the representative of all those hungry spectres in the outside world that she had steadfastly ignored in order to preserve her empire. The comic details of Amos's escapades in her household, his expulsion, subsequent moral decline and absurd death (shot as a burglar in a final case of 'mistaken' identity), are sombrely matched by details of Daniel's imprisonment 'Under Earth's Deepest Stream'.

There is an austere symmetry in the fates of Amos and Daniel. Whilst the youth is clothed only in the outward guises of love, Daniel strips himself bare to a bodily torture that travesties sexual union. The dream world that engulfs Amos is interwoven with nightmarish messages from Daniel to Eustace which describe how he submits to the 'offices' of Captain Stadger, Reuben Masterson's demonic counterpart. On the very night of his arrival at the Southern camp, the soldier sleepwalks naked into the officer's tent, seeking out the 'army' within the army. His presentation of his body for 'duty' denotes his submission to that Manichean force he feels has dogged him throughout life. At first unconsciously, but later deliberately, he hunts down his persecutor. Stadger is like Daniel's double, his 'secret-sharer'; it is as if each had conjured the other out of the very depths of his being as the final exorcist of that body's tormenting aspirations. The sleepwalking soldier provides the officer with a vision of 'fulfilled hope' and offers him the 'perfect instrument' by which he can express his own self-hatred. As the days go by, Daniel is relieved of all routine duties to become the single conscript of Stadger's private army. In ghostly settings, alive with memories of Indians, childhood picnics and other tokens of a lost innocence, the two men conspire to repeat those ceremonies announced in a newspaper clipping with its headline 'Funeral Rites for Slain Youth', that had brought Daniel news of Amos's death.

If Daniel seems the answer to all the officer's dreams, so the soldier takes a grim satisfaction in being 'hideously injured by Stadger for no purpose or meaning. It confirmed somehow everything he felt about man and life' (p. 215). Pain is taken to an extreme where it offers a blissful release from the struggle to understand the suffering that is part of life. Just as Daniel had been so entirely trapped between his love for Amos and his inability to act upon it, so he now desires to be punished for failing and yet for persisting in that love. This secret stalemate drives Stadger wild, for the soldier both contradicts and confirms his own homosexual despair, accepts and subtly resists his punishment, offers and retracts the hope that he could love Stadger, too. For in his heart the Captain wants to be preferred to Amos, but he cannot make Daniel renounce this first love even though, causing his victim to relive all the underground hell of his coalmining days, he would drill into the very core of his being.

If the actions of the two men are so shocking as to invite the description 'homosexual Gothic', then this should not be understood in a trivial sense. Purdy does not set out to depict some inevitable homosexual agony where by tragic endings serve a conventional if not compulsory 'warning', or to sensationalise his subject with a lurid bloodbath. Instead, he creates a heightened realism, poetic and chilling in the intensity of its images, that conveys his own outrage at the recurrent 'crucifixion' of love. The horror and lingering impact of these events stem not so much from the sickening details of physical suffering but from their simultaneous, ironic testimony to the power of love which the two men struggle in vain to extinguish. In fact, their actions fall into the homosexual stereotype of sado-masochistic role-playing, and Purdy brings out and takes to its logical conclusion the underlying mixture of self-hatred and repressed longings in such behaviour. The destructive impulses to which Daniel and Captain Stadger give expression invert some of the very acts that signify love and dedication between two men; the merging of twin souls symbolised in the blood-letting ceremony of *blutbruderschaft* takes on a gruesome literality when they slash their chests and embrace in a frenzied compact of annihilation; the final act of penetration by some medieval-looking torture instrument is a cruel mockery of phallic intercourse, resulting in disembowelment and agonising death. Daniel hangs himself on his own cross; unlike his biblical namesake, he throws himself into the lion's den, a bewildered, self-made martyr who bears witness, nevertheless, to the ferocious power of love and to those lines Purdy quotes from Dryden's translation of Virgil: 'I know thee, Love! in deserts thou wert bred, And at the dugs of savage Tigers fed. . . .' (p. 240).

The pity of it is that both men have a physical beauty which contradicts their belief in life's ugliness. And although when Daniel sleepwalks into Stadger's tent it is to seek out his executioner, on another level his rebellious body is making the same plea it extended to Amos. Their relationship reiterates in purgatorial form

70

all the tensions and denials of the relationship between the landlord and his lodger. There are moments when they lie naked in the flowers like exhausted lovers, for Stadger not only resembles Amos but he fights against the same fierce longings to give himself to the soldier. Neither man can act on or eradicate these aspirations —except by becoming partners in a suicidal undertaking whereby the roles of sadist and masochist become one:

> In his extreme suffering, Daniel finally turned to his own torturer for sympathy. It was this action of the soldier that Captain Stadger himself evidently required, in his own despair, for without Daniel's turning to him, he might not have been able to find the strength to inflict the last and most consummate of the punishments he had ready for the man elected for them.
>
> (p. 224)

Eustace acts as a chorus upon these events and their wider significance is made apparent because of the changes they bring about in him. To begin with, his literary enterprise thrives as he pours all communications from or about the ill-starred lovers into the Works, thinking of the correspondence that comes to him from Daniel and also from Amos's Cousin Ida as an unexpected stroke of luck. But as he drinks in the full bodied 'stock' of life and literature, he comes to think of himself as 'hooked' on Daniel's story alone. The precedence the one correspondent takes over the other suggests a fracturing in the dialectic of hope and despair that he valued in life and now is unable to express even in his art. Cousin Ida stirs hopeful memories in many of the characters, and is almost unique in that, with no hint of a loss of belief in love, she can nonetheless speak openly of the suffering it involves. Yet the two subjects, Amos and Daniel, that Eustace had thought 'one', are now deprived of the axis of faith. He loses interest in his narrative poem as the artist's vision becomes a 'curse' from which he longs to be cured. He thinks of the whole U.S.A. where history is veering from economic disaster to world war as, 'nothing but Daniels and Amoss whispering and muttering to him in the falling darkness' (p. 172). Once a figure that stood out against the historical background, he now shies away from the pain of telling the 'real' story, abdicates as guardian of 'original stock' and fades into his surroundings. His narrative poem goes up in flames, coinciding with the larger conflagration of human hopes in society's 'economic burnout'. In a novel that seeks its own definitions of manhood,

71

Eustace's final reconciliation with his wife does not imply the dawning of some heterosexual 'light'. On the contrary, he seems more like a child seeking the comfort of its mother. Even so, Purdy insists to the last that there can be no escape; the subject Eustace flees is part of him, for what he offers Carla is still 'a kind of *ravening* love'.

Underlying the themes in Purdy's fiction is a feeling of a universal breakdown in the unity of family and community life. Bereft of any innate identity, if not mysteriously orphaned by the world, his isolated individuals turn to one another for comfort, or seek the guidance of a surrogate parent. These alternative 'families' abound in passionate relationships between men, whether this involves an overt sexual dimension or not. In particular, the love of two brothers exerts a continuous fascination on Purdy's imagination, from early writings such as the novella, *63: Dream Palace* (1957), to recent novels such as *The House of the Solitary Maggot* (1974) or the plays, *A Day after the Fair* and *True* (1977). In each of these works, two brothers are hemmed in by an alien, predatory world which, in tightening its grip, causes their love to seethe in murderous turmoil and sacrificial slaughter. Elsewhere, brotherhood is explored in a wider sense and with a homosexual significance reminiscent of Whitman's plea for intense loving relationships between men. Purdy gives imaginative endorsement to the philosophy of male fellowship that Whitman sums up in *Democratic Vistas* when he remarks,

> It is to the development, identification and general prevalence of that fervid comradeship . . . that I look for the counter-balance and offset of our materialistic and vulgar American democracy and for the spiritualization thereof.

But Whitman's exuberent prophecies have given way to the voice of lost opportunities in Purdy, whose tone ranges from the elegiac to the satirical. *Cabot Wright Begins*, for example, includes a sardonic epitaph on Whitman's dreams of 'adhesive love' when Bernie Gladhart, a modern Ishmael, is driven to such desperation by his alienation from fellow Americans that he seizes the chance of making acquaintance with an impressive looking Congolese, similarly adrift in the melting pot of New York: 'Taking Winters Hart's left hand in his, Bernie held his friend's dark finger on which he wore a wedding ring, and pressed the finger and the hand. Far from being annoyed at this liberty, Winters Hart was, to tell the truth, relieved and pleased. Isolation in a racial democracy, as he was to tell Bernie later that night, as they lay in Bernie's bed together, isolation, no thank you'. The two men sleep blissfully—'spoon fashion'.[9]

The comradeship of lonely outcasts is also portrayed in many of Purdy's short stories. Typical is the haunting simplicity of 'Some of These Days', where James De Salles, a young delinquent and drifter, tells of his desperate search to find the one person who ever cared for him: his landlord. Like the character Benny, in another story, 'Daddy Wolf', whose loneliness drives him to 'emergency' telephone calls to complete strangers and who longs to be 're-connected with a certain party', James feels that he has lost his only link to life. Injured in prison, on his release he struggles with his damaged memory to recall the name of the man who had taken him off the streets and given him a home. As his landlord sometimes frequented 'porno-theaters', James comes to spend day and night there in a fruitless search which leads only to his complete breakdown. There is a sombre irony in the religious fervour of his quest to be 're-connected'; he tells us that, 'even disliking it as much as I did, it gave me some little feeling of a resemblance to warmth and kindness as the unknown men touched me with their invisible faces and extracted from me all I had to offer, such as it was. And when they had finished me, I would ask them if they knew my landlord (or as I whispered to myself, my lord). But no-one ever did'.[10]

Loving fellowship and brotherhood are often no more than fading dreams of some other time and place in Purdy's fictional world, which is full of characters like James whose progress through life describes an attenuation as opposed to an accretion of being. Alongside and often overlapping with images of brotherhood, relationships typically fall into the Platonic scheme of an adolescent youth seeking the love and guidance of an adult. Yet the reappearance in work after work of a dazzlingly beautiful youth is far from being the hallmark of an 'effete' imagination dealing in pederastic daydreams. Instead, these youths are the vehicles for Purdy's savage satire against society's betrayal of the very ideals to which it pays lip-service; 'Applicants' on the threshold of adulthood, seeking directions and a 'home' in the world, they are the author's image for the undefined potential of existence, for some promise of love or transcendental spiritual purpose. Most frequently, they are denied true attachments; others 'extract' what they have to offer, feeding on their tenuous reality without giving anything in exchange. James asks 'Have you seen my lord?' and is ushered into a 'porno-theater'; Fenton Riddleway, in *63: Dream Palace*, is led deeper into a 'not-right' world after he has asked despairingly to be shown the 'way out'; the young hero of *Malcolm* (1960), looking for some clue to his identity, is given (and subjected to) 'addresses' that are nothing but 'dead ends'. When the Greek schema is specifically homosexual, there is no special pleading on its behalf, for, as always, it is the quality and not the character of a relationship that causes Purdy to approve or condemn it. Thus Fenton Riddleway is destroyed by being treated as a 'mechanical doll' which other people dress or undress according to their fantasies, in both worlds that prey on him—homosexual and heterosexual alike.

The themes of brotherhood and Platonic homosexuality come together in Purdy's two most recent novels, *In a Shallow Grave* (1976) and *Narrow Rooms* (1978). The first of these tells the story of a Vietnam war veteran, Garnet Montrose, who comes back to the living after an exploding bomb had buried him in a shallow grave. Now resembling some 'abortion' or 'nightgoblin', to the extent that people retch at the mere sight of him, Garnet would seem supremely qualified for the role of 'gothic monster'. Yet Purdy delights in the challenge of compelling our belief in his strange hero and making us recognise ourselves in his predicament. In this parable of rejection, the soldier's skin-deep disfigurement is a mirror of mortality and, given his past as a trained killer, it is also like the mark of Cain upon him. Until two equally desperate characters, Quintus and Daventry, enter his service, his appearance had driven away all 'applicants' for the post of watching over him. But through the mutual dependencies that spring up, this curious trinity perform acts of atonement and redemption by which they reconcile one another to life and death. Mutual sacrifices cause disfigurements to heal as they give one another proofs of their love. Unlike that other soldier, Daniel Haws, who by his own admission was not 'man' enough to love Amos, Garnet refuses to accept the finality of his own experience and forgoes the role of 'ordinary soldier from Virginia' to accept and to return the love of another man.

Narrow Rooms is, however, Purdy's most explicit treatment of sexual love between men. In synopsis, the plot has all the ingredients of a bizarre melodrama: in a remote West Virginian town, a character known as the 'renderer' (since his grandfather's trade was to boil down carcasses), the possessor of almost supernatural powers, is the fiendish, dope-smoking 'master' of a ring of homosexual 'slaves', comprising three youths of respectable families. Their involvements result in murders, accidental killings, male rape, grave-snatching, and mutilations that culminate in a gory sadomasochistic crucifixion. Yet, such is the power of Purdy's dark poetry, that these events take on the allusive resonance of ballad or myth.

The true significance of the story of Roy Sturtevant, the renderer, and his three 'pupils', Brian McFee, Sidney De Lakes and Gareth Vaisey, is hinted at through the character and choric utterances of the old doctor. His willingness to face life's realities contrasts with the more prevalent desire to escape them, a desire which ironically is itself seen to be responsible for the tragic shape life often assumes. At the close of the narrative, when the four principal characters are dead, Dr Ulric concludes that their little community has 'had its veil torn away', recognising the contemporary form of a recurring tragedy, that in his day had been enshrined in folklore by the story of Ruthanna Elder and the jealous passions that had led to the deaths of the two young men who loved her. In each generation, it would seem, tragedy is destined to erupt, as if some Calvinist God exacted periodic sacrifice among those whose youth symbolises the community's hope, as an exemplary punishment for their conversion of love from blessing to curse. Far from escaping into gothic fantasy, Purdy takes on this admonitory role, shaping his fictions in a manner calculated to shock and terrify, though only in order to dramatise that mysterious fatality which, in his view, causes life's promises to be repeatedly betrayed.

In characteristic manner, he first presents us with the bare bones of an extraordinary story that outrages conventional realism, then proceeds to flesh these out in details so hypnotic as to compel not only our attention but our belief. The sombre imagery of imprisonment in 'narrow rooms' is underlined from the outset by the notion of individuals being caught up in some preordained ritual. When Sidney De Lakes returns from prison, having served a sentence for the killing of his one-time lover, Brian McFee, he tells Vance, his younger brother, 'There are these people I suppose who are destined to play parts in our lives' (p. 16). Certainly, there was nothing accidental about his involvement with Brian McFee, nor does chance determine the renewal of his acquaintance with Gareth Vaisey. Irene Vaisey believes Sidney to have been 'called' to a new vocation as companion and nurse to her adored son, who has been a corpse-like invalid ever since the family truck collided with a train, killing his father and two younger brothers—a catastrophe brought about by the fact that Gareth, who was at the wheel, had been challenged to a race by Brian McFee, who was riding on horseback, alongside. Destinies continue to intersect with violent impact in the novel's present, and if the three youths seem 'prisoners' of fate, then Roy Sturtevant would appear to be the agent of this malevolent force. His nickname suggests his sinister ability to reduce materials to new shapes and Sidney likens him to some 'goblin' who has watched and 'dogged' him throughout life, as if Brian, Gareth and himself were mere 'envelopes belonging to Roy Sturtevant inside of which was concealed a message only the owner understood' (p. 131). The idea of life being fixed in patterns is embodied in the plot; Roy's power had reached out to Sidney through the intermediary of Brian McFee, causing the relationship between these two youths to culminate in disaster; the past is then made to repeat itself when the love that springs up between Gareth and Sidney is steered on the road to destruction.

One might suppose Roy Sturtevant's hold over his three 'victims' to place him in the old tradition of homosexual as villain, symbol of evil and corruptor of youth. But when we are treated to Roy's story, it is clear that Purdy uses him to present homosexuality as one of those realities of life that people refuse to acknowledge, thereby casting out a potent source of love. Its confinement to 'narrow rooms', in society or in the individual psyche, stores up fierce energies that inevitably burst forth in retribution. Furthermore, Roy's story offers glimpses of a peculiarly American fable, drawing on the traditions of the western, in which Gareth, Brian and Sidney are familiar heroes: clean-cut and manly, sportsmen and hunting companions, like young gods, they inspire worship in others and in one another. They are the 'cream' and 'quality' of local society, 'pure American stock right back to the Revolution'. The renderer's son, on the other hand, is everything that is outlawed from their pristine version of life. Trapped in the stigma of his ancestor's grisly trade, treated like a ghoul, denied his individual name, he is likened variously to all the outcast elements of American culture—a savage, dirty Leatherstocking, both Indian and 'nigger'. Hedged around by superstition, prejudice and taboo, he is 'lost' to society, contact with him 'soils' and 'stains'; he is Huck Finn, Heathcliff (to import a comparison) and Homosexual rolled into one. At the same time, he is the poignant hero of Purdy's personal mythology—the orphan and outcast child of love, in search of some connection to life. As the name 'Roy Sturtevant' also suggests, he is the exiled king of all those disturbing, impulsive forces that have been denied kinship in the larger world. Whereas his ancestors boiled down the carcasses of dead horses, Roy runs the StarLite Stables, schooling his three young horsemen in the forces of life's natural energy. This power can turn them into agents of destruction, like the Four Horsemen of the Apocalypse, or, as the curious symbolism of 'rendering' suggests, Roy is potentially a Christ-like figure, son of that ultimate 'renderer' of human flesh, in touch with realities and able to reveal to others their true nature, to teach the love of man for man.

Roy falls in love with Sidney when they are at high school together, entering into a helpless bondage as the youth torments him by both resisting and responding to his passion. Subconsciously, Sidney invites Roy to 'command' him to acts of sexual love which he can afterwards violently deny. Yet their mutual dependency is expressed by the fact that whilst Roy 'slaves' to help the dull-witted Sidney through school, the latter is inspired by such admiration to excel as an athlete, becoming a star football player, champion diver and swimmer. It is as if each had the power to bring the other to life. But whereas Sidney acknowledges that Roy stares at him 'like he seen Jesus', he gives his worshipper the character and tempting power of the Devil, telling how when Roy made love to him he feared he 'would pull the guts and soul out of me' —and so he kicks him to the floor or on another occasion slaps him in public after Roy has gained the honours of the valedictorian, solely out of love for the football player.

Sidney's rejection of his homosexual self with which Roy confonts him is eventually repeated with Brian McFee, who is fated to act out the very character of the love between the other two men—and its 'murder'. Realising and accepting his homosexuality early on, Brian seeks out a fellow spirit in the renderer. But Roy, embittered by past rejection, can invest this new relationship only with his feelings for Sidney, 'enslaving' love to murderous ends.

Directing Brian as an instrument of revenge, he urges him to trap Sidney into a sexual relationship in order to make him suffer, and finally to kill him. Yet his attempt to rid himself of his obsession only endorses his continuing love. As his mutinous 'pupil' cries out, 'It's you sendin' me to be *you* with *him*, ain't it?' (p. 81). Ironically, Brian takes his master's part in earnest, falling in love with Sidney, until history repeats itself and he too is rejected as 'soiled' because of his connection with the renderer—who likewise casts him off for failing to carry out his command. Between them, Roy and Sidney conspire to murder their outlawed love. Sidney's sexual shame is such that he applauds the dodge of hunting trips to provide a cover for his affair with Brian, and when the latter begins sending him passionate letters pleading to be taken back, Sidney is terrified 'to see his secret life put down in black and white, as if pictures of him naked were circulating through the mail' (p. 91). It is Sidney's fear of homosexuality together with Roy's goading of Brian to complete his 'assignment', that leads to the shooting; after half-heartedly stalking his prey during one of their hunting expeditions, Brian catches up with Sidney in a local tavern and makes a public declaration of *love*—the shock of which causes Sidney's gun to go off in his hand.

On his release, Sidney admits his homosexuality to his brother, but does so in a fearful way, alluding to 'terrible things' that were done to him in prison—though we eventually learn that Sidney himself had initiated and enjoyed those sexual experiences. Vance, like the puritan guardian of his brother's 'better self', cannot bear to think of any 'blemish' in his idol. He declares: 'I don't believe you're queer anyhow, or gay, or whatever they call it. . . . Prison made you think that' (p. 41). Vance would shut his ears to the truth, he had 'never begun or never wanted to understand' the feud with Roy Sturtevant, nor does he encourage Sidney to further confession about his prison experiences, telling Irene Vaisey (during a 'mission' to save his brother from the 'wrong kind' of happiness with Gareth) that such confidences would be to the advantage of neither. Nevertheless, Vance himself offers proofs of the love between men which he seeks to deny; as the Doctor notes when Vance is lacing Sidney's hunting boots: 'There was a peaceful expression on the boy's face which recalled the look some people have when receiving the host' (p. 6).

Love, in all its forms and guises, is the overall 'master' in this novel and the narrative takes shape from a dialogue between those who fear its calling and those caught up in a contrasting pattern of service and atonement. The Doctor sets an example in this last respect. Daily acquaintance with the realities of birth and death brings him 'too close' to life, he sometimes feels, yet he is humble before its mysteries. A priest-like figure, 'he toiled from early to late with the sick and the discouraged' (p. 4). He is an example of a true 'teacher', and encourages Vance to become his 'helper', an apprentice to his vision of life, as it were. Confiding secrets to him is like 'whispering it to the river by midnight' and when Vance confesses his shame over his brother's homosexuality, Dr Ulric retorts, 'I don't think of people as queer or straight. Not when you are as old as I. And I don't think God does either' (p. 18). Despite his intimacy with life's tragedies, the doctor never abandons his labours. His elusive faith in a cycle of renewal is conveyed by his habit of walking into the golden cornfields where he 'listens' to the moving stalks, absorbing a restorative calmness. The doctor, Vance, and Irene Vaisey establish a background of devotional service, the love of a 'father', mother and brother setting up contrasts to the more turbulent sexual passions of others. But these idealised loves betray some of the same fears and jealousies of the principals in this drama—as when Irene Vaisey comes across Sidney and Gareth, 'naked, holding one another in furious embrace' (p. 55), and dismisses the man who, by her own admission, had performed a 'miracle' for her lifeless son.

Love, then, is the ultimate 'renderer', with power to give or take away life. Both Gareth and Sidney were instrumental in spilling the blood of their 'brother' and can begin to expiate these crimes by serving one another. Irene Vaisey almost uses the word 'keeper' to describe her expectations of Sidney, who, accordingly, sets himself to 'feed a dead boy', making reparation to Brian in the person of Gareth. But although he declares that he is no longer ashamed of his sexuality, he has still to face up to his deepest self when his expulsion from the Vaisey household leads him back to the renderer. For when Sidney 'reports in' to Roy, it is not so much an act of repentance for the past as a surrender to despair. His masochistic submission to 'the man who in the end directed his every move' is a way of shirking responsibility for himself and can only fire the other's sadism to bring about a deadlock like that between Daniel and Captain Stadger. Instead of the Platonic ideal of mutual love and inspiration, a 'master' and 'slave' situation is recreated, with the ironic twist that each is doomed to play both roles, to be at once gaoler and prisoner of the other. Thus the past repeats itself with nightmarish vengeance as Roy renews his plots to rid himself of Sidney, reaching out to him through Gareth, just as he had through Brian. Gareth relives the agony of the dead youth, becoming another broken symbol of the thwarted passions of the other two when, in an hallucinatory, demonic scene, he is brutally raped by Roy in answer to his entreaties for Sidney's release from his power. Yet the renderer's sadistic frenzies are matched by an equally gruesome masochism; he slashes and mutilates the body that imprisons him by its continuing desire for Sidney. Nor is there any escape for Sidney as, in a further shift in this symbiotic pattern, he is drawn inexorably back to Roy and obliged to act out the part of Brian McFee. Now under command from Gareth to avenge his humiliation at the renderer's hands, he is—like Brian before him—goaded to kill the man he really loves.

In trance-like statements and in dreams, Sidney has grasped the identity of his twin self and outcast 'Maker'. Appropriately, his final visit to Roy has all the atmospherics of 'Judgment Day'. But both men are still driven by Brian McFee and Gareth Vaisey, the ghosts of their own love, to avenge its desecration. This deadlock of murderous passion is what Roy hopes to break by his ultimate command to Sidney: 'Nail the son of the renderer to the barn door' (p. 150). It is as if by the suffering of a mock crucifixion, he would absolve them from further punishment, redeeming and 'rendering' their true selves. For Sidney De Lakes, this act is like diving into the depths of his soul. Just as his school coach had inspired him to accomplish the impossible, so this incredible proof of love spurs him to obey its call. His lifelong picture of the 'dirty renderer' fades, leaving only 'this new coach bleeding and heroic against the barn door . . . waiting for his pupil's return' (p. 152). Sidney has a vision of how, when his task is complete and even Brian has been brought from the grave to 'witness' this atonement, then he and Roy

> would not part from one another ever after having only at last been united pursuant to so many devious detours and windings, as souls long separated from each other by the world's vicissitudes are said to enter paradise linked arm in arm.
>
> (p. 153)

But this vision can only be purchased at the expense of life itself. As events move to their dream-like climax, Gareth voices the fear and despair of one who perceives a perfect love that excludes him and seems not to belong to this world. Just as Sidney had been shocked into shooting Brian because of the 'perfect words' he uttered, so Gareth is shattered by the sight of Sidney tending his lover's mutilated body. He shoots them and is himself caught up in a hail of bullets from the besieging police.

The idea of a sacrifice necessarily repeating itself throughout history is built into the narrative structure. When the story switches from its focus upon Sidney to the griefs of the renderer, we are told,

> Behind this story so far is another story, as behind the girders of an ancient bridge is the skeleton of a child which superstition says keeps the bridge standing.
>
> (p. 58)

This principle is further expressed in the author's use of language, explaining the curious conjunction of modern colloquialisms, the lovingly reproduced speech rhythms of the Mid-West, together with archaicisms and poetic utterances that suggest the impingement of the past upon the present, the re-enactment of an ancient story. In a similar way, the 'skeletons' of the four youths, like those of Ruthanna Elder's two lovers before them, will sustain the spiritual fabric of community myths. Just as the renderer was able to reduce carcasses to materials useful in soaps or tallow candles, so these sacrificial deaths are potentially converted into sources of renewal, into agents of cleansing and illumination.

Purdy dramatises homosexual passions in this highly stylised moral fable with violent and shocking images to portray the consequences of turning away from one of the realities of life. Irene Vaisey could not bear to look on the famished embraces of two youths; at Sidney's trial, his lawyer advised him to conceal his actual relationship with Brian; the officer at the bedside of the dying Gareth wanted to shut his ears to the youth's confessions. And yet Gareth's story is told and has its effects—the doctor and Irene Vaisey agreeing that Vance De Lakes, for one, 'had no more strength in any case to keep away the truth' (p. 183). It is as if Purdy believed that the truth is only revealed when people are shocked by some sacrificial spectacle into an awareness of opportunities that have been denied—in this case, the 'perfect love' that might exist between two men.

NOTES

1. Leslie Fiedler, *Love and Death in the American Novel* (1960; New York, 1975), p. 476.
2. See, for example, Warren Coffrey's remarks in *Commentary*, XLIV (September 1967), pp. 98–103.
3. Truman Capote, *Other Voices, Other Rooms* (1948). (London: Penguin, 1964), p. 113.
4. Carson McCullers, *Reflections in a Golden Eye* (1941). (London: Penguin, 1967), p. 7. Subsequent page references are to this edition.
5. Roger Austen, 'But for fate and ban: Homosexual Villains and Victims in the Military' special issue of *College English*, 'The Homosexual Imagination' (Vol. 36, No. 3, November 1974), pp. 352–59.
6. Martin Seymour-Smith, *A Guide to Modern World Literature* (London, 1973), p. 143–44.
7. Henry Chupack, *James Purdy* (New York, 1975), p. 104.
8. James Purdy, *Eustace Chisholm and the Works* (1967). (London, 1968), p. 195. Subsequent page references are to this edition.
9. James Purdy, *Cabot Wright Begins* (1964). (London, 1965), p. 213.
10. James Purdy, 'Some of These Days', included in *A Day after the Fair* (New York, 1977), p. 146.

4

Terminal Sex: JOHN RECHY and William Burroughs

American literature celebrates images of manhood that draw nostalgically upon myths of the earlier pioneering society. But although the frontier virtues of physical strength, emotional toughness and violent self-assertion—brought together in the figure of the cowboy—retain their allure, this fantasy of male power has progressively narrowed to one of sexual dominance; Norman Mailer, for example, with his view of homosexuality as moral cowardice and as a desertion of the honourable battle with Procreative Woman, turns *machismo* into a new existential imperative.[1] Most writers who portray male homosexuals sympathetically value tenderness and emotional sensitivity in preference to aggression, yet some, like John Rechy and, to a lesser degree, William Burroughs, have cast the homosexual male in the role of new frontiersman, glorifying in his outlaw existence. Their fiction turns away from dreams of a perfect, redeeming love between men, to depict sexuality in a manner which precludes romance and the search for an enduring relationship. Instead, they celebrate an anarchic sexuality in which defiance and not the plea for tolerance forms the keynote.

Significantly, both have associations with the Beat writers of the Fifties—Burroughs as their mentor and Rechy as one of their imitators. Rechy's first novel, *City of Night* (1963), adopts the hipster idioms and the pattern of frantic journeying given classic expression in Jack Kerouac's *On the Road* (1957). As is the case with Kerouac, Rechy's fiction deals in romanticised versions of himself; likewise, he retains from his Catholic childhood a haunting sense of death, together with a compulsion to confess and account for his deeds. But whilst Kerouac continues the American tradition of covert homosexual romance, extolling the 'buddy system' as infinitely preferable to the domestic unit, the odysseys

83

of his hipster heroes do not seriously challenge sexual norms—the homosexual 'omissions' from his 'buddy system' having only retro-spectively been repaired by Ann Charters' biography[2] and Allen Ginsberg's *Gay Sunshine* interviews.[3] With Rechy and Burroughs, however, Beat delinquency takes an aggressively homosexual form. Nevertheless, despite their frankness and apparent radicalism, there is also something curiously negative in their treatment of sex.

City of Night has acquired the reputation of an underground classic. Certainly, Rechy gives a more detailed description of the homosexual subculture than does either Vidal or Baldwin, and whereas they present this world as one which threatens the in-dividual and lends a desperate impetus to the search for some romantic alternative, Rechy, drawing freely on autobiographical experience, writes from the point of view of an insider, identifying with the outlaw existence and investing it with heroic values— in his later works, more and more shrilly. But if this is the arche-typal novel of the sexual ghetto, it also exhibits something of a ghetto mentality. Although the author champions this subculture's defiance of persecution and conventional morality, there is also a deep and unacknowledged conflict between his hero's progressive involvement in homosexuality and his frantic determination to contain this within a traditional male identity.

A hustler's journey to the 'Lonesome' end of the American night would seem an apt subject for a documentary novel in the lurid popular genre. This aspect is checked, however, by a framework of self-analysis which re-interprets the (unnamed) narrator's life in terms of a rebellion. But even in retrospect and despite the con-fessional glow of his enterprise, the narrator finds it difficult to 'come clean'. His choice of lifestyle is presented as having its origins in a religious crisis, yet in a manner which obscures the question of sexual identity and its role in his development. The myth of a loving God is savagely contradicted by his childhood circum-stances, and thus,

> The God that would allow this vast unhappiness was a God I would rebel against. The seeds of that rebellion—planted that ugly afternoon when I saw my dog's body beginning to decay, the soul shut out by Heaven—were beginning to germinate.[4]

Childhood traumas furnish the philosophical clichés with which he decks out his adult existence: death is held to negate all meaning in life, to make a mockery of his innocence, and to justify his dedicated pursuit of what temporary homage he can exact from a world that promises only his annihilation. There is no convincing explanation as to why homosexuality should be singled out as the form of this revolt and the celebration of the existentialist Now! Surprisingly, the narrator makes no reference to the constricting sexual norms and expectations of a Catholic upbringing, and the rejection of religious myth scarcely seems sufficient motive for exiling oneself from conventional society in search of a 'substitute for salvation' in the homosexual underworld. Of course, Rechy wishes to persuade us that his narrator's choice of lifestyle is essentially symbolic—a pursuit of the negative heroism of self-destruction in an attempt to eradicate the innocence into which he was duped.

The domain of 'lost souls' the narrator seeks out is specifically that of America's sexual rejects, drawn like him to the anonymity of the large city. But if, according to the tenets of masculine orthodoxy, such individuals are 'damned', the narrator's own 'substitute for salvation' is to strike an 'angelic' pose of unsullied virility. One of his clients, an ugly old Professor, unwittingly holds up a mirror to the prison the hero devises for himself. The former seeks to cast a spell of words over the sordid reality of his dealings with prostitutes and conducts 'interviews' which consist in fact of his own breathless eulogies of this fraternity of 'angels'. His pathetic devices match those of the narrator, for, in his own series of 'interviews', the latter contrives always to bask in the temporary Heaven of another's admiration. Just as the Professor's rhetorical flights are grounded by the rejection of a (non-contractual) hug, so the narrator is apt to plummet from euphoric heights if his narcissism encounters any rebuff.

The narcissism which is held to explain his prostitution is interminably corroborated and given the respectable parentage of religious rebellion and a protest against the world's indifference to his fate. Nonetheless, it assumes such paranoid proportions as to be more comprehensible as the unacknowledged reflex of homosexual shame. The narrator flees any relationship that would exceed the strict rules governing the camaraderie of the streets and becomes inordinately depressed if his pose is challenged in any way, as when a client or 'ordinary' homosexual implies he might be capable of reciprocating their desire. His vocation as a hustler has no economic basis, it merely allows him to practice homosexuality without incurring any of its opprobrium, particularly the presumption of effeminacy. The hustler is the sexually available cowboy, the epitome of the 'tough guy', attractive according to the illusion of heterosexuality he contrives. The exchange of money is a symbolic, though necessary, token, by which his masculinity is 'absolved'. But although the narrator caters to the self-contempt by which an apparently 'straight' man is deemed infinitely more desirable than one's fellow faggot, he also conserves 'manly honour', ironically, by casting himself in a role from which women have been struggling to escape. He pursues a 'career' as a sex object, moulding himself to the fantasies of others and cultivating a 'dumb manner'. His passivity has the advantage of transferring all responsibility for the sex act upon some other male, yet it could never extend to the full submission of penetration as this would entail the adoption of the despised feminine (and presumed homosexual) role 'for real'.

The loneliness the narrator bewails is the self-fulfilling prophecy of the hustler's mask of indifference. His promiscuity brings him into contact with so much human misery that it is increasingly difficult to maintain the uncaring stance, but at the same time the heightened awareness of his own vulnerability reinforces his need for disguise. This establishes a pattern of guilty withdrawal from and inevitable return to a lifestyle which he sees as the only fulfilment of his narcissistic needs.

It is in Los Angeles that his apprehension of the crushed hopes in other lives begins to exacerbate his own sense of a dwindling capital which has been wholly invested in youth. He imagines,

> All the world was pouring into Pershing Square in a tidal wave of faces—that frantically each person would shout his Loss—into Eternity—to an uncaring Heaven! (p. 123)

But such sentiments, endlessly repeated, seem no more than existential pieties, not to say mystification, when the hero's vision of his doomed passage through a symbolic Night is so evidently the price of the self-image he has manufactured. Time is his enemy because he has narrowed life's meaning to those moments when an illusion of eternal youth is procured by the homage he receives and, more importantly, because it threatens to expose his sexual hypocrisy. However desperately he throws himself into the present,

86

there are constant reminders of decline: the proximity of Skid Row, the panic of being replaced on the streets by younger faces, and his acquaintance with characters like Skipper and Lance O'Hara who provide glimpses of what his own future might hold. Skipper both fascinates and frightens the narrator, for,

> Behind the sullen look with which he nailed the people who bought him was the unmistakable awareness that he was on the brink of facing his doom: of facing Death. . . . And Death for Skipper was the loss of Youth. (p. 156)

For Rechy's hustler too, 'death' is simply the state of being no longer desired; youth is a saleable asset, an essential adjunct of masculinity, and of paramount importance because its passing will bring him face to face with the question of his own sexuality—a 'doom' that as a 'seller' he can postpone but not altogether ignore, since the underworld provides him with many examples of those who become 'buyers' having once occupied his own proud position.

Because of this, the narrator's compassion is selective and, at times, suspect. The poignancy he would impart to Skipper's 'heroic' resistance to his fate is coloured by self-pity, and his contempt for those who take advantage of the ageing hustler's weaker bargaining position is coloured by his own panic. His sympathies are more easily aroused by those who offer no threat to his masculinity and heterosexual pose. Thus he is able to comfort the distress of a drag queen like Miss Destiny, and to admire the rebellious defiance with which she confronts her history of rejections. In fact, the hustlers establish a flirtatious, easy accord with the drag queens; each provides a flattering and necessary prop to the other's impersonation of a male or female role, and together they engage in a heterosexual charade, a tacit conspiracy to evade questions of homosexuality and gender role. For example, the narrator says of Trudi, the 'sweetest-looking queen in L.A.'—'youd have to be completely queer not to dig her' (p. 101). He also shares the drag queens' scorn for the merely effeminate male, the homosexual who in their eyes is neither 'man' nor 'woman'. This is evident in the portrait of a fat man and his thin friend in which he ridicules the effeminacy he fears when he imagines the latter,

> mincing in a tight olive-green suit as if his legs were tied at the knees; carrying a pencil-thin umbrella as affectedly as he carries

—and he carried it—the cigarette holder; entertaining, in the evenings, his equally closeted friends—with Cocktails.

(p. 150)

The narrator can ill afford to moralise on the 'closetry' of others.

Just as the fat man relished the evidence of Skipper's decline, so Hollywood's 'faggot chorus' delight in the downfall of their reigning beauty, the legendary Lance O'Hara, who promises to fulfil all their jealous fantasies by the scandal of his love for a street boy. Again, the narrator's sympathies are sharply divided as he identifies with the fallen idol and presents his detractors with vindictive satire. Lance is notorious for having defrauded and rejected a doting old man, an act of cruelty which is to haunt and finally to overtake him when he too comes to endure the public humiliation of youth spurning age, 'male' spurning 'faggot'. His case-history elucidates Rechy's implicit thesis that love (if not age) is the slippery slope to faggotry. According to this, to love, to reciprocate sexually, is to admit weakness and 'feminine' vulnerability, to court the possibility of rejection. These evils can be warded off by the spells of beauty, youth and the pose of manly indifference, yet the 'faggot chorus' waits eagerly in the wings for the moment when those who exulted in their power over them must cross the 'boundary' that comes with age, to feel the whip they once wielded, to become a 'score'—literally, someone marked down by another's success.

Despite his awareness that such characters reflect his own dilemma, there arises an effective stalemate between the narrator's growing interest in individuals and the fear that accompanies his equation of homosexuality with effeminacy. He flees the spectacle of love's debilitating effects on Lance, only to recoil once more when Dave, an attractive, *masculine* homosexual, not involved in the 'scene', offers a friendship unlike any the narrator has previously known. He pities Dave for 'the paradoxical fact of him in a world of furtive contacts; he should be married, the father of adored children' (p. 217), and when Dave remarks upon the sadness of a male elephant at a circus, painted pink and with a flowered hat, the narrator describes his feelings of impotent helplessness before the naked self-revelation of another person. But more especially, he reveals by this comment his own view of homosexuality as necessarily degrading to one's masculinity. It is as if a consummation of his relationship with Dave might render both as ludicrous as that same elephant or the pair of effeminate lovers living near Dave, the sound of whose whining voices helps precipitate the narrator's clumsy severance of this friendship.

If pity and compassion threaten his persona, the narrator's flight to San Francisco is an attempt to repair the chinks in his armour. Appropriately, he is drawn to sadomasochistic rituals which seem a logical extension of his exultation (albeit passively) in wielding (hetero-) sexual power over others. Neil, a pathetic character, with a collection of manikins, costumes and photographs that forms a sinister contrast to the Professor's album of 'angels', makes an appeal to the narrator's narcissistic vision of his own masculinity which proves irresistible. But instead of facing up to the homosexual significance of his behaviour, he presents the experience in abstract terms as a symbolic attempt to crush whatever of innocence remained within him. Neil worships neo-fascist images of masculinity, the props of boots, insignia, leather jackets, uniforms and whips. This idolatry of brute strength renders all tokens of weakness contemptible: love, compassion, femininity—and homosexuality. The role-playing in which he and the narrator collaborate underlines the homosexual self-contempt that unites them. 'Strong' and 'weak' partners correspond to 'straight' and 'faggot' stereotypes, and in their relationship hatred is exploited as an aphrodisiac with the result that they perversely imitate their oppressors, eroticising the values that tyrannise their own lives. When Neil's confession about his hateful weak father and dominating mother places his behaviour in perspective, compassion and shame do finally overwhelm the narrator. Nonetheless, his self-enlightenment proceeds with no reference to his sexual identity. Instead, his wanderings through the hellish underworld of Chicago's outcasts renew his allegiance to those who suffer life's 'uninvited, unasked-for pain' and reveal to him that, 'It's possible to hate the filthy world and still love it with an abstract pitying love' (p. 280). His compromise is to retain the mask of the hustler to assure his safe passage through the 'filthy world' without inwardly identifying with the moral indifference it projects, thereby securing for himself the self-esteem of 'abstract pitying love' with none of the disadvantages of actively putting that into practice.

The Mardi Gras Carnival in New Orleans is presented as the climactic symbol of what lies beneath life's disguises, so concentrating the narrator's sense of the world's ugliness that he is overtaken by a feeling of spiritual death. As an old gypsy woman tells him, Mardi Gras is the one day in the year when everyone appears *without* their customary mask. But for the narrator, the riotous festival seems itself a facade, a giant analogue of his own fate which this time he cannot ignore. New Orleans strikes him as a rotting city, whorishly painting its cadaverous face; its Carnival of life is overshadowed by death, by Ash Wednesday, the inevitable day of reckoning. His process of self-judgment is set in motion through his acquaintance with the proprietress of a gay bar. Like the narrator, Sylvia has searched out the homosexual subculture for 'symbolic' reasons. However, her outward toughness does not prevent her underlying compassion from taking a practical form, in that she counsels and criticises those who frequent her bar. When she reveals that her self-imposed exile is in fact a penance for casting out her homosexual son, the narrator, in listening to her sorrows, marks his new willingness to atone for those faces that haunt him, 'as if in judgment for nothing really given, nothing really shared' (p. 362). Since his experience with Neil, he is more ready to accept the priest-like role of 'hearing confession' which is one ironic concomitant of the anonymous mask he wears. But since communication (like desire) is strictly one-way in hustler territory, he can neither 'absolve' himself nor others by shared experience; to listen is momentarily to alleviate loneliness, but to expose one's own vulnerability in return is to destroy the desired illusion of strength. When the narrator blurts out to two prospective clients that he is not the way he pretends to be but like them is 'Scared', predictably, they turn their attentions elsewhere.

Jeremy, who witnesses this outburst, offers an alternative to the role-playing world of the streets: that of a loving affair. His instant psychoanalysis of the frightened hustler constitutes the day of reckoning that he has always fled. Jeremy has all the makings of a homosexual *deus ex machina*: handsome, intelligent, masculine, madly in love with the narrator, and ready to whisk him away for a 'lasting relationship'. But love, even if it is only a question of 'accepting' it with the same intensity with which it is given, is rejected as a myth

> which could lull you again falsely in order to seduce you—like
> that belief in God—into a trap—away from the only thing which

made sense—rebellion—no matter how futilely rendered by the fact of decay, of death.

(p. 366)

Therefore the narrator forces the encounter back into the safe formula of hustler and client, this time taking a dominant role as if to reassert the maleness he was in danger of losing. Having defeated temptation, he returns to the streets, committed to his 'heroic burden', emerging 'mythless to face the world of the masked pageant' (p. 369), having, in the euphoria of self-revelation, evaded altogether the question of his sexual identity.

At the height of the Carnival, Miss Destiny's evil angel makes an appearance (courtesy of J. P. Sartre), to sentence everyone to spend eternity repeating their present motions, for living the only way they 'could'. So, in the frenzied, accelerating tempo of the Carnival's 'gaudy funeral', the narrator repeats the characteristic movement of his life, whirling anonymously from partner to partner until some point of saturation is reached, the nightworld collapses around him and Ash Wednesday ushers in the feeling of 'spiritual death'. As ever, flight is his only reflex, and his journey ends where it began, with his return to El Paso and his mother, though the retrospective voyage of his writing marks an attempt to break the circularity of his experience and to atone for 'nothing really given, nothing really shared. . . .'

But Rechy also turns repetition into a stylistic device, with tiresome results. He would persuade us of the lonesome nature of his world by mere incantation of the word—'lonesome'; images of Heaven and Hell cram every page, and 'angels' drift in and out of his prose as if the Professor himself had had a hand in its composition. Not only does this religious rhetoric seem contrived (if compared, say, with the poetic vision of Jean Genet), but it also obscures the actual roots of suffering in the subculture which is described. The complex social and cultural pressures that affect sexual identity are glossed over by the simplistic myth of universal expulsion from an Edenic realm of love. The novel has all the moral complexity of Sylvia's *cri-de-coeur*, when she gestures towards the occupants of her bar and sighs, 'All—all, all . . . all . . . my . . . saintly . . . children. All flung out by something—or someone!' (p. 313). Rechy portrays rejection as some inevitable and unchangeable fate, according to which all and yet none are guilty, each is saint and sinner alike: Sylvia 'slaughtered her son and he

slaughtered her because they each *had to* (p. 326, my italics);
similarly, when Chi-Chi, a hopelessly 'butch' drag queen, turns on
a jeering tourist, Rechy must wonder whether the latter glimpses
in her,

> the hopelessness of his own sad fate . . . whatever shape that fate
> may have assumed for him, whatever destiny hovering over him
> —over us—like a dreadful cloud?
>
> (p. 333)

It is a pity that he dissipates the power of such scenes by the attempt to make homosexuality symbolic of some more universal
condition with which his narrator may safely identify, for his drag
queens have more evident claim to heroic status than the hustler.
Whereas the latter takes refuge behind the *status quo* of masculinity, the drag queens take on to the point of parody the visible
stigma of homosexuality; object lessons in the petrification of
available sexual roles, their confrontations with 'straight' society
produce some of the novel's most dramatic moments.

Numbers (1967) and *The Sexual Outlaw* (1977) mark subsequent stages in Rechy's portrayal of the homosexual as hero.
Numbers is, in some respects, a more skilful novel than *City of
Night*; its symbolic structure is designed to reveal rather than conceal its protagonist's sexual dilemma. Johnny Rio, ex-hustler and
'butch number' (whose beauties include 'almost ridiculously long
lashes'), driving from Texas to the 'foggy city of dead angels', is
the familiar autobiographical persona. The third person narration
is more than a narcissistic mirror, however, and although Rechy's
writing is singularly humourless, he does, in this instance, allow
himself ironic observations on his hero's sophistries. In a key passage, we are told:

> Always before, at each crisis of his life, the only salvation Johnny
> Rio has found from total shattering anarchy has been the grasping
> for and finding of a reason for his actions . . . a frame to contain
> his fantastic existence.[5]

In the framework of the novel itself, the author plays devil's advo-
cate to the elaborate self-defences of a younger, more ingenuous
version of himself, countering each move in the desperate game
that is played. For three years, Johnny Rio has disciplined himself
to break his dependence on sexual adoration, but,

Precisely one day after he told himself he was completely rid of the need for the life he'd fled—that day, as he stood looking at himself in the mirror, he felt curiously that he had ceased to exist.

(p. 23)

Rationing himself to ten days, he returns to Los Angeles, the scene of former triumphs, to confront and defeat the outlaw self. But just as this 'frame' promises success, it too collapses and, with a neat symmetry, the novel completes its own 'frame' of the hero's 'fantastic existence'.

Having fled his former life as a hustler after catching a glimpse of some 'depraved distortion' of his lovely self, the mirror has driven him into motion once more. A cross between Dorian Gray and the Lone Ranger, he studies his own reflection for solace and judgment after each tryst in the wild west of sexual outlaws. People and places act as 'mirrors' and 'frames' too, and are equally capable of treachery. Noting the ravages the years have wrought on his old hustling territories, Johnny seeks in other people confirmation of his own untarnished looks and masculine charms— for these are the weapons with which questions of homosexuality can be held at bay. In fact, his sexual practices are hedged around by so many rules and qualifications that the necessary combination of circumstances resembles a complex mathematical formula. He will neither initiate nor reciprocate any advance, for this would fatally compromise the heterosexual illusion he contrives and which is the basis of his power. Nonetheless, his behaviour is elaborately codified: his own time and motion expert, he calculates each exhibitionistic move so as to obtain maximum gratification in the least possible time. Casual encounters pose less of a challenge to his self-image, therefore he frequents locales with a rapid turn-over of likely worshippers: darkened cinema balconies, toilets, areas of certain parks. Such places have symbolic advantages: hints of danger and lawlessness act like an aphrodisiac; as territories with distinct boundaries they coincide with his effort to compartmentalise life; they also offer the cover of anonymity, contacts being strictly limited and conversation eliminated—except for those welcome eulogies of his assets ('You blew my mind baby . . .').

A section of Griffith Park becomes the focal point of the 'game' he plays. The territory to be conquered is overgrown and jungly, the perfect hunting ground and setting for a homosexual 'western'.

After a scouting expedition to colonise this frontier remnant with invented names, he stakes his claim to absolute ascendancy in its pecking order with the strutting bravado of a cowboy making his 'kills'. There is much unintentional comedy in this jockeying for position: by and large the natives trample one another in the rush to genuflect before the newcomer's 'weapon', but war has to be declared on rival beauties, hysteria mounts behind the studied mask of indifference, and showdowns occur. In awed tones, the commentator tells us that, 'One rejection—real or imaginary—can slaughter Johnny Rio, even among 100 successes' (p. 83). Rules that test his charms to the fullest take shape; he selects the handsomest, most masculine looking 'scores' (not that *he* desires them) since their reduction to a 'homosexual' role will make victory all the sweeter; he cannot 'count' the same person twice, and only actual sexual contact is eligible for addition to his total. By playing for such high stakes he flirts constantly with defeat, especially when others fail to reflect back at him his ideal self ('if he tries to rub against me or acts like he thinks I'll touch him, I'll bust him in his mother-fucking face' [p. 118]). The ludicrous and pathetic nature of this hypersensitivity is typified by the incident where, having carefully selected a mound as the pedestal from which to flex his muscles at passers-by, he is outraged when someone takes him for a *dancer*.

But although it is difficult to accept Johnny Rio at his author's evaluation as a tragic hero, neither is he simply a narcissistic clown. There is something genuinely sad about him. If for many homosexuals, the hypocrisy of daily disguise could at least be set aside in the act of sex itself, Rechy's hero takes himself so seriously that there is neither joy nor honest lust in his promiscuity; for all the purely physical nature of his contacts, they are merely the outward signs of a self-regarding spiritual longing, and for all his readiness to display his wares he is the helpless victim of physical inhibition.

The game he plays and the rules he improvises seemingly rise up from unknown depths in himself, as if some design of fate lay hidden there. And so:

> The horror that he *is* counting, accumulating numbers aimlessly, strikes his consciousness like a sniper's bullet. . . . And so it is a game—but a game which can't be won because it's limitless. Only *It* can win—the game itself . . . and the Park. The Park,

which is suddenly his enemy—his opponent in this mysterious game.

(p. 190)

From the beginning the Park disturbed him with its atmosphere of 'eternal, sad twilight', corresponding ominously with his mood on the road outside Phoenix when groups of birds seemed to court death by stationing themselves in the path of his car. If the Park allows him to flirt with and appear to triumph over his own definitions of death, it is also playing a game with him, paying out rope. . . .

'I'm alive', he tells himself, notching up the first conquest of the day; like the child he once was, counting the beads of his rosary to ward off fears of darkness, so now he spins a desperate litany of orgasms. Yet the game seems to be taking him over, as if the Park were folding him into its spectral trance. He retaliates by placing his own limit on the contest and hits upon the number, thirty, as the symbolic target by which his three years' absence can be redeemed in the space of the ten days he has allowed himself. He achieves only a Pyrrhic victory over his outlaw self and, by extension, the Park. For, when celebrating with friends, someone tells him that thirty is also a printer's symbol for The End; an attempt to make love *with* someone fails, and so the morning of departure finds him back in the Park, numbers accumulating in hallucinatory frenzy. The trap is sprung: to leave the Park is one kind of death, to stay is another—but at least his outlaw existence is a protest against the terms of his confinement, and thus he thinks in terror and excitement, 'This is what I'd like to do all my life! Until— . . .' (p. 248). 'Terminal sex' is at once his defiance and his chosen mode of death, that ultimate 'number'. If the Park is his prison, then he turns on its ghostly Sheriff, a man in a red convertible who has dogged him like a shadow throughout these days; but the man, who never removes his mirrored glasses, merely returns Johnny's accusations, confirming his role as hunter and hunted. Finally, cocking an imitation rifle, he pings upwards in protest at the 'Heavenly Sniper' who holds all the numbers, and concludes, 'There never was a reason, I'm just here and that's all', thereby resigning himself to a 'craving that expects no surcease' (p. 255). That taste for the limitless which defined the frontier energy of the archetypal west has its ironic counterpart here: the treadmill of sex in a corner of 'macho country'.

95

In an interview with James R. Giles, Rechy claims, 'The homo-sexual is the clearest symbol of alienation and despair. And nobil-ity.'[6] But however one might sympathise with these sentiments, *Numbers* remains unconvincing in its attempt to impart an exis-tential glamour to its hero's revolt against 'fate'. Johnny Rio more insidiously symbolises the tyranny of *machismo*. There is pathos but little nobility in an addiction to power which depends on the ephemeral combination of looks and manly charisma and causes the hero to snipe not so much at 'Heaven' as at fellow homosexuals who are reduced to mere numbers in his solipsistic codification of sex as power-play; their subservience is both the price he now charges and the fuel of his revolt.

In *The Sexual Outlaw* (1977) Rechy seeks to ornament his pro-totypical hero's existence by a more revolutionary frame, up-dat-ing his image, as if anxious to be identified with the radical liberation movements that more especially since the late 1960s worked to transform the self-concepts of homosexual men and women. The work is described as a 'non-fiction account, with com-mentaries, of three days and nights in the sexual underground', and combines the narrative of ex-hustler, Jim, with documentation of gay oppression (by police, judiciary, media and religious organ-isations) and the author's statements on his life, writings and view of homosexuality. Jim's narrative gives a cinematic account of a self-indulgent, exhibitionist marathon, a race against time to cram as much sex as possible into one long weekend. This latest incarna-tion of Rechy's fictionalised persona is something of a veteran, seeking, as ever, mirrors for his continuing desirability and tri-umphant survival of the years. His chain of furtive encounters in toilets, parks, garages, and alleys, testifies interminably to his stamina, his superstud charms—and to those characteristic fears whereby the merest hint of rejection plunges him into suicidal despair.

It is understandable that Rechy feels the need to place expository frames around this account which in itself would scarcely display Jim as an unsung hero and courageous freedom fighter in the very vanguard of the sexual revolution. Admittedly, the narrative is adorned with the rhetoric of heroism—but as a 'gladiator' on the brink of the 'arena', Jim is not about to do battle with some Goliath of oppression—merely to swagger into the shadows of a rotting pier to hold impromptu court with a circle of eager admirers. Rechy makes the point that *any* assertion and celebration of one's homosexuality is, in our society, still a rebellious stance, but although Jim's energies and monumental score may well inspire amazement, he is hardly the model of 'liberation'. Nonetheless, the author makes the following observations on his kind:

> Promiscuous homosexuals (outlaws *with dual identities*—tomorrow they will go to offices and athletic fields, classrooms and construction sites) are the shock troops of the sexual revolution. The streets are the battleground, the revolution is the sexhunt, a radical statement is made each time a man has sex with another on the street [my italics].[7]

Yet the 'battlegrounds' to which Rechy refers are only nominally public and one cannot imagine that many unsuspecting matrons stray into them to have their consciousness raised by witnessing the 'shock troops' at work. Indeed, their very invisibility to all but the cognoscenti is what makes the police raids on behalf of an outraged (but absent) populace so hypocritical. In themselves, Rechy's attacks upon the methods of police and judiciary are justified, but as the basis for his 'promiscuity-as-revolution' stand they carry less weight. He rails against the crude mechanics of oppression but not the 'hidden curriculum' of society's sexist values that lend them their authority, for, paradoxically, the repressive forces he criticises are precisely those required to maintain the 'sex in dark corners' arena for his hero's gladiatorial triumphs. The separation of sex from the individual's everyday world and its relegation to the safety-valve of 'outlaw country' is a dubious model of revolutionary freedom. Whilst tradition may lend a 'silently symphonic, intricate, instinctively choreographed beauty' (p. 196) to these Dionysian revels, the liberating affirmation of sexuality is, at the same time, a balletic ritual of oppression where the individual (though even here he must be young and attractive) is simply a figure in an orgiastic tableau, a number.

At times, Rechy seems aware that Jim's activities are hardly likely to bring the message home to the people and is led to fantasise about televised orgies and High Street sex. Yet secrecy and invisibility have themselves been eroticised in his anonymous world, and it never seems to occur to him that instead of settling for a 'dual identity', his 'shock troops' might do battle within the everyday world, in the 'offices and athletic fields, classrooms and construction sites' to which they return on Monday mornings. In fact, the 'fight' in which Jim engages is always being won—as Rechy reveals by his war cry, 'Board one place, we'll find two more' (p. 300). The 'hunting grounds' can scarcely be defeated by the forces of repression, to which they cater. As Rechy's heroes are themselves so hedged around by their own vanity as to be incapable of initiating or forming relationships, incapable even of expressing desire, his revolutionary fervour is little more than an exhibitionist's desire to *épater le bourgeois* which, in the absence of televised orgies, can be transmitted only by the most graphic written account. Rechy is committed to the maintenance of an underground, demanding only 'better conditions for the workers', not the overthrow of the system.

William Burroughs, a writer of much greater stature, addresses himself to many themes outside the focus of this study, but his images of male homosexuality do suggest certain comparisons with those of Rechy. The explicit physical detail which characterises both writers' treatment of this subject has provoked scandal and controversy; while some dismiss them as pornographers, even organising threats under obscenity laws, they have in other quarters acquired the reputation of 'freedom fighters'. Although their defiance of traditional taboo has been courageous, it seems strange that they should be regarded as 'homosexual heroes' when the type of liberation presented in their work is so limited—or, in Burroughs' case, so limitless.

In his *Gay Sunshine* interviews, Allen Ginsberg—apostle to the great God of the underground—advances Burroughs' claim to the revolutionary's laurels, stating,

> He's one of the few gay lib 'heroes', one of the few homosexual theorists who has theorised up to the point of outside-of-the-body, and detachment from sexuality. In fact, the cut-ups were originally designed to rehearse and repeat his obsession with sexual images over and over again . . . so that finally the obsessive attachment, compulsion and preoccupation empty out and drain from the image.

He adds,

> The body itself may be the by-product of a large scale conspiracy by certain forces as Burroughs says, trying to keep people prisoners in a prison universe made out of parent matter.[8]

98

It would seem, therefore, that while the rest of us are still struggling to reclaim our bodies and our sexuality, Burroughs, the trail blazer, urges us to be free of the whole process.

Hammering everything into his visionary metaphor of addiction, Burroughs depicts sex as a debilitating craving of vulnerable human flesh, a craving that enslaves just as much as does heroin. In his paranoid version of reality as science fiction, the pilgrim's progress runs along the path of excess. He devises recipes for a 'naked lunch' whereby we can see what is on the end of the collective 'fork', 'stuff' ourselves to the point of nausea and so hope to cure our dependency and 'habit'. Of course, this could all be regarded as a wonderful joke: like an alcoholic committing himself to a brewery, Burroughs can indulge all his favourite fantasies again and again, an addict of his own medicine. Semen jets crazily and voluminously in work after work, the 'cure' seeming as far away as ever. Yet in some quarters, patience is running out, as exemplified by the magisterial pique with which one reviewer greeted *The Wild Boys*:

> Indeed, assuming Mr. Burroughs has a point to make at all, one is left wondering how many close ups of sodomy and masturbation will be needed to make it obvious.[9]

Certainly, Burroughs seems engaged in endless battle with himself; his anarchic sexual drives are in combat (or is it collusion?) with a censorious self which is graced with the cunning of the *avant-garde littérateur*. The fantasist embarks upon a masturbatory spree, whilst the censor obliges him to take a scalpel to this image bank of 'dirty' pictures, to cut up, shuffle, repeat, rearrange them and thereby erase their erotic hold. At times, though, this censorious self that desires to break the bonds of the body and soar into some blissful, empty, silent plane of being seems kin to the Green Nun in *The Wild Boys*, who orders her victim to write out '*i am a filthy little beast* ten thousand times in many places',[10] only to feed vicariously on such confessions and go at night (in 'Christ drag'!) to visit a young nun in her cell. Ironically, the attempt to obliterate the images by sheer force of repetition is only partially successful, and though none of the novels is allowed to form a coherent whole in any traditional sense, the fragments, emblazoned on our consciousness by an exquisite command of language, continue to exert a subliminal spell. One is reminded of the fate of Johnny Rio whose attempt to subdue his appetite by the surfeit of 'numbers' left him prey to a 'craving that expects no surcease'.

Johnny Rio's fear of being 'taken over' by the Park is a dread of the vulnerability and possibility of rejection that he associates with homosexuality. Burroughs, likewise, sometimes presents homosexuality as an alien force that can nest, cuckoo-like, in the individual consciousness. Whereas Rechy's hero comes to choose this fate, he strives nonetheless to impose his own shape upon it by seeking endless confirmation of his superior power. Ironically, this reproduces an aspect of the very phenomenon he fears: that is, by reducing himself and other people to the narrowest of sexual dimensions, his individual self is subsumed by his homosexuality. This is a fate Burroughs obviously fears, and in *Junky* (1953) homosexuality is imaged as an invasive power that 'takes over' its 'host'. The narrator confides:

> A room full of fags gives me the horrors. They jerk around like puppets on invisible strings, galvanised into hideous activity that is the negation of everything living and spontaneous. The live human being has moved out of these bodies long ago. But something moved in when the original tenant moved out. Fags are ventriloquists' dummies who have moved in and taken over the ventriloquist. The dummy sits in a queer bar nursing his beer, and uncontrollably yapping out of a rigid doll face.[11]

The contempt Burroughs shows for his fellow homosexuals in this passage betrays a fear of vulnerability analogous to Rechy's own. The homosexual is presented as a symbol of passive manipulation, the prey of some 'virus' as it were (recalling those old theories of a disease, 'caught' in adolescence, usually from an older man or too much masturbation!). Burroughs does not appear to consider that the 'fags' he sneers at here might have been 'living and spontaneous' until society and not homosexuality 'moved in'. And if individuals are deadened by stereotypes, then the viciousness of his parody in this instance ignores the social context that makes *spontaneity* impossible for many homosexuals. His simplistic view of the self as infinitely malleable by forces that lie always *outside* denies the naturalness of homosexual experience and the fact that for many individuals it is the very expression of their autonomy and personal freedom.

Burroughs' homosexual paranoia is encapsulated in more comic terms by a parable in *The Naked Lunch* (1959) which relates how a man is 'taken over' by his anus—it learns to speak, develops teeth, bites through his clothing and eventually encases him in a suffocating, film-like growth. Since anal eroticism is the staple theme of this author's personal fantasies, the story gives farcical acknowledgement to the potential treachery of this orifice—the point of pleasure being also the point of entry of that 'alien force', and what better image of power than the phallus? There are many variants on this idea in his work: if in the realm of drugs he found himself looking for the 'final fix', similarly he is obsessed by the notion of 'terminal sex'—that final orgasm which releases one pleasurably from the whole messy business of living. Although Burroughs declares his horror at these parallel death routes, they also exert a hold over his imagination which it seeks continually to exorcise, as if there is no final point of liberation from the body's tyranny, only the endless attempt to liberate oneself. He is fond of relating instances of people literally dying of sex; in *The Naked Lunch* we are told of a malady known as 'Bang-utot' whose victims are obsessed by the idea that their penis will enter their body and kill them—Burroughs surmises misplaced sexual energies to be the cause of death, possibly an erection of the lungs! And in the 'Blue Movie' section of the same novel, he repeats and rearranges his most ghoulish images of sex as demonic possession when Johnny, Mark and Mary, the three guests at a 'naked lunch' are themselves devoured by a monstrous lust which plays sadist to each masochist self; a hanging forms the main course and the cannibalism of genitals an impromptu dessert. The author's fascination for the image of the hanged man recalls that of the 'fags' jerking about like puppets on invisible strings, and the notion of sex as the noose around one's neck is his most extreme metaphor of its tyranny. It conveys his fear of (and, one suspects, his delight in) the involuntary nature of sexual arousal—the brute response of the phallus to stimuli beyond conscious control. Thus, the basis of his 'horror' at the flesh's shameless subservience is the reduction of the whole complexity of social and sexual relations to biological fact. Burroughs claims that this section was written as a tract against capital punishment,[12] the ultimate symbol of society's addiction to power—yet there is little internal corroboration of this. The scenes convey more obviously the way sex is envisaged as leading to the 'death' of the autonomous self—and the fact that Burroughs eroticises this very tyranny. The earlier sequence describing the 'Mugwump' confirms this impression; the grotesque creature is like some imaginary incarnation of the homosexual 'virus', forcibly entering a blond youth and obliging him to go 'all the way' before a delighted audience whose 'cocks ejaculate in silent "yes"'. Such masturbatory fantasies are spun on a dubious didactic thread which equates homosexuality with the deadliest pact of sadist and masochist: 'The boy looks into the Mugwumps eyes blank as obsidian mirrors, pools of black blood, glory holes in a toilet wall closing on the Last Erection' (p. 95). In such scenes we are never sure whether, to use Burroughs' own analogy, the ventriloquist or the dummy is speaking to us.

In *The Wild Boys*, A Book of the Dead (1971), the eroticist joins forces with the 'outside-of-the-body' theorist, or, as one of the novel's many voices puts it: 'This is the space age and sex movies must express the longing to escape from flesh through sex' (p. 82), which seems a comic formulation of Burroughs' own paradoxical ambitions. Here, he comes closer to projecting male homosexuality in heroic terms, as may be gauged from one critic's complaint that,

> He dwells so lovingly on each piece of rectal pleasure one would think it was paradisiacal sex amongst the angels rather than aberrational acts he was describing.[13]

Ironically, the 'Wild Boys' *are* more like angels than ordinary mortals, or at least they are demon saints, abstractions, mutants, forerunners of a sexuality which has broken free of the manipulators of human flesh, lifting them on to some other plane of being, some ante-chamber to the 'Blue Desert of Silence', which is Burroughs' desired nirvana.

The novel might be described as a futuristic 'western' where the 'cowboys' and 'indians' of the author's fantasies run amok in global conflict. On one side are the 'Controllers' of the human species with their diseased Pentagon minds, familiar villains in his demonic mythology; they are opposed by the 'Wild Boys', a kind of collective hero, an underground guerrilla movement, spreading out from their base in North Africa. The armies of 'civilisation' are thus directed against some science fiction 'Sodom and Gomorrah' or international 'vietcong' of homosexual hippydom. It is soon apparent, though, that those who pass themselves off as defenders of the world's purity are themselves manufacturing and manipulating sexual 'depravities' as the justification of their police states and totalitarian controls. They have 'pictures' on everybody.

Running like a motif through this warfare is the 'story' of Audrey, a 'thin pale boy his face scarred by festering spiritual wounds' (p. 32). Like an incarnation of Burroughs' youthful self, he haunts the environs of St. Louis, a spectre, a 'dead child' of the suburbs. The 'Penny Arcade Peepshow' of his mind is a world of sexual fantasy in which images of his future whirl in kaleidoscopic profusion. There are many versions of Audrey's 'story', just as Audrey himself fades and blurs into other characters, in particular into one called Johnny. This duplicates the process of the main narrative, which seems to be made up of innumerable 'films', spliced in surrealist confusion, breaking into and incorporating one another. If the 'Controllers' have their 'pictures' on Audrey, then Burroughs retaliates with the tactics of the 'Wild Boys', sneaking behind enemy lines to 'explode' those pictures. If society issues one with a 'ticket', a programme, a manufactured version or 'film' of reality, then this can be fed back into the machine to destroy it. There are a number of exemplary demonstrations of this idea; at one point, for instance, Johnny and Mark are programmed as all-American astronauts,

> playing the part of American married idiots until the moment when they take off on a Gemini expedition bound for Mars, disconnect and leave the earth behind forever.
>
> (p. 83)

They offer a blueprint for the 'escape from flesh through sex' in the trail of 'image dust' left in space, delirious fragments of remembered adolescent love-making that 'explode' the heterosexual 'ticket' with which they were originally issued. Elsewhere, Audrey/ Johnny, as the drifting offspring of a junkie and an alcoholic, haunting a Mexican golf-course, tells us,

> What happens between my legs is like a cold drink to me . . . I know that other people think of it as something special to do with how they feel about someone else and there is a word love that means nothing to me at all. It is just a feeling between the legs, a sort of tingle.
>
> (p. 105)

This is all that tethers him to the earth—otherwise, like a toy balloon, once released he might blow away across the sky. If love is just another blackmailing fabrication through which society maintains its 'prison universe' and prevents one 'streaking across the sky like a star' (p. 102), then Burroughs is endlessly engaged in severing the cords that restrain him, bidding (a spectacular) farewell to all his favourite pictures, so as to anaesthetise and release himself from their erotic hold.

If sexuality is monitored by the 'Controllers' ('Operation Little Audrey on target', one of them smugly remarks) and harnessed to Machiavellian ends, then their films can be subverted—just as Audrey smashes through the screen that tracks his progress, wiping out the Green Nun and other luminaries who are gathered in conference. And if Johnny's departure to join the 'Wild Boys' is part of their plan too (his farewell note is beamed into each suburban heart as proof that 'vile tentacles' of evil are reaching into decent American homes), and if the 'Wild Boys' themselves are included in this strategy, then these larger films can also be smashed. The gangs of 'dead children' feed death back into the system, slaughtering and butchering those armies that come to 'liberate' (and film) them, blessed with an emotional anaesthesia that renders them as pure and blank as space itself. Like harbingers of that 'outside-of-the-body' realm Burroughs craves, they can move through time, venturing into the 'Blue Desert of Silence' and reproduce themselves, picturesquely, by conjuring will-o'-the-wisps out of the air and fucking them into fleshly form. This is the ultimate in jockstrap brotherhood, a total escape from the confines of human existence, yet one which does not forfeit the benefits of homosexual eroticism. It is like a crazy wish-fulfilment of all Rechy's dreams: a mass insurrection on the part of his fellow outlaws and the establishment of a Peter Pan world of eternal orgy.

Burroughs imparts his own fantastic interpretation to the gay liberation concept of 'coming out'; he offers no hope or model for reshaping existing patterns of identity, only the injunction to destroy all patterns and constricting moulds, to release the entrapped spirit to some netherworld that lies, necessarily, beyond the scope of definition. If one conceives of sex as a form of communication and a way of defining feelings that break the circle of self, then neither of these two authors achieves such a liberation. Rechy's heroes communicate only with themselves, whilst Burroughs wants to break free of the self altogether, to escape into a psychic nowhere. Both reject love as an imprisoning myth that seduces one away from rebellion; both portray sexuality as a protest against the confines of physical existence, yet succeed only in reducing life to the merely physical and in dramatising the death of the individual personality within a perspective of 'terminal sex'.

NOTES

1. Norman Mailer, *The Prisoner of Sex* (1971).
2. Ann Charters, *Kerouac* (San Francisco, 1973).
3. Allen Ginsberg interviewed by Allen Young, *Gay Sunshine* 16 (January, 1973) and *Gay Sunshine* 17 (March 1973).
4. John Rechy, *City of Night* (1963). (New York: Ballantine, 1973), p. 17. Subsequent page references are to this edition.
5. John Rechy, *Numbers* (1967). (New York: Evergreen Black Cat Edition, 1968), p. 117. Subsequent page references are to this edition.
6. John Rechy interviewed by James R. Giles, *Chicago Review* 25 (Summer, 1973), p. 21.
7. John Rechy, *The Sexual Outlaw* (New York: Grove Press, 1977), p. 229. Subsequent page references are to this edition.
8. See Note 3. (*Allen Ginsberg Gay Sunshine Interview, with Allen Young*, Bolinas, California: Grey Fox Press, 1976), pp. 37–8.
9. *The Times Literary Supplement* (January 2nd, 1972), p. 622.
10. William Burroughs, *The Wild Boys* (1971). (London: Calder & Boyars, 1972), p. 28. Subsequent page references are to this edition.
11. William Burroughs, *Junky* (1953). (London: Penguin, 1977), p. 72.
12. William Burroughs, *The Naked Lunch* (1959). (London: Corgi, 1968), Introduction, p. 14. Subsequent page references are to this edition.
13. J. J. Murray, *Best Sell*, Vol. 31 (November, 1971), p. 352.

5

Only Connect: E. M. FORSTER and J. R. Ackerley

The posthumously published writings of E. M. Forster offer an interesting perspective on the fortunes of the homosexual hero. *Maurice*, written in 1913–14, revised in 1919, 1932, and 1959–60, finally appeared in 1971; the stories on homosexual themes in *The Life to Come* date from 1922 to 1958, yet were not published until 1972. Although their social background may now seem remote, the open affirmative spirit in which they were conceived is more characteristic of the present day. Undoubtedly, Forster might have published these works in his lifetime, though at what precise point is a matter for conjecture. Novels which deal frankly with homosexuality still tend to be construed as self-exposure and likely to endanger a reputation. In 1965, forwarding Donald Windham's novel, *Two People*, to Forster, J. R. Ackerley quotes from its author's letter to him:

> I had a terrible time finishing the book—a moral block about it—which I think you must be familiar with and will understand. Times have changed since Morgan wrote *Maurice* (and publishing since you wrote *We Think the World of You*, I dare say), but my relatives haven't.[1]

The practices of other writers place Forster's self-censorship in a more favourable light, for if timidity plays its part in the long-delayed publication of these writings, then so does personal integrity and defiance of convention. Fellow homosexuals such as Siegfried Sassoon sublimated their most personal feelings in their public work, whilst privately confessing to 'unpublishable writings'. Others, like Vita Sackville-West, adopted the old expedient of transposing the sex of a principal character, *The Challenge* (1924) being a disguised version of her love affair with Violet

Trefusis. Another contemporary, Osbert Sitwell, makes merely a 'safe' reference in the five volumes of his autobiography to David Horner, his life-long companion. D. H. Lawrence, whose idealisation of male friendship was, like Forster's, in part inspired by Whitman and Carpenter, destroyed his treatise on homosexuality, *Goats and Compasses*, and suppressed the revealing Prologue to *Women in Love* where Birkin is depicted as homosexual ('it was for men that he felt the hot, flushing, roused attraction which a man is supposed to feel for the other sex'[2]).

It is too easy to complain, as many critics have, of an excessive timidity on Forster's part. Those who nowadays applaud the wildest fantasies of Burroughs or Genet must find Forster's homoeroticism tame by comparison, but it is worth recalling that the writing of *Maurice* and *The Life to Come* extended from a decade which saw the banning of *The Rainbow* to one which began with the prosecution of *Lady Chatterley's Lover*—by which time Forster was in his eighties. If amorous, heterosexual gamekeepers could still, in 1960, cause a public sensation, then one appreciates an old man's reluctance to launch his own less orthodox gamekeeper and upper-class lover into the fray. Furthermore, until the 1967 Sexual Offences Act freed some homosexuals from the fear of criminal prosecution, individual 'offenders' were faced with savage punishment and social disgrace for relations which *Maurice* earnestly recommends. The wonder is that the novel came to be written at all, or that it survived its author's impulse to destroy his 'indecent' writings, a practice only partly accounted for by artistic dissatisfactions, as he was also careful to omit any reference to homosexuality in his biography of Goldsworthy Lowes Dickinson, despite the frank sexual confessions available to him in his old friend's manuscripts. The survival of the homosexual writings illustrates, albeit belatedly, that insistence on 'connecting' and truthtelling, however painful or unpopular, which is pitted against respectability and conformity in Forster's work. To some, they are an awkward and embarrassing legacy with a nuisance value akin to the quirky heroism with which Adela Quested, in *A Passage to India*, brings the pageant of tribal honour to a muddled halt.

Reaction to these stubbornly preserved writings has been generally unfavourable. It is important to note, however, that irrespective of their artistic merit, the mere revelation of the author's homosexuality has been sufficient to throw doubt on the stature of his earlier work. The reviewer of *Maurice* for the *Times Literary Supplement* thought fit to pontificate on the limitations of the 'homosexual imagination' as follows:

> Most obviously, Forster could not imagine any aspect of the range of experience between men and women—heterosexual attraction, heterosexual relations, marriage were mysterious to him. No wonder he resented having to write 'marriage novels'—the subject was quite beyond his range . . . No doubt this is why one feels in so many of Forster's novels a kind of transference at work, as though one were reading a different story, but translated into socially acceptable terms.[3]

But it is arrogant to suppose that homosexuals are 'most obviously' disqualified from any understanding of heterosexuality (indeed, they are among its most assiduous students), or that they cannot help but codify their own predilections. Elsewhere, George Steiner applies the technique of 'code-breaking', to proclaim, somewhat wildly, that

> The encounters between whites and native, between emancipated rulers and 'advanced' Indians, in *A Passage to India* are a brilliant projection of the confrontations between society and the homosexual in *Maurice*.

He also maintains that the very centrality of *Maurice* in Forster's work and private life,

> may narrow or specialise the sum of his achievement. In the light of an intensely spiritualised yet nervous and partly embittered homosexuality, a number of Forster's most famous dicta—'it is better to betray one's country than a friend', 'only connect', take on a more restricted, shriller ambience.[4]

By curious logic, universal relevance is deemed synonymous with heterosexuality, but if Forster's 'connections' include the homosexual, should this be presumed to exclude all others, to be 'more restricted' and 'shriller'?

'Narrow' and 'dated' are the words most commonly used to describe *Maurice*. Superficially, it is indeed dated, with its Edwardian setting and occasional lapses into the sexual ignorance it criticises (as Lytton Strachey pointed out, its views on masturbation are decidedly quaint). But to dismiss it as Jeffrey Meyers does by asserting that in 1971 it had lost 'all its moral and social significance',[5] or as John Sayre Martin does, saying that, 'In today's world Maurice could have been an active and happy homosexual as well as a stock broker',[6] is both to display a complacent optimism about the present day and to ignore the fact that homosexuality involves not just a minor issue of law reform but a wider challenge to conventional lifestyles, in relation to which Forster's novel is still relevant. Certainly, *Maurice* is more limited in theme and structure when compared with *Howards End* or *A Passage to India*, but this narrowness of focus is inevitable in a novel which concentrates on the inner life of a single individual who must necessarily seek his destiny outside ordinary society. Its central proposition that homosexual fulfilment is incompatible with conventional involvement in society is borne out by most contemporary treatments of the theme for, as has been suggested, the homosexual novel is typically a description of a journey away from the everyday world. And although Forster's 'greenwood' was already a nostalgic conception in his own day, it has its modern equivalents: Vidal's pastoral idyll on the banks of the Potomac; Baldwin's France, Isherwood's Berlin or California; Burroughs' adventures in North Africa and 'outer space'; and Rechy's Griffith Park, where the greenwood has shrunk to a miserable oasis of outlaw sex.

The novel opens with a vivid prophecy of the sexual hypocrisies from which Maurice must struggle to disentangle himself, when he is taken aside by a well-meaning schoolmaster, Mr Ducie, who is determined to 'enlighten' the fatherless boy on the principal 'connection' of life. During their stroll along a beach, Mr Ducie sketches a diagram in the sand with his walking stick but is later stricken with panic to think that his graphic message has been left for the edification of passers-by. The boy is filled with distrust for the 'lies' he has been offered, and the diagram that falls apart like 'an impossible sum' in the 'darkness'[7] of his mind, anticipates the impact of his homosexuality on Maurice's place in the ordered social structure and the programme to make him into a replica of his father. The scene introduces the imagery of light and darkness that runs throughout the narrative; it prefigures the ignorance of other father figures, such as Dr Barry, and the shame of other educators, like Clive Durham, who theorises enthusiastically on Platonic love yet squirms with embarrassment when asked for a kiss and who, after his miraculous conversion to heterosexuality, would dearly like to erase the signs he too has left in the sand. The scene also sets up an ironic twist of the plot, for Mr Ducie invites Maurice and his 'wife' to dine with him ten years hence, but when they do meet quite by chance in the British Museum, Maurice is busily wooing a male partner and his old schoolmaster has forgotten his name, not to mention his invitation.

Outwardly, Maurice has more in common with the robust virility and practical energies of the Wilcox males in *Howards End* and none of the qualities that the author satirises in himself, perhaps, in the timid, cosseted Schlegel male, Tibby. As with Vidal's protagonist in *The City and the Pillar*, Forster's hero is emphatically ordinary—a tactic which is used similarly to stress that homosexuality is not confined to rare creatures or to unusual circumstances. But whilst it is important that his hero should seem on the surface unremarkable, Forster labours this to the point of dullness. The early chapters are very short and rely heavily on generalisation and summarised information; at times, they read more like a synopsis or set of notes on character and plot. The account of Maurice's subconscious life is more compelling. His journey from darkness to a 'painful dawn' is conveyed in terms of a metaphoric landscape; his adolescent years are spent like a somnambulist, groping in the fog of the 'Valley of the Shadow of Life' toward two dreams which shine like beacons. In one, he tries to superimpose the naked image of George, the garden boy of whom he was so fond, on to some 'nondescript' whose existence he resented, but as physical contact is about to occur, the 'nondescript' reappears; in the other, he is in the presence of an ideal friend who, he senses, will transform his life. These hints of the struggle to choose a natural as opposed to a conventional mate are the disconnected fragments of an inner 'diagram' which promises to undermine the orthodox schemes set out for him.

Until Maurice's second year at Cambridge, other people are little more to him than, 'flat pieces of cardboard stamped with a conventional design' (p. 32). It is only by stepping outside convention and making an impromptu call on a new acquaintance, the exotic Risley, that Maurice is touched at last by a 'breath of liberty', since it is then that he meets Clive Durham. Under Clive's tutelage, Maurice is introduced to the Ancient Greek ideals of male friendship, but a declaration of love proves too premature for his 'suburban soul' and his response is comic in its priggishness: 'Durham, you're an Englishman . . . it's the only subject absolutely beyond the limit as you know, it's the worst crime in the calendar' (p. 56).

Forster's fiction typically organises itself around those symbolic moments when instinctive and conditioned reflexes are in conflict. Both men fail the test of such a moment, for when Maurice subsequently tells Clive that he returns his love, he is met with apologies for 'criminal morbidity' and the demand not to be 'grotesque'. It is only by short-circuiting their conventional, conscious selves that they are united, as when Maurice, in despair at his rejection, climbs through Clive's window and hears his name being called 'out of dreams', or when, owing to another impulsive action on Maurice's part, they spend their most perfect day together careering about the countryside on a motorbike.

Our initial impression of Clive as the liberated homosexual who coaxes Maurice out of his stuffy, hypocritical lair is progressively undermined and finally destroyed in the last scene of the novel in which Clive whimpers with disgust at the news that Maurice has 'shared' with his family's gamekeeper (in the Russet Room at Penge!). In the course of their friendship they exchange roles completely, so that Maurice emerges as the healthy, down-to-earth homosexual lover, and Clive as the neurotic, guilt-stricken renegade who opts for 'safety'. The plot performs its own revisions on the 'symbolic moments' in their relationship. Most obviously, the incident where Maurice climbs through Clive's window to declare his love—whereupon they kiss 'scarcely wishing it' and part—is ironically reformulated when Maurice leans out of the Russet Room window to deliver the invitation, 'come!', to the open countryside and is miraculously answered by another figure out of dreams: the garden boy of old, in the shape of the gamekeeper, Alec Scudder— who stays the night. But Forster is inconsistent in his presentation of these ironies. His own comments seek to place an interpretation on the love between Maurice and Clive which is contradicted in its dramatisation. When they stay together at Penge, the scene that is intended to proclaim the triumphant, daring nature of their intimacy is a comic failure. Clive, who boasts of being an 'outlaw', goes crimson when Maurice speaks of his physical attraction to him and switches the conversation to the subject of aesthetics. Forster comments:

> And their love scene drew out, having the inestimable gain of a new language. No tradition overawed the boys. No convention settled what was poetic, what absurd.

(p. 86)

But when this 'new language', which gaily flings 'tradition' and 'convention' to the wind, inspires Maurice to ask for a kiss, we are told: 'Clive shook his head, and smiling they parted, having established perfection in their lives, at all events for a time' (p. 87). Maurice's gaucherie inadvertently deflates Clive's intellectual bravado, yet Forster does not falter in his own flight of sentimental rhetoric and shows a blatant disregard for the unresolved sexual tensions of the relationship whilst talking coyly of its 'perfection'. The 'Golden Age' they are said to enjoy fails singularly to live up to Clive's élitist formula for, 'a particular harmony of body and soul that I don't think women have even guessed' (p. 84). But Forster continues to endorse in high-flown phrases Clive's shrewd management of the affair, attributing their bliss to the fact that by denying the sexual impulse Clive is 'sensible' and able to lead 'the beloved up a narrow and beautiful path' (p. 91). Maurice, humble and adoring, accepts what is offered and submits meekly to the veto on physical passion.

In his Terminal Note, Forster admits the possibility of personal animus in his later characterisation of Clive. The fault lies, however, not in the satirical portrait itself, but in the sudden switch from an indulgent attitude to one which is sharply critical. The elements in Clive's character which sustain the satirical contrasts between his youthful and mature self were always evident. Notwithstanding his intellectual rebellion, Clive never progresses beyond an adolescent fear that his sexual nature is sinful. The acute nervous strain and the determination that his desires must never become 'carnal' result at sixteen in a breakdown. The liberating rejection of religion and the discovery of the Ancient Greeks do not fundamentally modify his shame. His neurosis erupts once more when the 'normal' Englishman rebuffs his love and the precarious 'greenwood' of his world of books and music is shattered. His final breakdown and miraculous conversion to heterosexuality come when his studies are complete and he is expected to take up his social duties. The broadening interplay between sexual and social themes marks the turning point in Forster's attitude towards him; the pressures on Clive to marry, provide Penge with an heir and assume the role of the young squire are sketched with a scathing irony when Mrs Durham cultivates the acquaintance of Maurice's family on the grounds that 'one ought to cross breeds a bit' (p. 92). But if Forster has rearranged in homosexual terms his typical scenario where prospective marriages hint at desirable coalitions between different levels of English society, no revitalising potential develops from the 'cross breeding' of Clive and Maurice. Outside the sanctuary of Cambridge their passionate relationship degenerates into a routine of weekly meetings which transform neither of their lives.

Forster glosses over Clive's abrupt reversion to 'normality' by attributing it to some 'blind alteration of the life spirit' (p. 106) (brought on by influenza!), whereas it is more obviously the expression of a nervous crisis which takes the shape of a renewed morbidity over his body's 'weakness' when he is forced to consider his future. Clive suffers a relapse in Maurice's presence, becomes hysterical when the latter kisses him, cringes from his fussy nursing, talks of the 'cleanliness' of death, and escapes to Greece. Mediterranean culture is usually the stimulus to the physical, instinctive self in Forster's fiction, but in Clive's case it brings only the vision of a 'dying light and a dead land' (p. 104). Such a reversal is not implausible for, as the whole novel makes clear, homosexual repression is too often the price of a 'safe' passage through life. But that Forster should present Clive's 'cure' at face value is all the more striking because he proceeds to satirise his passionless and conventional marriage in vituperative terms. Clive betrays his youthful ideals and turns into the stuffy, pompous bore that Maurice starts out as, becoming the 'nondescript' of that adolescent dream. His choice of security over passionate fulfilment is seen in the 'symbolic moment' when he confronts his friend on his return from Greece. There is prophetic irony in the contrast between Clive, who is cocooned in bandages, the guinea pig of the Hall sisters' first aid practice, and Maurice, who is 'like an immense animal in his fur coat' (p. 112).

Cast out into the darkness again, Maurice becomes a more sympathetic character. His bitterness gives way to a calmer, stoical outlook which is obscurely prompted by his dying grandfather's cryptic reference to some 'light within' to be released in the serenity of 'evening'. But although Maurice too seeks a refuge in outward respectability, his homosexuality is depicted as an educating as well as an alienating force, causing the flesh to develop 'the sluggish heart and the slack mind against their will' (p. 133). He comes increasingly to question the values of his class, thinking of himself as an 'outlaw in disguise' and nurturing dreams of how in the time of the greenwood two men like himself might have defied the world. His yearnings subtly undermine the attempt to find peace in conformity: he is horrified to find himself lusting after Dr Barry's young nephew; he responds in an unguarded moment to a lascivious old man on a train, then knocks him down as if to erase the image of what age might do to him; he avoids a handsome young French client, and begins to suspect his interest in a youth at the charity settlement where he works in his free time. Forster uses Maurice to illustrate the sexual ignorance of the society that condemns him to loneliness and suffering for when he casts around for help, one doctor speaks of homosexuals as 'asylum work' and Dr Barry, a family friend, declares it to be an impossible delusion on the part of a 'decent fellow' of Maurice's class when the latter confesses, amid sobs, to being 'an unspeakable of the Oscar Wilde sort' (p. 139).

The concluding chapters have a complexity and a dramatic intensity which are sometimes lacking in the earlier episodes. The scenes at Penge revolve around the idea of 'cures' and fresh starts, drawing together in ironic contrast images of past and present, nature and society, rebellion and conformity, dream and reality. Both Maurice and Clive look on the visit as a last experiment: Maurice clings to the hope that his friend might yet save him from misery; Clive, from the safety of marriage, is prepared to offer a helping hand—but only to establish relations on a new, 'mature' footing. Whereas Clive once scorned the values of Penge, he now epitomises them, playing the part of the local squire in a manner which reminds Maurice of how Penge's inhabitants always seemed to be 'rearranging' England in their own image. But just as their political enthusiasms are called into question by the disrepair of the estate itself, so Clive has schemes to 'reform' Maurice but not the time to put them into practice. Yet in an indirect and ironic manner he does help Maurice. He interprets the curt manner by which Maurice disguises his hurt feelings as evidence of that hoped-for maturity and end to 'sentimentality'. In fact, his neglect engenders in Maurice a mood of 'biting recklessness' which determines him to consult the hypnotist and prompts the announcement that he hopes shortly to marry, too. But this impulsiveness has itself stirred ghostlier roots, for soon after their talk, Maurice is pictured kneeling at the windowsill dreamily issuing his 'proposal' to the empty air, entreating someone to 'come!'. Furthermore, wishing to encourage his friend's marital negotiations, Clive urges him to use Penge as his base. This coincides with Maurice's desire to imbibe its atmosphere as an emetic, 'to get rid of the old poisonous life that had seemed so sweet' (p. 106)—thereby opening himself to a more radical cure than the one he imagines.

Forster skilfully correlates the intrusion of Alec Scudder upon Maurice's consciousness with the methods and prescriptions of the hypnotist. Initially, Alec is identified with Maurice's irritation towards Penge; he glimpses the keeper flirting with two maids and is envious; he is associated with the dismal hunting trips and there is bad feeling over a tip. But as he leaves for his consultation, Maurice is stunned to see the keeper's face peering out from a hedgerow. Reflecting despondently on the bedraggled, spoiled blooms, evidence of nature's incompetency, 'He leant out of the window to see whether she couldn't bring it off once, and stared straight into the bright brown eyes of a young man' (p. 156). One hypnotic encounter precedes the other. The boyhood dream of an ideal friend—'sort of walking towards me through sleep' (p. 159) —is all that the consultant manages to revive in him, and this is what finally overtakes him on his return to Penge, where

> he was supposed to lie fallow to the suggestions sown during the trance, and never wonder whether they would germinate or not.
> (p. 166)

Following the doctor's advice to take exercise in the fresh air, and spurred on by his host's neglect, Maurice wanders the grounds, newly receptive to their beauties. His boyhood dreams had been described as growing within him 'like plants that are all leaves and show no sign of flower' (p. 27); now he is entranced by the evening primroses, which recall his grandfather's references to evening and the release of the 'light within'. Flowers are associated with his loves: Alec's face springs from their midst; Clive taught him to appreciate the form of the primroses, but he discovers their scent for himself. Just as he brushes against the corduroys of Scudder, who materialises from the shadows like some natural spirit, so he brushes against the flowers, returning to the house with his black hair dusted with golden pollen.

Although he exchanges the potent magic of the open air for the stuffy formalities of the drawing room, events continue to focus Maurice's thoughts upon Scudder. The local clergyman irritates

115

him by prying into the keeper's affairs, causing Maurice to see in Scudder a symbol of the freedom denied by the society Mr Borenius personifies. The clergyman's emphasis on the keeper's likely 'emigration' and need of 'confirmation' is ironic in view of what becomes a covert battle between the two men for Scudder's errant soul. The 'seeds' of rebellion that have been developing in Maurice's consciousness finally 'flower' when, in a trance-like state, he flings open his bedroom window and repeats his forlorn cry—to be answered this time by Alec Scudder, who appears as if summoned out of that boyhood dream.

If the ending of the novel is open to a charge of sentimentality, then this is not so much the result of Forster's handling of the relationship between Alec and Maurice as his blithe insinuation that they 'lived happily ever after'. The scenes leading up to their disappearance emphasise conflicts which might realistically be expected to take time to resolve. With the dawn, 'class calls', and although Maurice's partnering Alec in a cricket match momentarily stirs in him the old vision of two men defying the world, the rest of the day brings guilt, remorse and the fear of scandal. The 'emetic' which Penge was to provide has taken an unexpected form, yet Maurice's agitated behaviour, illness and sudden departure are attributed to the strain of his marriage negotiations, as his hosts look on him benignly as an 'official lover'. Maurice's panic, exacerbated by the pleas and veiled threats of Alec's letters, is convincingly presented. It recreates the pattern of his original response to Clive's declaration of love; the reflex of social conditioning causes him to denounce the passion in 'criminal' terms, but as terror subsides, his body yearns nightly for Alec, and something of his former spirit of recklessness returns to mock him for his desire for safety at any price.

Alec's reactions to their situation are equally convincing. He is not just the *deus ex machina* of Maurice's dreams, and Forster is careful to supply plausible reasons for his magical appearances. Likewise, his romantic image as 'an untamed son of the woods' is revealed to be an accident of circumstance and is replaced by a more realistic picture of a man also enmeshed in the expectations of his class. Indeed, Alec is the one who continues to feel the weight of social obligations and with a shrewd practicality opposes Maurice's plans for them to break away and make a life together. Just as the young Clive first rejected Maurice's repentant

116

approaches, so Alec, hurt and humiliated by the lack of response
to his letters, takes time to recover his trust. When they meet at
the British Museum—against a backcloth of the heroes of antiquity
—Alec's crude threats of blackmail are the equivalent of the panic-
stricken measures Maurice had adopted to protect himself from
the anarchy of his feelings. Having plumbed the depths of his own
'muddle', Maurice is able to sympathise with Alec's own, to disregard the surface meaning of words and trust to his intuition of
what lies beneath. Their underlying harmony emerges as the
Museum distracts them from their ostensible purposes, 'They
would peer at a goddess or a vase, then move at a single impulse'
(p. 195). That the misery Maurice perceives beneath Alec's 'brassi-
ness' when they part after spending another night together,
should lead the latter to renounce his plans to emigrate, disappoint his family, elude Mr Borenius, and risk all, is not beyond
the bounds of credibility—what does fail to convince is Forster's
suggestion (to the accompaniment of a magnificent sunset) that
their difficulties are all over and that journeys end in lovers meeting.

The author endorses Maurice's rousing heroics without giving
any indication of how they will be put into practice. When Alec
lets his ship sail without him, Maurice reflects: 'He had brought
out the man in Alec and now it was Alec's turn to bring out the
hero in him. He knew what the call was, and what his answer must
be. They must live outside class, without relations or money; they
must work and stick to each other till death. But England belonged
to them. That, besides companionship, was their reward. Her air
and sky were theirs, not the timorous millions 'who own stuffy
little boxes, but never their souls' (p. 208). Although the England
spawned between Penge and the suburbs is discredited for its
oppressive values, its 'poisons', and its addiction to safety, and is
opposed to the (Carpenterian) natural world of freedoms, 'cures',
healthy impulses and simple living, at the same time, homosexual
pantheism is scarcely a viable alternative. Maurice admits to the
hypnotist that the England of the greenwood is 'all built over and
policed' (p. 185); Alec maintains that there are no 'openings' in
woods; and Forster discarded his epilogue which portrayed the
two men living happily together as woodcutters. Apart from its
anachronistic air, it is difficult to see the greenwood as the heroic
antithesis to 'safety', when Maurice values it above all as a refuge.

117

Forster evades these anomalies in the last scene where Maurice bids a defiant farewell to Clive, severing his connections with the world in which he has moved, just as he tears petals from the evening primroses to leave a little pile of expiring light before melting back into the darkness. In some ways, it is an appropriate note on which to end: Clive, like a caricature of Maurice's old pompous self, expresses horror at the 'grotesque' conclusion to the 'marriage negotiations', retreats behind a wall of platitudes and plans to rescue his friend from the 'cesspool' into which he has wandered. Their reversal of roles is complete when, in subsequent years, Clive is visited by Maurice's old dream of an ideal friend:

> Out of some eternal Cambridge his friend began beckoning to him, clothed in sun, shaking out the scents and sounds of the May Term.

(p. 215)

It is significant that Maurice vanishes into night and reappears only in a dream, for this also pinpoints the romantic oversimplification of Forster's prophecy of bliss for his two outlaws. He freezes his picture of them in the first flush of passion ('I was determined that in fiction anyway two men should fall in love and remain in it for the ever and ever that fiction allows'[8]) and, by insisting that this is the end and not the beginning of the story, obscures their hopeful 'signs' in the 'sand', to leave us with the dream and not the reality.

However, it is not surprising that Forster should have been unable to imagine a social context which would happily contain his two lovers; their obvious difference in class would create a scandal even if they were simply to set up house together. But although unconvincing as a realistic alternative, the greenwood does symbolise the need to break uncompromisingly with a hostile society, which is in itself a brave and heroic message. Indeed, Forster's novel has been charged with sentimentality as much for its positive attitude towards homosexuality as for the inadequate presentation of the basis upon which its hero's relationship might be expected to survive. Jeffrey Meyers criticises *Maurice* severely (in *Homosexuality and Literature 1890–1930*), and his arguments deserve comment. The subtlety, allusiveness and symbolism he admires in treatments of homosexual themes are suspiciously similar to those moral imperatives of 'caution', 'reticence' and 'sublimation'. Certainly, he dwells on the fact that, with the exception of Forster, the writers with whom he deals (Wilde, Gide, Mann, Musil, Proust, Conrad, T. E. Lawrence and D. H. Lawrence) present the homosexual experience as 'extremely negative'. He approves of Forster's first three novels since they dutifully codify a homosexual theme; *The Longest Journey* is 'oblique, ambiguous and interesting', but *Maurice*, where the theme surfaces defiantly, is 'flat, banal, dull' (p. 106). We are called upon to admire the treatment of the relationship between Rickie and Stephen Wonham, where he supposes homosexuality to have been cunningly disguised in terms of bastardy and a lame foot, and to condemn *Maurice* for revealing 'virtually nothing about male love' (p. 106). What this in fact means is that in *Maurice*, Forster is to be censured for not toeing the pathological line and depicting homosexuality as a deformity or crippling handicap, thereby disappointing Meyers' predilection for convoluted sexual symbolism (he is reduced to sniffing out anal symbolism in the bad drains of the Penge dower house, and masochism in Maurice's cleaning of a bed-pan:

> Maurice's connection with Clive's 'filth' is the symbolic equivalent of the 'self-condemned feeling' that impels Maurice towards a lower-class lover, with whom sex replaces shit.
>
> [p. 104])

What Meyers would like Forster to reveal about male love is typified by his complaints about the scene where Maurice knocks down the old man in the train; he laments both the brevity of the episode and the author's failure to learn from the 'superb example' of *Death in Venice* where a similar incident prophesies Aschenbach's degeneration into just such an old man:

> Unlike Forster, Mann portrays Aschenbach's yearning for Tadzio ambiguously and suggests that a *homosexual love*, though modelled on Hellenic idealism, *is a degrading and destructive passion.*'
>
> (p. 106, my italics)

Many of the stories in *The Life to Come* are variations on the themes of *Maurice*, homosexual idealism providing the implicit base for satirical treatments of society's corrupting influence on natural impulse. The title story (1922) locates the greenwood in the more plausible setting of some pagan continent and describes with sombre wit the desecration of its values by the encroachment of white 'civilisation'. The four-act drama develops out of a Forsterian 'muddle' conceived in a spirit of bitter farce: Paul Pinmay, a zealous young missionary, is sent deep into the forest to test his talents on one of its wildest, most stubborn tribes; Vithobai, their boy-chief, misunderstands, placing his own literal interpretation on the invitation to 'Come to Christ', whereupon the missionary responds in a night of passionate love-making. Remorse turns to horror when the news that the whole tribe has subsequently 'embraced' Christ creates a sensation, makes Pinmay's reputation, and causes him to be appointed administrator of Vithobai's district. Whereas once the forest was an enchanted place, sheltering a way of life that was innocent and joyous, Pinmay proceeds to stamp out all the romance and gaiety—his importunate convert being ordered to 'wait'. As the years pass, civilisation increases its stranglehold, bringing disease and the clatter of industry, felling trees until the woods are pervaded by 'a whitish light that seemed to penetrate every recess',[9] and Vithobai's entreaties for Pinmay to 'Come to Christ' with him in the last piece of forest are haughtily rejected. The dénouement comes when Vithobai, pensioned off in a modern house and dying of consumption, is visited by the missionary, eager to smooth his passage into the next world—and so, more importantly, to facilitate his own. But in an ironic repetition of their original 'muddle' spontaneity has its revenge over hypocrisy when Pinmay's placatory references to love's fulfilment in the 'life to come' are taken literally by the chief, prompting him to stab his former lover in the heart and, with the plea to 'wait' for him in the next world, to hurl himself from the roof.

In 'Dr Woolacott' (1927) and 'Arthur Snatchfold' (1928), the conflict between nature and society is symbolised (as in *Maurice*) by a chance encounter between the inmate of a stuffy country house and an incarnation of the healthy outdoor life, a free spirit of the greenwood. Clesant, the sickly young squire in 'Dr Woolacott', is imprisoned in a child-like existence, as if cradled in cotton wool —hence the title—on the orders of the mysterious doctor who seems to personify all the repressive forces of upper-middle class life. In the circle of Clesant's thoughts, or in reality, a rescue bid is spawned when a young farm worker, 'fresh as a daisy, strong as a horse', incites him to fight Woolacott's regime. He embraces Clesant, but the sound of approaching voices, the panic, guilt and ex-

120

citement of intimacy, bring about the young squire's relapse. But before Woolacott can arrive to 'save' him, he has drawn new courage, hidden the intruder in the bed, given himself to him and died in his arms.

If homosexuality is Clesant's 'disease', then society, in the shape of Dr Woolacott, promises to arrest its progress and guarantee its victim a niche in the world; by renouncing music, intense feeling and personal relations, its symptoms can be contained. But the farm worker asserts the 'disease' to be Woolacott's own creation, for which nature has its cure; he informs his bewildered disciple, 'that was the word—love—why they pursued me and still know I am in the house' (p. 125). The ending is ambiguous: if homosexual love can be consummated only in death, then, as in the previous story, all hope of fulfilment is transposed to the 'life to come'; alternatively, there is something courageous in preferring to 'die' to society rather than to accept a niggardly life of self-denial. Clesant might also be thought of as an image of the author, similar to Melville's persona, Bartleby the scrivener, who 'prefers not to' carry out the writing tasks prescribed for him, and in the end, prefers the silence of death. Denied his theme by a public—or by a part of himself—that does not want its peace of mind disturbed, Forster must wonder whether, by evoking his heroes in the private (and unpublishable) recesses of his imagination, he is not exacerbating his creative paralysis, and whether complete silence might not be preferable to self-torment. Such questions find expression in the beautiful passage describing the intrusion of the household into the private world where Clesant greets his saviour:

> The voices entered. They spoke of the sounds of a violin. A violin had apparently been heard playing in the great house for the last half hour, and no one could find where it was. Playing all sorts of music, gay, grave, passionate. But never completing a theme. Always breaking off. A beautiful instrument. Yet so unsatisfying . . . leaving the hearers much sadder than if it had never been performed. What was the use (someone asked) of music like that? Better silence absolute than this aimless disturbance of our peace.
>
> (p. 123)

Although it is quite different in tone, 'Arthur Snatchfold' also concerns the potentially destructive repercussions of a brief homosexual encounter on social position. Sir Richard Conway, a smug,

121

well-to-do business man, spends a dutiful weekend at the country house of an associate, Donaldson. His temper, strained by politeness and fake amusements, is restored, however, when he contrives a quick tumble with a milkman, whose bright shirt and cheery manner have attracted his attention. But the Forsterian virtue of seizing opportunities for fulfilment has in this character shrivelled to selfish cunning. For Sir Richard, who believes pleasure to be won by coolness and daring, the moment of uncomplicated lust is neither spontaneous nor liberating. He schemes to encounter the milkman in a nearby wood, getting up early to procure his morning 'delivery': 'There was probably nothing the lad wouldn't consent to if properly handled' (p. 133). His calculations are correct; they enjoy a romp in the bracken and go their separate ways—to what extent, a sequel ironically unfolds. Conway's self-congratulation turns to cowardly dismay when he subsequently learns from Donaldson of a scandal concerning 'indecency between males'. Conway, whose affairs have since prospered at his associate's expense, is amused by the latter's hypocritical reasons for 'preferring' to give up his country house—one of these being the case of indecency. But his pursuit of this amusement, like his tumble with the milkman, leads him unwittingly to the brink of disaster when he presses for more details. It becomes clear that Conway is the guilty party whom the authorities would dearly like to apprehend. A conversational slip even betrays his complicity, but well practised in the art, he is able to bluff his way out of danger. His selfish cunning contrasts with the naïve courage that the milkman had shown by stubbornly protecting Conway's identity and by refusing to show any shame in court. Incapable of such heroism, Conway is left pondering the name of his saviour and the double miracle of his being 'snatched' out of and back into the social and heterosexual fold without anyone being the wiser.

The four stories, 'The Classical Annex', 'The Obelisk', 'What Does It Matter?', and 'The Torque' (1930–1958) all elaborate fantastic homosexual incidents that exact a sweet revenge upon middle class prudery. In 'The Classical Annex', 'connections' to pagan sexuality have been severed, the more suggestive artefacts of past cultures being relegated to a dusty side-room of Bigglesworth Municipal Museum. Yet some 'obscene breath from the past' causes a loutish nude of the 'non-intellectual variety' to exhibit a Priapic development which proves too much for its municipal fig leaf and for the nerves of its prim curator. Its animation climaxes with the rape (amid giggles) of the curator's son, and can be halted only when the resourceful father makes the sign of the cross from the shelter of an Early Christian sarcophagus—thereby freezing their impromptu connection for posterity! 'The Obelisk' expounds another bawdy joke, 'poking' fun at the hypocritical respectability of a married couple on a dreary seaside outing. Dutifully, they set out to visit a local monument, only to be waylaid by a pair of mischievous sailors, separated, and brought to wander from the straight and narrow path of propriety—each to enjoy an educational experience of a more vigorous kind. As a precaution, the wife goes to buy a postcard of the Obelisk they are both supposed to have seen, only to learn that the monument in question had fallen into a ravine as the result of a landslip. Thus her prissy husband is toppled from his pedestal, like the crudely phallic symbol itself, and his reinvigorated, self-satisfied expression is noted with new awe. In 'What Does It Matter?' the whole moral edifice of a nation comes tumbling down, spy systems and all, when a scheme to frame its President in a sex scandal backfires and ushers in a Golden Age of free love, causing the country to be sealed off by the 'civilised' world. An earthy young gendarme, who instructs the Head of State in the delights of 'poking', sparks off the revolt against the kill-joys by the simple declaration, 'What does it matter?' which is taken up as a national catchphrase and call to revolution. An act of buggery also alters the course of history in 'The Torque', where a little pagan community must rear the cuckoo's egg of Christianity in the monstrous shape of the Virgin Perpetua. With her rise to power, the ease goes out of living and tolerance gives way to tyranny. But the proof of her sainthood— the golden torque which hangs in the basilica as symbol of her miraculous delivery from a marauding band of Goths—is also the sign of her hypocrisy and the cause of her downfall. We learn that Marcian, her brother, had in fact saved her from the horse-like member of the chief Goth by cheerfully resigning himself to the fate which, by the sheer volume of her prayers, she had inadvertently courted. The torque, given to Marcian as a mark of affection, is claimed by his insufferable sister as the reward of her virtue. But at night it fills the basilica with flashing lights, and Perpetua, eager to perform another miracle, hurries to 'save' her people from false gods. Salvation comes in the guise of a thunderbolt that strikes

the tyrannous virgin dead and under her brother's carefree, hedon-
istic example the community relaxes and returns to its old ways.

'The Other Boat' (1913 and 1957–8) is perhaps the most ambitious and successful of this group of stories. It contrasts with
sombre effect two boat journeys: the return of Mrs March and
her children from India, with the outward passage in later years
of her eldest son, Lionel. Seen in retrospect, the events of the first
voyage provide a blueprint for the tragedy of the second. Home-
ward bound, the children are allowed to play with Coco, a half-
caste boy who, charmed by Lionel, is 'good at dying' in their soldier
games. Mrs March becomes agitated when Coco leads her brood
to another part of the boat; fearing sunstroke, if not some
obscure contamination from the 'other boat' into which they have
wandered (her fierce colour prejudice derives from the scandal of
her husband 'going native' with a Burmese girl), she sets out to
rescue her 'doomed' children. A strange incident occurs; a sailor
draws a chalk circle around her as a sign that she has trespassed
into the crew's own territory and must pay a forfeit. Figuratively,
this also signifies the penalties she will pay for the inviolable circles
that she draws—according to class or colour—around herself and
other people. Momentarily dumbfounded, the traditional prank
unleashes her own superstition, and she sows the seeds of fate
when she turns her anger on Coco and accuses him of being 'unmanly'. When her baby dies of influenza in England, Coco and
sunstroke are blamed: that the child died from 'cold' and not from
'heat' is prophetic, however, for Mrs March's icy taboos and her
husband's passion combine to disastrous effect in Lionel.

Years later when on an outward passage, he and Coco share a
cabin (a result of the latter's scheming), Lionel writes to his mother
that their paths seldom cross:

> He has more than a touch of the tar-brush, so consorts with his
> own dusky fraternity, no doubt to their mutual satisfaction.
>
> (p. 207)

But Lionel, a real soldier now, is himself prone to 'whitewash';
above deck he consorts with his own kind, entering into their racist
chatter, yet below deck (as if at a deeper level of his psyche), he
embarks on an affair with Coco which slowly recreates the fraternity of that 'other boat'. Once more Coco proves the ideal friend;
he offers genuine companionship and an awakening to sexual

passion. He draws Lionel into the charmed circle of his love, weaving a strange magic around him, plotting to defeat the example of the mother with that of the father—until the Englishman's horror on finding that the cabin door has been left unbolted while they made love (perhaps deliberately) breaks the spell and brings his 'above deck' prejudices flooding in upon them. Lionel is only 'half-caste' too, his self splintered by the clash of personal passion with tribal and military prejudice; the charmed circle is converted to a noose and, re-enacting the shameful frenzy in which he slaughtered a native in a desert war, he strangles Coco as the climax to a last brutal love scene and, 'with the seeds of love on him', dives into the sea. Coco's body, confirming the superstitions of the native crew, moves northwards against the prevailing current—in the direction of his lover and that 'other boat'. Thus homosexual love is once again consummated in violent death and fulfilment is bitterly deferred to some 'life to come'.

In all of these stories, be they comic parable or social tragedy, a chance homosexual encounter is developed into a symbolic clash of values between a white, Christian, middle class code complete with its guilts, inhibition, hypocrisy, and emphasis on self-control, and those of some other ethnic or social group whose tribal, pagan, peasant or working class code stresses impulsive action, passion, sexual pleasure and simple living. But if the men representing the first group tend to be the 'villains' and those in the second the 'heroes', this is not due to a simple contrast between heterosexual poseurs and frank homosexuals. Admittedly, there are some poseurs: Pinmay, Sir Richard Conway, and the schoolteacher in 'The Obelisk', but their hypocrisy—typified by their 'snatched' homosexual pleasures—is part of an entire way of life. Equally, the men in the second group are not idealised for taking a stand on sexual preference; none, with the exception of Coco (and perhaps the 'loutish' statue!), are portrayed as confirmed homosexuals. Homosexuality is envisaged as a more varied phenomenon than in *Maurice*; it is presented as a test and not a type of manhood. This view posits a utopian world where there are no rigid sexual categories but a healthy eclecticism of response, ranging from a momentary, uncomplicated lust for another man to the idealistic dedication of two partners in a love relationship. Indeed, the idea of sex as 'fun' is something of a relief from the apologetic air of *Maurice*, where physical passion is hedged around with austere vows of lifelong devotion. These stories presume a bisexual potential in all men, one which is perverted by social, religious and cultural regimentation. In this way, Forster subverts sexual stereotypes by presenting conventional taboos as an emasculating force, so that those who rebel or are furthest from the reaches of society are the more manly. Obviously, there is an element of wishful thinking here: those whose sense of their own manhood remains unperturbed by a homosexual encounter and can cheerfully ask 'what does it matter?' are provisionally answered in the tragic social realities presented by 'The Other Boat'—the only instance where Forster imagines a developing homosexual relationship in convincing detail. Nonetheless, those stories which have often been pronounced semi-pornographic and degrading to the author's reputation engage in wishful thinking of a potent, polemical kind, bringing a welcome breath of comedy to a subject long overburdened with confessional gloom.

Forster's homosexual writings invite comparison with those of Joe Ackerley, his close friend. Ackerley's difficulties confirm that the pressures of censorship on frankly homosexual literature were not confined to Forster's generation (or to his temperament). Though bolder and more forthright about his preferences, Ackerley was nevertheless obliged to compromise his ideals of honesty. The portrait of the boy-loving Maharaja of Chhokrapur in *Hindoo Holiday* (1932) had to be toned down for publication. Similarly, he was persuaded to omit sexually explicit scenes from *We Think the World of You* (1960), despite earlier resolves not to alter them ('I fancy that they are what people actually want, something free and natural and uncomplicated by guilt or psychology'[10]; but after Leonard Woolf had accused him of 'sexual naïvety' and Frank Warburg had warned him of possible prosecution, he accepted that the book had to be 'castrated'.[11] His frankest writing, like Forster's, was only to be published posthumously. In Ackerley's case, however, the pressures of censorship were more of a nuisance than an impediment to creativity; his token concessions did little to bowdlerise the unashamedly homosexual heroes of *Hindoo Holiday* and *We Think the World of You*.

As in Forster, Ackerley's search for the Ideal Friend comes closest to fulfilment among men of the working classes. In British homosexual literature, the erotic image of the working man is created variously from the reaction against middle class values and the search for sexual encounters that do not compromise social position; the underground tradition of working class prostitutes; socialistic ideals of breaking down class barriers; and the nostalgia for a simpler way of life which invests the physicality of the working man with redemptive power. These characteristics emerge from the writings, diaries and memoirs of figures such as D. H. Lawrence, Carpenter, J. A. Symonds, Oscar Wilde, Roger Casement, Lowes Dickinson and others, and establish a tradition which has continued to the present day.[12] Forster exemplifies the tendency to romanticise the working class man; he focuses his irony on the reaction to homosexuality of the middle class partner, absolving his would-be deliverer from similar scrutiny, so that the latter remains more of a symbol than a realistic social type. In *Maurice*, the hero comes to terms with himself over a long period of time, whereas Alec's commitment to their relationship takes place with undue rapidity and is too easily endowed with an air of permanence. Though it may be true that working class men have fewer sexual inhibitions, the stigma of homosexual 'effeminacy' might be supposed to be at least as strong as in any other social stratum.

In Ackerley's work, the ideal is weighed against the lessons of extensive sexual experience. The comic and often sad discrepancies between dream and reality are anticipated in the portrait of the Maharaja in *Hindoo Holiday*. An ugly, tiny, endearing man, he is endlessly thwarted in his efforts to secure the Ideal Friend: he dreams of a lover like the Sun, but has to purchase what companionship he enjoys. The Maharaja is like a character out of *Le Petit Prince*, the comic lord of a small planet; and the state of Chhokrapur, a self-contained world yet one hemmed in by watchful neighbours, provides Ackerley with a metaphor of individual behaviour which is developed throughout his work. The national dilemmas are duplicated in its individuals—worlds within themselves yet ones which crash helplessly and comically against the recalcitrant reality of others, resulting in perpetual muddles and failures to 'connect' as each strives to maintain his little kingdom.

In *We Think the World of You*, Ackerley laughs at himself in the person of Frank, his narrator, who is doomed to play Maharaja to the elusive Sun of a working class boy. The novel shows how Ackerley is able to deal with homosexuality matter-of-factly and to treat sexual frustration in a comic manner which emphasises problems common to any relationship. Johnny, a feckless youth, is patently incapable of reciprocating Frank's affectionate devotion, and what superficial fund of tenderness he has must be shared between his benefactor, his wife, and his mother (Frank's ex-charwoman, Millie). Only his alsatian dog, Evie, arouses any passionate feeling in him and she, as the surrogate for her master, becomes the centre of an emotional tussle between Frank and Johnny's family for the duration of the latter's prison sentence. Again, we have the feeling of entering into a foreign country—a strange obsessional world where individual efforts to shape reality are at comic cross purposes and characters might well be talking different languages. The novel dramatises extended comparisons between human and canine behaviour; each character 'thinks the world' of another and jealousy expects that devotion to be returned single-mindedly. Johnny 'thinks the world' of his dog, a vision Frank comes to share since Evie has the vitality and physical beauty of her master but also the fierce need to receive and return affection that he lacks. In addition, she mirrors Frank's dog-like relation to Johnny, for Evie is condemned to her own prison sentence in Millie's back yard, to the 'hoping and waiting for something that never comes'.[13] Frank would 'adopt' her, as he would Johnny, and entertains fantasies of springing them both from their prisons. But enthusiasms backfire; in separate misunderstandings over 'visiting times', he succeeds only in losing the 'remission' of both dog and her master. Frank regresses from a reasonable, good-tempered if patronising human being, to the state of a rabid animal, foaming with absurd rages at the 'unreasonableness' of others. Yet he has looked on Johnny and his family in dog-like terms—taking them for granted and expecting them to defer to the bountiful nature of their would-be master. He is made to recognise that their devotions are as complicated as his own, since all are imprisoned in their separated worlds, prepared, like him, to fight 'tooth and nail' to secure the love of a chosen mate. This is the lesson Evie finally teaches Frank, for when he does win possession of her, conceding Johnny to his wife, the dog becomes the very image of his former self—a creature possessed by love and a jealous maniac who succeeds (where he failed) in winning her master's exclusive devotion —to the extent that all Frank's friends are driven away and he is left puzzling over a new kind of imprisonment with an unexpected Ideal Friend.

My Father and Myself explores, ruefully, another set of dramatic correspondences between individual worlds that had once seemed far apart. The author describes his long search for the Ideal—working class—Friend in cheerful, self-questioning fashion. The impossible demands made on prospective candidates may be gauged from the fact that his love life begins with a golliwog and ends with an alsatian bitch—standards of uncritical devotion that are hard to match. He admits:

> It may be thought that I had set myself a task so difficult of accomplishment as almost to put success purposely beyond my reach; it may be thought too that the reason why this search was taking me out of my own class into the working classes, yet still towards that innocence which in *my* class I had been unable to touch, was that guilt in sex obliged me to work it off on my social inferiors.[14]

In preferring only the 'normal, manly boy', Ackerley in effect restricted his choice to the world of male prostitutes—however genteelly this may have been toned down by the face-saving traditions of patronage. But neither the obsessional nature of his quest nor its failure should be taken as an image of 'homosexual reality' which negates Forster's contrasting idealism. Both the salubrious metropolitan underworld and the pastoral idyll are more properly seen as a measure of the frustrations society imposes on its homosexual members and cannot be held to represent any definitive 'truth' about homosexuality. Although neither escape route provides any real solution to his problems, each of these two writers embarks on a therapeutic process of self-analysis which does begin to liberate him from the obstacles to fulfilment that have been internalised from his social sphere.

Only in retrospect does Ackerley begin to 'connect', to discover the secret worlds of those around him. This is symbolised above all in his re-acquaintance with his father, who, like his son, had compartmentalised his life and lived in comic muddle. Not only is he discovered to have maintained a mistress and a separate family, but to have been in his youth one of those very guardsmen whose favours the son was later to court. Ackerley concludes from the story of a broken love affair between his father and a Count: 'it looks like one of those bitter lessons so many of us learn who try to buy the human heart with cash' (p. 38). The Count's failure to find in Ackerley's father his Ideal Friend, has been repeated in the failure of father and son to enter into the reality of the other. From this unexpected vantage point, Ackerley must re-examine all those other potential friends and lovers who passed through his life, and wonder whether he ever did them justice or whether, as was the case with his father, he related only to his own preconceived images of them. If Forster's opportunities belong to the 'life to come', Ackerley is the sad clown of opportunities lost.

NOTES

1. Letter from J. R. Ackerley to E. M. Forster (1st February 1965). Included in *The Letters of J. R. Ackerley*, edited by Neville Braybrooke (London, 1975), p. 257.
2. D. H. Lawrence, A Prologue to *Women in Love, Phoenix II* (London, 1968), p. 104.
3. *The Times Literary Supplement* (8 October 1971), p. 1215.
4. George Steiner, 'Under the Greenwood Tree', *New Yorker*, xlvii (9 October, 1971), p. 166.
5. Jeffrey Meyers, *Homosexuality and Literature 1890–1930* (London, 1977), p. 99.
6. John Sayre Martin, *E. M. Forster, The Endless Journey* (London, 1976), p. 164.
7. E. M. Forster, *Maurice* (1971). (London: Penguin, 1972), p. 19. Subsequent page references are to this edition.
8. E. M. Forster, 'Terminal Note' to *Maurice*, p. 218.
9. E. M. Forster, *The Life to Come* (1972). (London: Penguin, 1975), p. 103. Subsequent page references are to this edition.
10. Letter to Stephen Spender (?/11?/55), *The Letters of J. R. Ackerley*, edited by Neville Braybrooke (London, 1975), p. 115.
11. This information is given in Neville Braybrooke's Introduction. *Ibid.*, p. xxix.
12. David Storey's *Radcliffe* (1963) is a prime example of this continuing tradition.
13. J. R. Ackerley, *We Think the World of You* (1960). (London: Penguin, 1971), p. 48.
14. J. R. Ackerley, *My Father and Myself* (1968). (London: Penguin, 1971), p. 110. Subsequent page references are to this edition.

6

Fellow Travellers: Christopher Isherwood and others

In British fiction the question of homosexuality is invariably considered from the point of view of the middle or upper class male; the working class male may well be an object of desire, but he is rarely the protagonist. Moreover, it is often considered in relation to the traditional formula for 'making a man' that is particular to the privileged classes: public schools, Oxbridge, commissions in the army. But obviously, none of these exclusive contexts allows the scope to explore an open and integrated identity in a continuing lifestyle. As Forster and Ackerley indicate, the pursuit of homosexual happiness usually entailed a journey away from the restrictiveness of the British class system. Other writers—most notably Christopher Isherwood—confirm this. Their heroes, not to say their authors, might be thought of as 'fellow travellers' since they are engaged in a rebellion against the values of the establishment, which is both political and—more covertly—sexual. They pass through the narrow portals of a particular educational system to seek the 'finishing school' of the world at large, but more especially to enjoy a licence that would be unthinkable at home.

Describing his experiences at Eton, Cyril Connolly remarks in *Enemies of Promise* that homosexuality was, 'the forbidden tree round which our little Eden dizzily revolved'.[1] His comment applies equally well to the type of fiction—almost a minor genre in itself—that traditionally flirts with homosexual themes.[2] Since Victorian times, the public school story has provided writers with an outlet for discreet homosexual sentiment and has frequently served to examine the 'hidden curriculum' of manhood in the upper classes, to challenge as well as to endorse its heterosexual orthodoxy.[3] It avails itself of a ready-made conflict between private and public morality, between the values and sexual tensions of a personal relationship and the group emphasis on character building of a rugged, competitive kind. As Connolly also suggests, one way of showing 'character' was to report your best friend for homosexual activities. The fate of the sensitive individual in such an environment has been a favourite theme in novels, ranging from Hughes' *Tom Brown's Schooldays* (1856) to Denton Welch's *Maiden Voyage* (1943) and *In Youth is Pleasure* (1944), as well as being a subject for countless autobiographical memoirs. In contemporary fiction, such as Simon Raven's *Fielding Gray* (1967), Michael Campbell's *Lord Dismiss Us* (1967) and Angus Stewart's *Sandel* (1968), the school story puts aside the language of reticence and indirection to deal explicitly with adolescent homosexuality.

Fielding Gray reworks the clichéd story of the 'golden boy' whose smooth passage towards the 'glittering prizes' is rudely interrupted by a homosexual scandal and his expulsion from the élite. Fielding Gray would seem to have every advantage: intellectual brilliance, sportsmanship, good looks and charm. But Raven uses the issue of his homosexuality to weigh these qualities against others which determine success in the new post-war society. The Headmaster, taking an austere stand on the need to atone for the evils of war, preaches to the effect that, 'we cannot retire into our pleasant gardens'. This, however, is precisely Fielding's ambition: a hedonist, he aspires to the 'pleasant garden' of Cambridge and to the old-fashioned lifestyle of the 'wining and dining don'. The way in which these prospects are jeopardised by his affair with Christopher, a fellow schoolboy, is presented as a sardonic parable. Genuine affection and self-interest are in opposition, the irony being that Fielding's single-minded devotion to either would have averted catastrophe. As it is, he wavers disastrously between the two; overwhelmed by his feelings, he seduces the other boy, but then beats a prudent retreat from the consequences. The result is that Christopher undergoes a nervous breakdown, is involved in a minor scandal, expelled from school, and commits suicide.

Fielding is caught not only between the standards of the old world and those of the new, but also in a deeper pattern of betrayals which makes a mockery of all standards. On one side there are those who wish him well, like Peter Morrison, the departing Head of House, who voices the 'practical' view of homosexuality when he warns his successor, 'It's not a question of morals, Fielding. It's just that you're now too important a person to be found out'.[4] On the other side are those who scheme to their own advantage, like Fielding, but without being 'found out': his mother and her cronies conspire to cheat him of 'unmanly' scholarly ambitions; and their fellow blackmailer, Lloyd-James, a rival for the position of Head Boy, helps turn the evidence of Fielding's liason against him. The arbitrators are the Headmaster who, despite keeping an eagle-eye on Fielding's morals, cannot quite penetrate his charm, and Constable, his prospective Cambridge tutor. Constable is a man of the present, ready to take a stand on the individual's right to intellectual and sexual freedom, ready to save Fielding from the philistines. Ironically, though, he is also ready to take a stand on homosexual ethics and, believing Fielding to have betrayed Christopher, reneges on his promise of support and condemns the 'golden boy' to an obscure life as an army officer. There are no heroes in the novel's world; Constable, the obvious candidate, like Peter Morrison, is disqualified because of his chivalrous prejudice where women are concerned. Both his and Morrison's insight into Fielding's moral character are in fact a product of their blindness to the equally scheming and unscrupulous nature of his mother. By contrasting attitudes to homosexuality, the author dramatises many varieties of hypocrisy and although there is no consistent moral justice in *Fielding Gray*, there is poetic justice of a kind. On hearing of Christopher's sexual scandal, Fielding takes secret pleasure in being able to relegate the boy to memory as nothing more disturbing than an image of 'vanished beauty'—which in effect is to be his own fate. In later life, Morrison tells him:

> To me, Fielding Gray is the beautiful and brilliant hero of the first summer of the new peace: an illusion as it turned out to be, but a bright and memorable one. After that—nothing.
>
> (p. 175)

Michael Campbell's *Lord Dismiss Us* is an endearing mixture of sentimentality and satire, moral seriousness and camp humour, self-consciously addressing itself to the whole genre of the school story, with one eye on E. M. Forster and another on Ronald Firbank. The characters are exaggerations of stock types: the stern new Headmaster engaged in a homosexual witch-hunt; the older masters snug in their ivory towers; the eccentric Chaplain, flouncing in lace, sniffing oranges and presiding over a chosen brood at tea-parties;

133

the rebellious intellectual whose temperament and tongue are a match for Jean Brodie; the dashing schoolboy hero and his angelic loved one. It is a nostalgic recreation of the rituals of public school life, the halcyon days of the long summer term, cricket, choirboys, sneaks, crushes, love letters . . . the only snake in this little Eden being sexual guilt.

The novel dramatises its thesis of the 'undeveloped heart' by conjuring up a recurrent cycle of emotional catastrophe which is as predictable as any other aspect of the school calendar. Ashley, the rebellious young master, himself an old boy, is the prime example of the system's cultivation of intellect at the expense of the emotions. His love/hate attitude towards the school sets the tone of the novel itself. For him, the place is sacred to the memory of adolescent love, and profaned by the Christian dogma and taboos which bring about the destruction of that love. Ashley is suitably haunted by those Forsterian goblins of panic and emptiness as his efforts to prevent his own history repeating itself in the love between Carleton, one of the senior boys, and Allen, one of the new entrants, prove powerless in the atmosphere of hysteria whipped up by the Headmaster. But although the novel takes a positive attitude to homosexual relationships, it is compromised by a melodramatic sense of despair—which again takes its tone from Ashley. He pours scorn on Carleton's vision of a permanent love affair, telling him, 'You haven't the faintest idea what the world's like outside here. . . . Do you know what you'd have to endure every single day of your life from other people—spoken and unspoken?' (p. 245), and, when his dismissal obliges him to face that outside world again, proves his point by committing suicide. In so far as Campbell's novel simply replaces schoolboy romanticism with the rhetoric of doom, its central satiric effect is weakened.

Whereas these two novels manipulate clichéd characters and situations to ironic purpose, treating homosexuality as a moral issue within a particular system of values, Angus Stewart's *Sandel*, which presents a relationship between a young Oxford student and a thirteen-year-old choirboy, draws a more individualised portrait. Concentrating on the inner tensions and the development of their love, the novel avoids both sensationalism and sentimentality, disdaining special pleading, apologies and propitiatory victims. Instead, it contrasts the subterfuges in which David and Anthony engage to protect themselves from others, with the honesty and comic complications of their own unique world. Thanks to a combination of courage and good fortune, they are not traumatised by exposure to society's categorical judgments and the ending escapes the obligatory melodrama when Anthony must go on to a new school and a new stage of growth. Having travelled the same road for a while, they accept the fact that they must part company, and our final image of David, as he drives away, reaffirms the trust in instinct which has so far guided them:

> There was strength in his wrists and he knew some live thing in his mind must keep him locked to the road. It was like an aircraft's blind-landing equipment perhaps.[5]

Like the public schools, Oxford and Cambridge have been mythologised through a range of literature. University life is represented as a time when friendships are all-important and, like the school story, the novel with a university setting allowed a celebration of intense romantic attachments between men which might have been thought suspect in other contexts. It is understandable that a homosexual consciousness should have expressed itself more openly here than elsewhere. In *The Longest Journey* and in *Maurice*, Forster indirectly presents Cambridge as the nearest social equivalent of his greenwood, paying tribute to the liberating effect on himself of the society known as the Apostles. However, the free lifestyles and homosexual sympathies of such university coteries in past generations have been made explicit only in more recent years—in the reminiscences of public figures, and more especially in the flood of biographies, memoirs, diaries and letters describing the Bloomsbury circles into which many of the Cambridge Apostles graduated. Evelyn Waugh's *Brideshead Revisited* (1945) evokes a nostalgic picture of Oxford friendships, and introduces a gay character, the outrageous 'aesthete', Anthony Blanche, who is shown in defiant skirmishes with the hearties. Although Charles, the narrator, is coyly heterosexual, his discovery of friendship with the eccentric Sebastian Flyte is suffused with the glow of a great romance and his description of his state of mind on first venturing into Sebastian's circle could equally well serve as an archetype of homosexual myth:

> I was in search of love in those days, and went full of curiosity and the faint, unrecognised apprehension that here, at last, I should find that low door in the wall, which others, I knew, had

> found before me, which opened on to an enclosed and enchanted garden, which was somewhere, not overlooked by any window, in the heart of that grey city.[6]

Julian Mitchell gives a picture of more recent university life in his novel *Imaginary Toys* (1961) in which one of the principal characters is openly homosexual and whose problems, when treated alongside those of his more conventional friends at Oxford, are made to seem equally as ordinary and unsensational. Nicholas is not part of any clique euphemistically portrayed as 'aesthetes', but is integrated within a circle of friends, both men and women, who accept him without fuss or condescension.

A more dramatic context for the exploration of male friendships is the army, where the pressures to conform to a code of hypermasculinity reinforce sexual taboos—which can in turn be threatened by the close relationships that spring up in closed communities, especially under the stress of war. It seems significant that two recent novels which deal with the love between two men should have chosen the distant setting of the First World War. Susan Hill's *Strange Meeting* (1971) and Jennifer Johnston's *How Many Miles to Babylon?* (1974) quietly undo all the usual trappings of 'macho' heroism to focus the horrors of war on its destruction of a single relationship. In Susan Hill's novel, Hilliard, a lonely individual, deeply shocked by his experiences at the Front and even more isolated since the loss of three quarters of his Battalion, is brought back to the living by the warmth and friendship of Barton, a fellow officer. When Hilliard admits that he loves him, 'as he had loved no other person in his life. The reason for this and the consequences of it were irrelevant, the war was irrelevant, something for them to get through',[7] he could well be speaking for Alexander Moore, the hero of Jennifer Johnston's novel, whose overriding loyalty is to his companion since childhood, Jerry Crowe. Rather than lead the firing squad which was to punish his friend's temporary desertion, Alexander chooses to curtail his misery by shooting him and by taking his place before a similar squad. No-one understands this sacrificial action, or indeed the love which prompts it. Both novels subtly subvert our notions of how men should feel and behave towards one another, without allowing us to label and perhaps dismiss the relationships as 'homosexual'; any such categorisation is held in abeyance by the muted treatment and the specialised nature of the setting.

Simon Raven's *Feathers of Death* (1959) and Mary Renault's *The Charioteer* (1953) deal directly with homosexuality in a military situation and exploit the inherent dramatic potential to the full. Alistair Lynch, the hero of Raven's novel, is involved in a scandal when, as an officer commanding a troop of soldiers under fire from native rebels in some far-flung colony, he shoots one of his men, who is also his lover. The novel builds up a detailed background to this event, a court martial serving as the focal point in a drama where in fact homosexuality itself is on trial. Lynch's open, genial personality, the circumstances and nature of his interest in the soldier, all contradict the official version of his 'foul affections'. Yet he is viewed without sentimentality as a complex individual whose good qualities are offset by his foolishness, greed and arrogance. His background resembles that of Fielding Gray, and this earlier novel addresses itself similarly to questions of the proper balance between the individual's pursuit of pleasure and his responsibilities towards the community at large. His regiment provides its own answer, striking a compromise between the stylish pretensions of some and the professional austerities of others, priding itself on being worldly, civilised and liberal. His fellow officers scorn 'middle class' prejudice against 'Etonian' goings-on, yet they take exception to Alistair's unrestrained appetite for the 'good life', his lack of diplomacy, his brazen and unrepentant attitude. As their commander, Lord Sanvoisin remarks,

> The open homosexual, however likeable to you or me personally, is just a pure bloody nuisance in the sort of world in which you or I are forced to live and run an army.[8]

Lynch tells a fellow officer how, ever since Harrow, he was fatally attracted by a combination of softness and masculinity in others. Drummer Harley is just such a man, a watered-down version of Billy Budd, set apart by his dreamy ways, his youth and immaturity. This renders him susceptible to Lynch's seduction, but also precipitates a crisis of identity for he is desperate to live up to the code of the other soldiers. Ironically, the camaraderie of the soldiers is not without ambiguities, and the narrator describes Harley's own friendship with Simes as,

> quite common between private soldiers a long way from home. It was a strong and apparently innocent bond between lonely men, but with passion and sexual inclination ever present. (p. 184)

Indeed, it is Simes's jealousy over his friend's affair with the officer that provokes the crisis; in a lunatic attempt to prove his manliness, Harley tries to join a party who have been detailed to fetch help, disobeys Lynch's orders, and is shot. By making fine discriminations between class types, Raven constructs a moral drama in which genuine ethical questions are set in conflict with social conditioning and prejudice. Lynch's failure to manœuvre discreetly within the double standard of private and public morality exposes the hypocrisy of others whilst confirming his own arrogance; his brave affirmation of his homosexuality simultaneously reveals his egoism in supposing that the soldier is able to make the same sophisticated distinction that he can between heterosexuality and masculinity. His scorn for conventional codes of behaviour combines disastrously with Harley's excessive respect for them, and the two men pay a tragic penalty.

In *The Charioteer*, Mary Renault uses the setting of a military hospital in wartime Britain to consider the stereotype of the manly hero. Two of her principal characters are conventional war heroes and homosexuals, and a third is a Quaker conscientious objector. On one level, the novel makes a familiar plea for tolerance by its detailed characterisation of the three men, placing emphasis upon their many positive qualities and the honourable nature of their conduct; yet on another level, it has all the hallmarks of a sentimental homosexual fantasy. Thus Laurie, wounded in the foot at Dunkirk, falls deliriously but chastely in love with Andrew, the Quaker orderly at his hospital. Their romance is developing suitably when fate strikes in the alluring shape of Ralph, the very Head of House for whom Laurie nurtured untold passion at public school, suddenly re-encountered in the unlikely context of a party held by a mutual gay acquaintance. Furthermore, it transpires that Ralph, now a dashing officer (but out of active service, having lost part of one hand), has retained his own secret passion for Laurie, though at school he dared only present him on his last day with a copy of *The Phaedrus*. As fantasy, this is reasonably entertaining: we savour the drawn-out pursuit of the sexy Andrew and are chastised for our lasciviousness by continuing proof of Laurie's wholesome intentions; we shudder with him at the dilemma of having to choose between two delectable men, between innocence and experience, as it were; we worry that, unless he stops dithering, both will elude him. More seriously, though, the novel overworks its attempt to show these as clean, responsible, *manly* loves, living up to their Classical ideals, particularly when this is achieved at the expense of a clique of local 'queens', the type that 'give homosexuality a bad name'. These local gays, with names like Bunny, Toto, Bim and Sandy, are hysterical, neurotic, lecherous, malicious, and above all, *loud*. Laurie's belief that they had identified with their 'limitations' is a give-away of the novel's conception of homosexuality as a handicap, albeit a minor one—like that damaged foot or hand, that need not radically alter one's life.

Fascination with the dramatic combination of homosexuality and conventional military heroism continues unabated. It has surely reached fever pitch in the literary industry devoted to T. E. Lawrence, whose sexual eccentricities now seem to stir the imagination more than his military crusades (was he or wasn't he raped, and if he was—heaven help us—did he *enjoy* it?). Other national military heroes furnish rich source materials for writers. General Gordon is the subject of Robin Maugham's *The Last Encounter* (1974), and is sympathetically portrayed as a man doubly besieged at Khartoum—by the encircling forces of the Mahdi and by the homosexual temptations that mass within. A further example is William Clive's novel, *Fighting Mac* (1977), which explores the character of Major-General Sir Hector Macdonald, who committed suicide when faced with a homosexual scandal.

However much they may lend themselves to the presentation of dramatic or nostalgic images of male friendship, none of the social contexts looked at so far can be used directly to suggest how the individual homosexual might achieve a satisfactory lifestyle and it is not surprising that the search for happiness has more frequently been depicted in terms of the escape route of foreign travel. Obviously, Britain does not have a monopoly on puritanism and prejudice: Isherwood's Berlin, Douglas's Capri or Corvo's Venice can be matched by Baldwin's Paris, Burroughs' Tangier or Horne Burns' Naples. And if one man's prison is another's sexual playground, this is further illustrated by the French writer, Yves Navarre, who shows his protagonist in *Killer* (1975) as finding sexual freedom at fifteen years of age in Oxford, whereas a central character in *Sweet Tooth* (1973) ends his search in the sexual underground of New York. But for the British upper class homosexual in particular, periods of travel and residence abroad coincided conveniently with the traditional pattern for the education of the gentleman. Of British writers who reject their homeland, Christopher Isherwood presents an intriguing example. The title of his recent slice of autobiogaphy, *Christopher and His Kind* (1977), refers generally to the scattered homosexual 'tribe' with whom he has come to identify, and at the same time to writers of his own class and generation whom he portrays as 'fellow travellers' in more than the political sense. It is interesting to consider his work in the light of other portraits of the homosexual as expatriate.

In past generations, homosexuals were faced with the choice of leading a double life or paying the penalties of society's hostility; some were able to opt out of that dilemma by taking themselves into voluntary exile, yet others, like Norman Douglas or Michael Davidson had exile 'thrust' upon them. As Davidson comments in *The World, the Flesh and Myself* (1962),

> plainly, unless I became a different person, I should be back in prison before too long. But I couldn't change into a different character; therefore I must change my domicile—get out of England.[9]

Both he and Douglas were able to make a living as 'foreign correspondents' of a literal or literary kind and, apart from necessitating that they live abroad, their sexuality had a direct bearing on their work in the sense that their involvements with native youths became a medium of communication with the culture and the locality itself. Isherwood's skills in evoking the spirit of place develop similarly out of direct contacts and relationships. A pioneering work in the new genre of 'confessions of a (famous) homosexual', Davidson's autobiography indicates a direction that Isherwood's writing has also taken.

Some of the merits and demerits of homosexual 'travel literature' are exemplified by Davidson's portrayal of his relationships with working class youths and youths of other countries (typically, he admits to a sense of sexual taboo with members of his own class): they lend themselves to the exposition of a cultural dialectic, to vivid insights into other ways of life, and often to the expression of sincere socialist sympathies for the underdog; but fundamentally they depict situations of sexual colonialism, however prettily these may be decked out with affectionate patronage and pedagogic ideals. Davidson himself, with his wry self-observations and criticisms, comes across as a fascinating individual, but his protégés are regarded with a sentimental, uncritical eye. In the absence of the interplay of personality and emotional conflict that is found in truly reciprocal relations between equals, we are left with descriptions of charming, beautiful, servile youths who make no permanent demands but blur into one composite impression.

Robin Maugham's autobiographical memoir, *Search for Nirvana* (1975) presents another abiding image of expatriate life—the utopian dream, the endless voyage to discover an earthly paradise. He uses the framework of a boat journey to a tiny island off Ceylon as a metaphor of his life's quest and an occasion for reminiscences of past moments when nirvana of a kind seemed within his grasp, as when he enjoyed an idyllic romance with a young Arab soldier, or with a German boy in Salzburg. Contrastingly, *The Wrong People* (1967), his first frankly homosexual novel, subjects such dreams to ironic scrutiny. Ewing Baird, a member of Tangier's international homosexual set, is taught that money cannot buy happiness when he tries to fulfil his own fantasies by manipulating those of another man. Arnold Turner, a timid master at an approved school, on holiday from repression in this mecca of cheap sex, is persuaded to deliver up one of his charges in exchange for a permanent home in Tangier and an Arab youth provided for him by Baird. The latter had left England owing to its stifling, conventional atmosphere and can buy as much sex as he wants in Tangier, yet he yearns to adopt some deprived English youth whom he can educate to share his way of life. The novel makes melodramatic concessions to the old idea of homosexuality as a corrupting force and a rich man's vice, whilst subtly endorsing dreams of homosexual happiness. This ambiguity is denoted by the title: 'The Wrong People' conjures up a vision of debauched predators, whereby Baird's Platonic schemes are explained by his guilt and self-hatred, and Turner is shown to lose all moral principles after a sodomitic spectacle sends him giddy with 'monstrous' passions; but at the same time it suggests that the dreams are valid and it is only a case of the wrong people having been matched—Baird's prospective partner *is* desperately in need of such a new life, but turns out to be in love with Turner, whose own prospective partner, the Arab boy, Riffi, is simply a little whore who goes off with a higher bidder.

The upper class homosexual's pursuit of 'foreign' pleasures is the subject of John Lehmann's 'confessional' novel, *In the Purely Pagan Sense* (1976), which he has described as 'a statement about what life was like for a homosexual during my lifetime'.[10] However, Lehmann's persona, Jack Marlowe, scarcely ranks as an average member of the 'tribe'—except in so far as he is representative of 'Christopher's Kind' in the narrower sense of those able to adventure outside their own class and society. His emphasis on the happy enjoyment of his sexuality is welcome, but needs to be balanced against accounts such as Ian Harvey's *To Fall Like Lucifer* (1976) if the precarious foundations of that happiness are to be appreciated. Marlowe takes the golden route from Eton to Cambridge to Bloomsbury, yet finds he must travel abroad to rid himself of his residual puritanism and his sexual inhibitions. This 'self-imposed exile' takes him to Berlin, where an Isherwood figure introduces him to the gay bars and tells him that the youths there are all 'pretty much on the rocks'. Marlowe is able to describe how, on his return to Vienna,

> Now that I knew the ropes rather better, I saw it would be easy to pick up boys, particularly at that time owing to the appalling unemployment, so many were ready to offer themselves.
>
> (p. 57)

History conspires to place him in a buyer's market and, as usual, the crude economics of these relationships are offset by the gloss of friendship, mutual enjoyment, and an element of 'cultural research' amongst the natives. Even so, there is something embarrassingly smug about Marlowe's happiness. He contrives to satisfy his pagan senses by abstracting sex from his social and professional world altogether and, although he thinks of his homosexuality as a passport to other levels of society at home and abroad, his excursions are so purely sexual, so numerous and so superficial as to be scarcely worth remembering at all.

Lehmann's attitude is one that Christopher Isherwood investigates more critically, and in his work the individual who ventures like a tourist into other lives comes to be seen as more of a parasite than a pioneer. If in his earlier books the narrator's detachment is used as a technique to portray the human picturesque, later he questions the neutrality of his persona, developing its character until it moves into the centre of the portrait, as in *A Single Man* (1964), or becomes the subject of an 'autopsy', as in *Christopher and His Kind* (1977), where he repairs the sexual omissions of his early work in a manner which contrasts sharply with Lehmann's self-satisfied confessions. Isherwood does acknowledge the deep conflict between his sexual and social selves, analysing how his socialist sympathies and his attacks on the stuffy puritanism of his own class had their roots in his need to assert his homosexual identity. His perennial themes of aloneness and separation, of the multiplicity of self, and the individual's search for a homeland, develop out of the homosexual experience. The social critic of the first novels, engaged in psychological warfare against the establishment, authority and the family, is the public persona of a sexual rebel fired by anger towards what he now calls the 'heterosexual dictatorship'. In Isherwood's pre-war novels he takes a mischievous delight in portraying individuals whom respectable society would shun, and he is released from the need to moralise on their sexuality by the ingenuousness of his narrator's fascination with their 'eccentricities'. In particular, he depicts the comic pathos of older men obsessed by heterosexual youth: Edward, in *The Memorial* (1932), Baron von Pregnitz, in *Mr Norris Changes Trains* (1935), and Peter, in *Goodbye to Berlin* (1938). In later novels such as *The World In The Evening* (1954) and *Down There On A Visit* (1962), homosexual characters are portrayed more fully as individuals and not just as 'naughty' pawns in the game against 'The Others'. Moreover, in these two novels the narrator moves into the foreground of events and is subjected to an increasingly critical scrutiny within the overall pattern of contrasts between the committed individual and the tourist in life.

Stephen Monk in *The World In The Evening* is the least sympathetic of Isherwood's narrator figures. It is as if the author had distributed the warring factions in his own experience—his 'sinful' European past and his 'redeemed' American (Vedantan) self—among the various characters. Stephen embodies the most irritating features of those fictionalised Isherwoods: the calculated 'little boy lost' appeal which disguises an inability to face up to himself; the dalliance with other people and their causes which never really impinges on his own privileged existence and pursuit of private pleasures; an infantile irresolution and a character trivialised by sexual hypocrisy. Brought up by Sarah, a saintly Quaker woman, he reacts against his puritan background by running off to taste the sexual freedoms of the European capitals and then, in guilty rebound, tries to anchor his existence by marriage to an older, motherly woman, Elizabeth Rydall, a 'Bloomsbury' novelist. After her death, he becomes an appendage to another woman, Jane, an American beauty from the pages of Scott Fitzgerald, with whom life is one long glittering party. They live on the Riviera until the shadow of fascism falls over Europe and then, as the old world veers towards its 'evening', prudently retire to the social whirl of California. When Jane's infidelity confirms his unimportance to her, Stephen flees to the home that Sarah keeps for him in a Quaker community in Pennsylvania. A fractured hip prolongs his stay, allowing him to imbibe the goodness of those around him and to make a 'clean break' with the past by a period of introspection, healing and purification.

In confinement with the 'better self' Aunt Sarah represents for him, Stephen can no longer postpone a crisis of confrontation. As he recovers his past through the task of editing Elizabeth's letters, he must face up to the accusations of conscience, one of which is sexual hypocrisy. His possible homosexuality is suggested by the recollection of Michael Drummond, someone with whom he satisfied a 'shameful physical itch' and then ran for the cover of his wife. Drummond, who is in love with Stephen (albeit mawkishly and hysterically), is a new kind of homosexual in Isherwood's work: he is self-accepting, proud and defiant, as well as being more politically committed than the butterfly Stephen. Stephen is given another chance to come to terms with homosexuality in his friendship with two local men—his doctor, Charles, and the latter's lover, Bob, an artist, 'lapsed' Quaker and ex-marine for whom, more so than for Drummond, homosexuality has become a cause. As another 'lapsed' Quaker, Stephen's predicament may be compared with that of Bob. Both rejected their puritan upbringing because it seemed to deny them sexual freedom, yet they retain a sense of conscience which in neither case can find any outlet for positive expression. As Charles suggests, Bob needs some 'heroic setting' wherein his Quaker self might be reconciled with his homosexual self. He invokes the concept of camp, defining it as 'expressing what's basically serious to you in terms of fun and artifice and elegance',[11] and when Stephen sees Bob's paintings, he reflects,

> I thought I could see in them the conflict between Bob's birth-right Quakerism and Charles' 'High Camp'. Perhaps the creation

of 'Quaker Camp' would be the only possible solution to Bob's problems, both as a human being and a painter.

(p. 131)

But Stephen, similarly, is seeking some compromise between the 'fun and artifice and elegance' of his past, and the wholesome dull goodness of his present. And by extension, Isherwood is evidently trying to present the serious business of conversions, commitments and causes in an artistically interesting and amusing fashion (one example of his artifice being that his literary 'better self'—Elizabeth Rydall—writes a valedictory novel, *The World In The Evening*). The attempt does not succeed. Whilst Sarah dispenses inner light like cocoa, the earnest cause of the homosexual lovers is enlivened by a merely facetious line in camp chatter, and Stephen, whose 'purification' is as effortless as the rest of his life, is too trivial to merit our interest. When at the close of the novel his second wife inflicts a few home truths on him and urges him to be more honest with himself regarding his latent homosexuality, his reply is significant: 'it takes so much character—more than I've got—to be a good one' (p. 130). The respect for 'character' in others, and the struggle to enter into possession of one's own, is taken up more forcefully in Isherwood's next novel, *Down There On A Visit*.

As a work of conscience, executed in stylish, self-deprecating fashion, this novel might be thought a further experiment in 'Quaker Camp'. It presents four acts in a theatre of self, where a narrator revisits his past and descends beneath the surface of his relations with particular individuals. Invitation and personal appeal (or their absence), journeys and sudden departures from routine, deliver to the narrator challenges to define himself that are properly met only in this retrospective enterprise. The first section describes the young Christopher's feelings towards a distant relative, a Mr Lancaster, who lives in some German port. Christopher scorns the other man as the epitome of respectability and, puffed up with indignation by Lancaster's clumsy patronising invitation, he sets out to refute the slur on his 'manhood' by venturing across the North Sea in one of his host's tramp steamers. But the crossing, like Mr Lancaster, proves to be dull, comically thwarting his efforts to convert experience into 'epic myth', and the visit itself is made memorable by nothing more than petty snubs and petty triumphs. The irony is that the pompous behaviour of each one disguises the

145

fact that he hopes to recruit the other as a 'character' in the compensatory myth he constructs from life. Afterwards, Isherwood learns that Mr Lancaster has killed himself and, further, that he had often spoken warmly of the 'nephew' destined to become a great writer. And so Lancaster does become a 'character' in Isherwood's personal mythology, but with a vengeance. The posturing of the past is abandoned in humble recognition of a fellow spirit for now, like Mr Lancaster, Isherwood has apparently ceased to believe in that 'epic song of himself'.

If Mr Lancaster anticipates the author's own journey into despair, Ambrose brings him face to face with his own rootlessness. Like Isherwood, Ambrose rejects England because of the constrictions it places on his life, but is more honest and specific as to what these are. Openly and matter-of-factly homosexual, he states simply that he does not 'belong' there, recalling how at university the rooms that were so expressive of his personality were totally wrecked by a gang of hearties. His tiny Greek island is his permanent refuge; it represents his self-sufficiency and his saint-like renunciation of the world. Other people come and go, leaving Ambrose unmoved, serene and sphinx-like. For Isherwood, the venture had seemed consistent with his heroic vision of himself, but this illusion is deflated by the comic reality and chaos of life on the island. Having gone there to fall in with the plans of Waldemar, his German friend, he then looks to Ambrose for reasons to stay or depart. By himself, he cannot meet the island's challenge to define where he 'belongs'. Apparently, he neither stays for the boys, as some do, nor leaves for a woman, as do others. In the end, Ambrose's polite indifference and refusal to take seriously Isherwood's game of exile combine to impress on the latter his status of tourist, whereupon he resorts to the old expedient of yet further travel. He retreats from his aloneness as it is reflected in the other man, and perhaps from the recognition of its source in their common homosexuality.

Waldemar, like Isherwood, is searching for some alternative life to that prescribed by his class, society and historical situation. When Isherwood re-encounters him in the company of Dorothy, a communist friend from his Berlin days, the treatment Waldemar receives at the hands of both the immigration authorities and Dorothy's family reinforces the narrator's hatred for the class-ridden society of his homeland and Waldemar's decision that he does not belong there reaffirms his own. But although both men are given to grand romantic gestures, there is also something absurd in the way they prudently keep their options open. When Waldemar interrupts his return to Germany in order to appeal to Isherwood to join him once more in a life of travel—and is turned down—it is revealed that he had been keeping a taxi waiting for him all the time. Similarly, whilst Isherwood is all a-quiver with pre-war hysteria, cutting a dashing figure about town and living from moment to moment, he is secretly intent on pursuing a love affair in America. If Isherwood resembles Mr Lancaster and Ambrose to the extent that he experiences some of the despair that leads them to 'die' to the world, he also resembles Waldemar in his opportunism, his instinct for survival and self-preservation.

In America these secret selves overtake him. Like Waldemar, he is stranded in a foreign country when a love affair fails; like Ambrose, he faces a lonely exile; and like Mr Lancaster, his epic song of himself has collapsed. He turns in desperation to an old friend, Augustus Parr, who helps him submit to the discipline of Vedantan philosophy. In this last section, Isherwood is contrasted with Paul—once a glorified male prostitute in highest European society, presently another jaded and weary traveller in life. If, in some sense, the author denied his symbolic kinship with those other selves, he finds in Paul a chance for atonement. The latter combines the characteristics of the others on a grand scale; both sexual adventurer and creator of his own legend, he is now utterly alone in the debris of his past and contemplating suicide. Isherwood plays the Good Samaritan, taking him into his home and introducing him to Augustus Parr's midwifery of the spirit. At the same time, he needs the support of someone like Paul to sustain him in his new way of life, to help him endure those rites of purification where 'Quaker' meets 'Camp'. But Paul's ability to throw himself completely into any undertaking, whether it be the life of a prostitute or that of a saint, also illustrates Isherwood's own lack of will power. Paul's experiments in self are pursued with utter dedication, whatever the heavens or hells to which they lead him. In later years he becomes an opium addict, and when Isherwood re-encounters him in Paris and attempts to ingratiate himself by offering to try a pipe of opium, Paul retorts:

> You're exactly like a tourist who thinks he can take in the whole of Rome in one day. You know, you know, you really *are* a tourist,

147

to your bones. I bet you're always sending post cards with 'Down here on a visit' on them. That's the story of your life.[12]

Paul, like the other 'fellow travellers' whom Isherwood depicts, shows no emotion on parting from him, and if this is consistent with those harsh words it also reflects a self-absorption common to all of these characters.

Isherwood's novel sets out both to accept *and* to refute this verdict on himself. Augustus Parr's maxim, 'open yourself', is enacted in the narrative strategy, the 'Quaker' self unpeeling the masks of the 'Camp' self to corroborate Paul's accusation. At the same time, by detailed and perceptive portraiture of these four individuals, by taking us *down* on a visit to the hellish underside of their lives, he seeks to clear his conscience and to demonstrate a reformed self. But though these portraits do retrospective justice to their subjects, Isherwood still fails to take us deeply inside himself. The novel's autobiographical striptease leaves its author clinging coyly to one last mask. Against a background of public events and historical issues, Isherwood presents himself as someone defiantly committed above all else to personal relationships. And yet he characterises his past selves by reference to individuals with whom he did not engage in any deep or reciprocal relationship and only flirts with self-revelation where more intimate affairs are concerned. The crisis of despair that overwhelms him in America and which has so much importance in his life, is glossed over, his lover designated by an initial, his sex concealed by the avoidance of personal pronouns. This lingering dishonesty is exposed in *Christopher and His Kind* where, in a further attempt to 'come clean', the crucial influence of his homosexuality on his life is analysed, and we go 'down there on a visit' all over again.

In fact, the homosexual reality underlying Isherwood's hostility towards England, the problems of his involvements with 'Waldemars', and his deliberate choice of the expatriate life, create a more powerful, dignified and poignant validation of his overriding commitment to personal relationships, to friendship and to truthfulness, than the posturing selves of this novel where the author taxes our willingness to share in his sense of his own importance—the private self of *Christopher and His Kind* being at once more human and more genuinely heroic. Isherwood's narrator figures have typically been weak men, fascinated by strength of character in others. Of course, this is also the popular image of the homosexual male, an image that Isherwood eventually sets out to contradict. As Stephen Monk maintains, it takes 'character' to be a 'good' homosexual, a theme to which the author returns in A Meeting by the River (1967) where the single-minded religious commitment of a man entering an Indian monastery is set against the 'visitor' mentality of his brother, whose weakness is illustrated by his spiritless retreat to his wife after an ecstatic homosexual affair threatened the foundations of his life. The courage to be oneself and to assume one's full character is an aspiration of Isherwood's fictional selves; they journey towards and develop *homosexual character* until they are able to stand alone, in the centre of the portrait, as in A Single Man where the hero's homosexuality is an integral part of his personality and a source of strength.

George, the hero of A Single Man, is a fifty-eight-year-old teacher of literature, of upper class, British, public school background, living in Los Angeles since the 1930s, for much of this time contentedly with another man—and so clearly bears a 'family resemblance' to Isherwood. Much of the novel's impact, its pathos and its humour, derive from the fact that the hero is set apart from others most obviously by his homosexuality, yet he cannot be reduced to the singleness of identity that the stereotype might imply. With ironic play upon the title, Isherwood uses the span of a single day to dramatise how 'George' is a whole variety of selves, past and present, all of whom are engaged in a complex discourse with one another and with the multiple selves of others. The fluidity of his identity is further suggested by the author's own Vedantan beliefs, which are presented by the metaphor of an encompassing 'ocean' of being that repossesses each individual 'rock pool' in sleep, or in death. These beliefs also hold the key to the strange sense in which George's ordinary, innocuous interactions with other people translate themselves on to a more abstract, universal plane: he is both a unique individual and a symbolic figure, an Everyman.

George's house is another version of the 'rock pool' in which he slowly re-emerges after the night's dissolution of identity to the constrictions of time, place and body. He must reconstruct himself with weary, almost perceptible effort, face the mirror with its ghostly reminders of past selves, face the descent into the house where the memory of his lover's death hits him each morning like a blow in the stomach. In this way his homosexuality is introduced, without explanation or apology, but simply as a fact of his life. A 'single man' both as a homosexual and as one whose life partner is dead, George is doubly removed from his neighbours' way of life. Appropriately, his house is dark and secret-looking, sheltering in the hillside, separated from others by a ramshackle bridge. But, far from being a hermit's retreat, it is revealed as an embattled position. George struggles to live in the present, not to dwell sentimentally on the past, and yet, as the survivor of a long partnership, he is determined to preserve its wider values. He stays on in the house as a defiant relict of the colourful, bohemian community that has passed away. Once a colony of artists and drop-outs, now it is a respectable suburb, a breeding ground for the TV family. George is proud of keeping its former spirit alive, of his own nonconformism. He plays the role of 'old story book monster' to the noisy, invasive children, making bad-tempered sorties to chase them back over his bridge; he is a disturbing outsider to the rituals of the grown-ups, a Cassandra to the Saturday Night Barbecue crowd that is typified by his immediate neighbours, the Strunks, who ration their invitations to times when their friends are absent. George prefers the husband's view of him as a 'queer', since at least that acknowledges his difference, to the wife's sweet-voiced denial of what he is. Mrs Strunk is 'trained in the new tolerance, the technique of annihilation by blandness'[13]—a 'disease' whose symptoms George sees everywhere in modern California.

George is not an idealised character, and his battle to survive is often pictured in a ludicrous light. His homosexuality has engendered in him a criminal complex which stirs wild fantasies; he takes an absurd delight in 'fooling' the authorities, in negotiating the hazards of ordinary living without being exposed as a 'Public Enemy'. This is summed up by his aggressive manner of joining in the 'mad, metropolitan chariot race' of the freeway system each day, defying the police patrols he imagines are prowling for individuals like himself whose age or criminality disqualifies them from the mainstream of 'Bland Country'. But George must also battle against symptoms of 'Blandese' in himself. As he drives, an automatic chauffeur persona takes over and though this allows him to indulge his pet hatreds and fantasies, he wonders what other functions it might not begin to usurp. Similarly, at work he employs a 'talking head' self and worries whether it might not be planning some kind of 'merger' with the chauffeur. The university is a smooth-running factory of 'Blandese' where people are reduced to 'singleness', to mere symbols and abstract functions. His objections to the substitution of codes and automatic reflexes for the fullness of self are illustrated by his reaction to two tennis players. Since his 'talking head' is busy elsewhere, he is free to enjoy a moment of pure lust for their beautiful, half-naked bodies. But as he is thrilled by their dissimilarities—one is a fierce looking, stocky Mexican and the other a tall blond youth—so he is presented with a revelation of how the 'rules of the game' have taken over intrinsic differences between individuals. He fantasises that the taller youth should 'throw away his useless racket, vault over the net, and force the cruel little gold cat to submit to his marble strength' (p. 42).

As a teacher of literature, George is intimately concerned with the complexity of form and the elucidation of symbolic meaning and, as a character in Isherwood's novel, he himself is offered as an example of that process. What seems no more than a touching, realistic portrait of a teacher trying to reach a class of students whose minds are usually elsewhere, presents itself simultaneously as part of a discourse on the multiplicity of self, on the problems of knowing and communicating those selves. In the classroom, George gives a performance that draws eclectically upon all the public and private facets of his personality, one that is calculated to elicit a reciprocal response from his students. He tries to break through the abstract, impersonal nature of their encounter by expressing himself far more freely than usual, touching on a subject close to his heart—that of minority groups, and the ways in which symbols have come to disguise and gloss over real differences and complexities. His speech emphasises the novel's overall attack upon 'annihilation by blandness'; George wants people to recognise and react to differences, not to smear them over with 'pseudo-liberal sentimentality', and by choosing the comic example of the minority of the 'freckled' he is able to rail against the notion that the persecuted minority should always be deemed 'spotless'. And his argument that minorities have their own retaliatory aggression is demonstrated splendidly in his own character, in all his diatribes against the family, the heterosexual dictatorship, the young, and the country of the Bland.

The different selves revealed in George at various points in his day are reiterated in the presentation of him as a member of different minorities: as a homosexual, as an old man in a country where

151

youth is deified, as a foreigner, as an intellectual in a philistine world hawking the 'real diamond' in which no-one believes, and, after his visit to a friend dying of cancer, as one 'of that marvellous minority, The Living' (p. 87). Sudden spontaneous gestures celebrate his simple joy in living and show him revelling in those symbolic contacts that alleviate his aloneness by including and acknowledging him in some common enterprise: he draws encouragement from the easy-going physical democracy of the gym or the friendly wave from two of his students, Kenny and his girlfriend, which is a token that, 'The old steamship and the young castaways have exchanged signals—but not signals for help. They respect each other's privacy' (p. 63). There are such occasions when George receives and returns the respects of his 'fellow travellers', others when he chooses to reaffirm his 'singleness', his unique personal history, his memories of Jim. Both these responses coincide in his relationship with Charlotte, an old friend whose outward circumstances resemble his own. She too is British, and something of a battered old survivor, stranded in her particular 'rock pool'. Charlotte's invitation to dinner, as George well knows, conceals her need for a shoulder to cry on, yet depressed at the thought of a long evening alone, he accepts. He can sympathise and enter into her sentimental talk of the 'old country' and of their individual 'tragedies' without inwardly participating in her brand of self-pity. He can be secretly amused by her wiles and conversational manœuvres to return to her favourite topics, and still be taught a lesson by her, 'in purest ignorance', namely that the truth of his life with Jim cannot be betrayed by her drunken, melodramatic version of it.

If, through the unwitting offices of Charlotte, George comes to terms with his past, his evening culminates in a confrontation with the present, in the person of Kenny, his student. Whereas Charlotte and George were only superficially united by familiar rituals and secret comforts, he and Kenny come together by spontaneous departure from routine, something which promises to fulfil itself in a deeper rapport. George, determined to make the most of his evening, changes his mind about going home and visits his favourite waterside bar where Kenny happens to seek him out. The latter explains his presence cautiously, however, pretending that he had wanted his girlfriend to spend the night in a motel with him in that part of town. At first, they fall into a 'symbolic dialogue' between age and youth, with Kenny wanting to know whether experience is any use. George's claim that in his case he has grown steadily sillier is put to the test when Kenny suggests a midnight swim and is astonished to find his challenge accepted. What George means by 'silliness' is that age and experience (as recapitulated in this one day) has taught him to value the present and to give himself up to its possibilities. So we see him in the surf:

> Giving himself up to it utterly, he washes away thought, speech, mood, desire, whole selves, entire lifetimes; again and again he returns, becoming always cleaner, freer, less.
>
> (p. 138)

These rites of purification, of dissolution of self, recall the opening passage where George is described as emerging from the 'ocean' of sleep to reconstruct himself to face the day. But this immersion is far from routine, bringing rejuvenation and an affirmation of the will to live, so much so that Kenny must rescue his lunatic friend from the waves and, nanny-like, scold him and rub him down.

But although the two of them can share experience in this impersonal way, the scene is not the prelude to the set piece seduction that Kenny, for one, might have expected, and their evening terminates without any intimate understanding. The drunken confrontation of 'sage' and 'disciple' takes place with Kenny sitting demurely, half draped in a blanket, Classical Greek style, yet refusing to face his real motives for being there. He is the one person out of George's day most interested in knowing *him*, but will not admit it. He prefers to wait passively for his curiosity to be satisfied in that moment when George will 'give himself away'. On the other hand, George is prepared to forego caution, to come out of his 'lair'. He tries to sum up what experience can achieve in his attempt to help Kenny solve his problems of finding a place to sleep with his girlfriend, offering the use of a spare room in his house on evenings when he will always be out. But when this shocks the youth and seems to supply him with the formula for which he was waiting, George launches into a long tirade against the attitude to life that Kenny displays. He thunders:

> Are we going to spend it (life) identifying each other with catalogues, like tourists in an art gallery? Or are we to try to exchange *some* kind of signal, however garbled, before it's too late?
>
> (p. 148)

He continues:

> Instead of trying to know, you commit the inexcusable triviality of saying *he's a dirty old man*, and turning this evening . . into a flirtation! . . . It's the enormous tragedy of everything nowadays. . . . All any of you ever do is flirt, and wear your blankets off one shoulder, and complain about motels.
>
> (p. 150)

Ironically, Kenny displays that tourist mentality Isherwood formerly diagnosed in himself. Kenny is prepared to flirt and to go 'down there on a visit'—but not to stay the night. George, on the other hand, is newly prepared to relate to people, and decides it is time he started looking seriously for a new partner. Indeed, we are left with the hopeful image of him masturbating, anticipating a new lease of life. Any suggestion of pathos in these 'solitary' pleasures is quickly dissipated, however, by the comedy of his own sexual tourism; he adventures among the sensual images of the day, before settling for the tennis players, slipping between and blending with the bodies he conjures up, and afterwards talking to himself,

> as if to an old greedy dog which has just gobbled down a chunk of meat far bigger than it really wanted.
>
> (p. 153)

Even death cannot be guaranteed to reduce George to 'singleness' and Isherwood concludes with the ironic hypothesis that even if his character were to die that night, doubtless some part of him would still be left voyaging out upon the larger waters of consciousness. His insistence that George is a 'non-entity' neatly summarises his importance: he is heroic in the sheer ordinariness and common humanity of his homosexuality, and in his courageous determination to embrace and live out *all his selves*.

NOTES

1. Cyril Connolly, *Enemies of Promise* (1938). (London: Penguin, 1961), p. 234.
2. But even the saintliest of devotions between schoolboys were liable to censure if physical contact were implied; thus the *Saturday Review* singled out a chaste kiss in F. W. Farrar's *Eric* (1858) as being, 'to the infinite indignation of all English readers', and when Alec Waugh's

The Loom of Youth appeared in 1917 its discreet suggestions of public school homosexuality were enough to cause a scandal.

3. Of course, the school story is not wholly the preserve of British writers; in American and European fiction some of the better known examples of its use to dramatise romantic friendships and adolescent homosexuality are: John Knowles' *A Separate Peace* (1960); Fritz Peters' *Finistère* (1951); Roger Peyrefitte's *Les Amitiés Particulières* (1944); and Robert Musil's *Young Törless* (1906).

4. Simon Raven, *Fielding Gray* (1967). (London: Panther, 1969), p. 47. Subsequent page references are to this edition.

5. Angus Stewart, *Sandel* (1968). (London: Panther, 1970), p. 238.

6. Evelyn Waugh, *Brideshead Revisited* (1945). (London: Penguin, 1974), p. 32.

7. Susan Hill, *Strange Meeting* (1971). (London: Penguin, 1974), p. 105.

8. Simon Raven, *Feathers of Death* (1959). (London: Panther, 1964), p. 175. Subsequent page references are to this edition.

9. Michael Davidson, *The World, the Flesh and Myself* (1962). (London: Quartet, 1977), p. 247.

10. John Lehmann interviewed by Peter Burton and Denis Lemon, *Gay News* No. 102, p. 17.

11. Christopher Isherwood, *The World in the Evening* (1954). (London: Whitelion, 1973), p. 120. Subsequent page references are to this edition.

12. Christopher Isherwood, *Down There On a Visit* (1962). (London: Signet, 1974), p. 269.

13. Christopher Isherwood, *A Single Man* (1964). (London: Magnum, 1978), p. 21. Subsequent page references are to this edition.

7

High Class Camp:
Angus Wilson and Iris Murdoch

Angus Wilson portrays homosexual characters within conventional, domestic contexts, in relation to their families and their work, and at those points where their own cliques overlap into the ordinary social world. By showing that they are caught up in the common problems of everyday living, he aims to represent homosexuals in a realistic and convincing manner, whilst the breadth and diversity of his canvasses of English life are authenticated by their presence. It is true, however, that Wilson's characters are drawn largely from the middle classes and so the 'visibility' of his homosexuals is partly dependent on their movement within a liberal milieu. But this is not to suggest a cosy utopia where gay couples add colour to enlightened dinner parties; on the contrary, one suspects that the author also introduces such characters into his plots and thematic structures in a spirit of mischief—relishing the comic possibilities of putting liberalism to the homosexual test, as it is put to so many others.

In his own life, Wilson has been willing to identify himself with the campaign for gay rights. However, his homosexual characters are never vehicles for propaganda. They are variously as comic, as pathetic, as wise, as foolish, as good and as bad—as human, in other words—as all of his other characters. In so far as homosexuality is treated as an issue, Wilson makes use of it to mock instances of superficiality and selectivity in the respect for and belief in individual freedoms within the liberal and humanist tradition. He delights in conjuring up situations of social embarrassment which dramatise a new uncertainty of response towards homosexuality and which expose an absence of principle or moral conviction. His satire is sometimes directed at the kind of prejudice which has become a mere reflex of respectability: in *Hemlock and*

After (1952), the homosexual contingent amongst those invited to the opening ceremony of Vardon Hall contribute to the general disaster by scampering about the corridors and bedrooms, 'like so many mating mice' (p. 154), and we are given a comic picture of the determination of other guests 'not to put two and two together lest they made four' when 'One solicitor's wife, having opened a bedroom door on the oddest embrace, cried loudly, "There's nothing *here*, to see anyway" ' (p. 155). The willingness to acknowledge the subject is sometimes made to look as ridiculous as the polite resolution to ignore it; in the same novel, guests at the party given by Bernard Sands' daughter-in-law have heard rumours of his homosexuality but, because he is a well-known novelist and local celebrity, they 'would have been glad to evidence breadth of mind, so long as the testimony were not asked too publicly' (p. 19). Similarly, in *Anglo-Saxon Attitudes* (1956), Elvira Portway is satirised for her 'radical chic'—professions of a tolerance which has been dictated by ideological fashion and opportunities for second-hand wit. When Robin Middleton declines to discuss his brother's sexual tastes, embarrassment prompting him to affirm the individual's right to privacy, Elvira retorts,

> Don't try to be broad-minded, darling . . . if we can't disapprove of our friends' sex-lives these days, at least we can discuss them to our heart's content. . . . It's the new liberalism.[1]

Wilson is fond of 'bringing home' the discrepancies between public ideals and private realities by dramatising the issue of homosexuality within the context of a liberal, sophisticated middle class family. In *Late Call* (1964), Harold Calvert is a secondary school headmaster with a gift for reclaiming 'lost causes' among his pupils, his remaining energies being devoted to the creation of a model community in Carshall New Town. In a novel that casts many a backward glance at *Hard Times*, he is the Mr Gradgrind of the Welfare State, while Sylvia, his ageing mother, supplies the contrast to his scientific rationalism, her inner grace and allegiance to the values of the heart recalling Sissy Jupes. Harold Calvert would like to run his family along the lines of his public philosophy but, just as Carshall New Town is bleak and soulless, so, with the death of Bess, his wife, his household has lost its inspiring force. Ray, his eldest son, has some of the 'character' and zest for life of which the community and his family stand in need;

described as Carshall's 'favourite son', the revelation of his homosexuality tests the ideals which the town and his father allegedly represent. After Ray prefers to leave home and make a new life for himself in London, his father declares,

> If a community like Carshall can't help a decent chap like Ray to make a more normal life for himself, then we've failed. We want him back and we want him in the family. I'll have no narrow-minded censoriousness in this house.[2]

However, the 'help' envisaged here is not support for Ray in his attempt to make a 'decent' life for himself in accordance with his sexual nature; all Harold Calvert can offer is 'decent up-to-date treatment'. But even this self-congratulatory display of 'modern' attitudes turns to petulant rage when Ray stands by his decision, whereupon his father acts the very part of the Victorian patriarch that he professes to scorn. Ray's brother, another ardent supporter of lost causes, also reveals his underlying conservatism when he argues, 'we ought to be grateful to him for not running risks in the town where we live' (p. 298). Only the 'old-fashioned' grandmother shows an unwavering, total acceptance of Ray, and opposes her son's tyrannical behaviour.

There is often a corresponding mixture of hypocrisy and egoism in the way other characters are seen to accept homosexuality in a member of their family. Inge Middleton, in *Anglo-Saxon Attitudes*, is a monster of selfishness and as much of a confidence trickster as Larrie, her son's Irish boyfriend. Having attracted John Middleton's affections by playing the role of a 'sad urchin', Larrie consolidates his position by allying with John's mother and hiding his mercenary nature behind a cooing manner which is attuned to the middle-aged little girl nursery talk with which Inge conceals her own lust for power over her son. But John Middleton is himself a good example of the way in which homosexual characters also are included as targets for the author's satire—particularly when their self-deception takes the form of a philanthropic liberal idealism that allows them to pursue sexual adventures in the guise of charitable works. John Middleton thinks of himself as

> a strong, individualistic social reformer with cynical good sense enough to make a nice career out of his genuine mission.

(p. 262)

But his ability to detect fraud and injustice in public affairs is thrown into doubt by his failure to do so in his private life. He is utterly, even eagerly duped by Larrie—another 'genuine' case with the 'cynical good sense' to make a 'nice career' out of it. John's subordination of truth to self-interest is ridiculed most thoroughly in the scene where his father descends on the ménage over which his estranged wife now presides, in the hope of extricating her from Larrie's criminal cunning. It is one of those occasions of acute social embarrassment that Wilson delights in imagining: Larrie, in his sugary whining manner, seeks first to ingratiate himself with their visitor and then to defy him in a slyly threatening speech; meanwhile John, convinced that his own homosexuality is on trial, can take a stand against his father only by endorsing his boyfriend's platitudinous drivel. Gerald Middleton, who has until now no particular prejudice on the subject, is left to muse,

> So this . . . is the effect of the love that dares not speak its name. He would have expected Inge to respond to such sentimental, insincere nonsense, but John. . . .
>
> (p. 193)

Critics have noted these excursions into homosexual territory and the world of 'camp' with some trepidation. As K. W. Gransden remarks,

> Wilson makes these venal and often sad relationships satirically explicit, repudiating the 'gentleman's agreement' by which they used to be regarded as unmentionable or disgusting or embarrassing . . .[3]

In a similar vein, Walter Allen speaks of *Hemlock and After* as having,

> a quality of nightmare intensity, especially in the description of the homosexual underworld, the world of 'camp' which is revealed with a terrifying brilliance that rasps the nerves.[4]

But it is quite wrong to suppose that Wilson intends to shock or to set our nerves on edge by the mere introduction of homosexual characters. His satire works to break down the initial impression of there being clear-cut divisions between 'respectable' and 'low life' elements in the social worlds that his novels evoke. In fact, the quality of camp—if this is taken to imply a theatricality often of a deliberately tawdry and embarrassingly comic variety—is often the unifying feature of these different social spheres, both a mode of criticism and an expression of the author's Dickensian relish for character. In an interview with *Gay News*, Wilson expresses regret that camp should have found a bad name among the present generation of homosexuals who seem to him too eager to lay claim to conventionality, and he values its 'extra invigoration of a rather over-genteel nation' and its licence

> to express yourself in a way which accentuated the theatrical and histrionic side of yourself; the life-loving side . . .[5]

Also, in *The Wild Garden* (1963), he describes his admiration for one of his brothers who combined an extravagant effeminacy with a sharp wit and a tenderness of heart, and remarks,

> His wit and his fantasy have both strongly influenced the texture of my free imagination, giving it an unusual quality of severely moral chi-chi and camp.
>
> (p. 140)

Wilson's delight in the surfaces and styles of behaviour, in poses, mannerisms, affectations, in the revealing detail and expressive function of dress, décor and material surroundings, in placing people by drawing attention to their attempts to place themselves —betrays an abiding fascination for the comedy of camp. To praise him for his naturalistic effects and the meticulous cultural research that seems to authenticate his social panoramas can obscure the fact that this characteristic wealth of detail is also organised and selected in a manner which is self-consciously exaggerated and artificial. Given that some of Wilson's perennial themes are immaturity, insincerity, play-acting and self-deception, his camp style, with its histrionics, mimicry, and fanciful conceits, is an effective means of exposing a corresponding artifice in human relations. In common with writers such as Gore Vidal and James Purdy, he contradicts the notion that camp involves a purely aesthetic view of the world, one which is incompatible with moral analysis.

Hemlock and After (1952), in which almost every character appears to be playing a part, is a good example of the relation between camp and moral satire in Wilson's work. The idea of life as a performance is explored most obviously in the character of Bernard Sands who, as a famous novelist and champion of liberal causes, prefers to cast himself in the role of 'Grand Enfant Terrible' rather than be trapped by or pensioned off in that of 'Grand Old Man of Letters'. He has a shrewd, if smug, sense of his audience:

> He must never allow them to feel they were indulging the court jester. They should continue to take from him exactly the pill they did not like, and take it without the sugar of whimsy.
>
> (p. 11)

Bernard prides himself on being an individualist and a free agent, able to operate in different social spheres without his identity being contained by any of them. Accordingly, he maintains a flat in London, passing freely from the cosmopolitan world (where he mixes in government and academic circles, smart theatrical and literary sets), to his family life in the country, where he observes the diverse elements that make up the small community of Vardon. His manœuvres in these separate territories show that in his public life, as well as in his art, he is a skilled image-maker. Content to have created a monument to himself in Vardon Hall, secured by his campaigning as a home for young writers, he relishes the idea that by refusing to play parent to this brainchild once it is launched, it will thereby become a subtler reflection of himself and his libertarian ideals. His vicarious identification with the younger generation is expressed more tellingly in his private life. Belatedly realising his homosexuality, he believes it to have been given an honourable shape in his relationships with Terence Lambert and Eric Craddock. Here again, he finds opportunities for 'creation', hoping to re-model and refine the two young men by his high-minded influence: Terence is to be dosed with principles so as to complete his graduation from 'golden spiv' to a self-respecting existence; Eric is to be weaned away from his over-bearing mother and set on the path to an independent, fulfilling life in London (. . . in Bernard's flat). However, Bernard's corresponding failure to act in an adult fashion towards his wife and children renders suspect his sense of mature parenthood in these other areas.

There is sly malice in the fact that Bernard Sands' latest artistic creation is entitled *The Player Queen*, for his hypocrisy is most apparent in his desire to screen his homosexuality from the family gaze. There is a comic scene where his daughter's determination to broach the subject coincides with his own decision to probe her 'bright disguised boredom with life', by means of the fatherly 'straight talking' on which he prides himself. There is genuine feeling behind their common desire to oblige the other to swallow the bitter pill of truthfulness, and yet the set scene of the problem novel is merely parodied as each is overcome with self-consciousness on realising that such is the stock situation in which they find themselves. Both are incapable of carrying off the sophisticated roles they had rehearsed and hypocrisies, instead of being swept away, are merely compounded. In his embarrassment, Bernard 'could only use flat words which sounded even to himself like the cant that others would certainly call them' (p. 59); and Elizabeth, who had been made to look foolish in public when an acquaintance made a knowing reference to her father's new life, is torn between a vindictive desire to treat the latter to some of his own moralising medicine and the fear of appearing ridiculously old-fashioned by doing so.

Bernard's crisis comes about not because of his homosexuality *per se* but because it leads him to an understanding of his own moral play-acting. Preoccupied by the problem of evil, he tries to decipher its workings amongst the disparate examples that present themselves to him in the course of his social life. A local character, Mrs Curry, is one target for this study, and Bernard sees her as his symbolic opposite, someone whose 'endless malevolence' is painted over with 'honeyed, lovey-dovey words of beauty from her cupid's-bow lips' (p. 15). He is more especially fascinated by the borderland between 'respectability and *loucherie*' that is represented by the camp contingent at a friend's parties. But Bernard's respectable motives for interesting himself in the 'moral anaemia' of the 'golden spivs' are matched by *louche* ones, too. Anxious as ever not to be placed, not to be classed with the 'twenties survivors' who make up the other group at Evelyn's gatherings, Bernard obtains a sexual thrill from the mere company of youth. Yet it is by investigating the moral ambiguities of camp that he is brought to a deeper understanding of himself.

In fact, the homosexual characters act as cyphers to the various social worlds which this novel explores, drawing attention by the conscious and calculated nature of their play-acting to the author's view of life as theatre. There is Sherman Winter, who 'had fallen into a conventional, caricatured pansy manner when he was quite

162

young and, finding it convenient, had never bothered to get out of it' (p. 88); a theatrical entrepreneur in professional and private life, he affects this soft-hearted manner as a cover for spiteful power games. He is a collector of people, glamorous props to his own performance, and his pursuit of Bernard's first boyfriend, Terence Lambert, lends an undercurrent of rivalry to their meetings. But the two men are revealed to be different in degree and not in kind—the benevolent mask which enables Winter to conceal his malice throws back a mocking, distorted reflection of Bernard's own self.

Terence Lambert is a theatrical designer on the 'social make' who shows an embittered understanding of what determines success by fabricating his own image, from the décor and furnishings of his flat down to the last details of personality, dress and accent. His cynicism is more comically expressed in his detection of frauds and in the roles which he allocates to people. Thus when Bernard remonstrates with him over his sarcasm towards Eric ('Miss Mouse') and forces him to admit standards of decency that ought to prevent his striking any pact with Sherman Winter, Terence retorts,

> Now I'm doing the golden-hearted tart. The boredom of you Bernard. As if I couldn't stand up to Sherman's second-rate little act of the Fairy Evil, if I haven't been sucked down into your sticky well of high-minded treacle.
>
> (p. 96)

Eric demonstrates a different variety of camp, compensating for his drab existence with baroque fantasies of being a Florentine page-boy or passing himself off as a homely choirboy with a simpering voice and 'nice' manner.

If homosexuals who aspired to 'pass' in society were once obliged to present a counterfeit image of themselves, here we see those arts of impersonation extended to other uses. Through playful fantasy, parody and self-parody, mime, mockery and sometimes malice, these characters are made to question stable notions of identity elsewhere as camp injects its own 'hemlock' into the novel's illusion of social reality and its solemn liberal theme. Sherman, Terence and Eric have an acute awareness of their own and of each other's role-playing, so that when they are brought together, appropriately, at the theatre, there is a mixture of kindly and cruel humour in their verbal skirmishes and attempts to upstage one another. Bernard, on the other hand, although fond of puncturing the pretensions of others, takes himself and the part he plays with utter seriousness. However, through exposure to Sherman's spite, Terence's 'hard clarity' and Eric's narcissistic whimsy, he is brought to see the flaws in his own performance. There are uncomfortable truths in their teasing caricatures of him: Sherman congratulates him on the 'versatility' of being both a married man and the escort of a beautiful youth; Terence compliments him on the impressive display of egoism which has brought to fruition the Vardon Hall scheme; Eric, wearying of Bernard's superior, moralising tone, quips, ' "I might just as well have made friends with one of those clergymen who make passes on trains" ' (p. 92).

Whereas such refusals to accept him at his own evaluation are irritating, Bernard's complacent idea of himself as a freelance observer of corruption in the world around him is put to a more conclusive test by an encounter with a male prostitute in Leicester Square. When the youth is arrested for importuning, Bernard is horrified to find that he experiences a frisson of sadistic pleasure. This glaring evidence of his own involvement in evil supplies the 'hemlock' that poisons his entire philosophy and his aspirations to a Socratic role. Having prided himself on being a benevolent reformer,

> He could trace now no kindness in his teasing exposure of Eric's ignorance or in his witty rebukes of Terence's vulgarity; he could see only the white frightened face of the arrested young man changing to the pink flush of Eric's embarrassment or the wincing tick of Terence's cheek, and could detect only his own answering shudder of pleasure.
>
> (p. 189)

But if the novel, exploring as it does ambiguity in motive and the inhibiting effect of introspection on action, has *Hamlet* as one of its obvious reference points, Bernard, fleeing from the glimpse of himself as 'Player Queen', goes from one extreme to another. For if his aggressive idealism and 'philanthropic homosexuality' were tainted by sadistic motives, so his melancholia and shame are also a form of pleasurable masochism—nowhere more evident than in the rambling soliloquy of guilt that he delivers at the opening ceremony of Vardon Hall.

Apologising for having concealed his homosexuality, Bernard

164

tells his daughter, 'Any attempt to merge two quite different social patterns is bound to have some embarrassing moments' (p. 58). Wilson, on the other hand, deliberately brings different social patterns into embarrassing conjunction. Initially, the novel creates the illusion of a spectrum of characters placed according to profession, class, and sexual type, in their material surroundings, their cultural and intellectual milieux. But the style and narrative movement combine to destroy this impression of social realism, to render it 'stagey', to 'camp it up'. The process discerned in Celia Craddock, who, 'If she suddenly felt that life was good, a mood came upon her quite genuinely but which she soon theatricalised out of reality' (p. 126), is parodied by the author himself, to the extent that quotation marks seem slowly to descend around his text. The novel's angle of vision is one which uncovers fundamental similarities amongst its characters, who are themselves *pattern-makers*, comically transparent in their attempts to fashion preferred self-images. Because of this pervading sense of theatricality, a character like Mrs Curry is no more than a monstrous exaggeration of all the other fakes and confidence tricksters. The narrative's destructive movement, exemplified in the collapse of the hero's persona, is extended in the farcical happenings at the Vardon Hall ceremony where, with many an embarrassing moment, 'respectable' and 'low life' characters are 'merged' in a staged spectacle which underlines family resemblances in the realm of camp and paves the way for subsequent moral discriminations. Whereas the occasion ought to have united the guests in a common benevolent cause, it releases instead a universal spirit of mischief, social decorum disintegrates and the self-interest of all parties is revealed in the worst possible light. The sophisticated are presented alongside outrageously vulgar versions of themselves: there is little to choose between the sluttishness of Mrs Wrigley and the preciosity of Mrs Craddock, between Ron Wrigley 'sexing' madly with his eyes and Sir Lionel Dowding giving distinguished leers, between Mrs Curry's pursuit of an alliance with Sherman Winter's mob and the attempts of Bernard's daughter-in-law to 'curry' favour with influential guests. As performances collide and crumble into sameness, Bernard Sands, who used to think himself unique, now sees only a grotesque mirror of self. But having once recognised his fellow performers, he must also re-establish his sense of moral difference; he must learn to distinguish between degrees of hypocrisy and malicious intent in himself and others, so to recover from his liberal, humanist ideals a more genuine basis for action. A truer moral strength is born of his humility and he does not allow the likes of Mrs Curry to presume that knowledge of his homosexuality has disarmed him as an opponent of evil.

Wilson's high camp is a mode of moral satire that operates in an unconventional manner—exposing and yet revelling in fraud. We never doubt that Mrs Curry is wicked, but at the same time we can relish her very 'awfulness', the sheer scale and exuberance of her malice. The author would seem to look on artifice in life as an endearing as well as a deplorable mark of human folly. Indeed, his own narrative exposes counterfeit characters by its own superior trickery, delivering its moral corrective in an entertaining form, coating its bitter 'pill' in the 'sugar of whimsy'. It draws its rhetorical energies from the camp qualities distributed amongst its homosexual characters: Sherman Winter's bitchery, Terence Lambert's unsparing vision, Eric Craddock's tender, playful fantasy, and Bernard Sands' 'severely moral chi-chi'. The serious and the frivolous combine in a comparable manner in some of Iris Murdoch's novels. There is a sense in which these two authors present erudite puppet shows for the amusement of an intellectual élite, a select audience of cult followers whose tastes they both parody and indulge. If Wilson's characters are set problems in liberal humanism, those of Iris Murdoch are put to the test of moral philosophy, and both authors demolish fixed patterns in their characters' lives by the ingenuity of their own encompassing designs. Love, in all its forms, usually shapes the attack upon those who reduce life to a structure of ideas, and yet their characters rarely move us when they are in the grip of an emotional crisis because love, instead of lending dignity and substance to their lives, is sometimes merely another puppet-master and illusions of freedom are sacrificed to the authors' own determined displays of cleverness.

Iris Murdoch treats homosexuality in a sympathetic manner as a dramatic instance of love's power to break down whatever system of controls is placed upon it. In *The Bell* (1958), the central character, Michael Meade, leader of a lay religious community adjoining a convent, is similar to Bernard Sands in that his public ideals are at variance with his private reality and the attempt to sublimate homosexuality rebounds on him. His past is presented in terms of exact reversals of feeling where his sexual nature is concerned. To begin with,

> It scarcely occurred to him that his religion could establish any quarrel with his sexual habits. Indeed, in some curious way the emotion which fed both arose deeply from the same source.[6]

But when he is considering the priesthood, this common source is seen as hopelessly corrupting. However, after one of his pupils, Nick Fawley, falls in love with him, Meade reverts in all sincerity to his original point of view, the passion (which is never consummated) inspiring in him ambitions of spiritual guardianship. Then, from a mixture of motives, the youth makes a melodramatic confession to the Headmaster, with the result that Meade is dismissed from his teaching post and falls back into his former guilt-stricken attitudes. (In *Henry and Cato* [1976], this schema of exact opposites is repeated in the dizzying and somewhat tiresome alternations of the priest, Cato, whose love for Beautiful Joe is like an electric current which, at the flick of an authorial switch, can run through its intricate circuit first in one direction and then in the other.)

The community Meade has founded is revealed to be a refuge for weak characters, for those in flight from the past, and it is satirised for its attempt to reduce life to neat and orderly dimensions. Even James Pace who, more than Meade, seems to possess the strengths that the other members admire, needs the support of a rigid framework of rules. A stern ascetic individual, his views on homosexuality are revealing. Sodomy is not deplorable, merely forbidden, he maintains, yet contradicts his own pat formula by an intense, irrational dislike for homosexuals. When Nick Fawley is to be rescued from a dissolute existence and brought within the community to which his saintly twin sister, Catherine, already belongs, Pace scorns him as a 'pansy' and (therefore) a troublemaker. And yet Nick arrives like a reminder of the homosexual self which would seem to have been outlawed by James Pace as well as by Meade—since the latter is conscious of,

> a certain clannish affinity with James, something nostalgic, crystallizing at a moral level distinctly below that at which he aimed to live at present.

(p. 84)

The calm surface of the community is as deceptive and liable to disturbance as that of the nearby lake. The lake provides an image of an element which is both shaped and shapeless, corresponding to a paradox in life that the community seeks to rule out. Character is elucidated by reference to the lake: a system whereby a boat runs along a fixed course between two points on its shores is a comment on the community's straight and narrow objectives; it is a magical element to be explored by Toby, a young visitor; it features in Michael Meade's nightmares and in those of Catherine; and it fascinates another visitor, Dora, who is pictured at the end of the novel freeing the boat from its tether and adventuring alone across the waters. It is also the focal point of the complicated plot which makes a mockery of the desire to ignore the past and live simply in the present. According to legend, a nun drowned herself when her refusal to own to a love affair caused the convent bell to fly miraculously down into the lake as a sign of God's wrath. The story of love's ambiguous power to be a curse or a blessing, to bring life or death, is unwittingly re-enacted by the members of the community. If love abdicates as the shaping force of events, then a destructive force is engendered in its place and, as if agents of a fate which that community brings down upon itself, Nick and Dora scheme separately to avenge themselves on the self-righteous residents at Imber.

Nick presents an opportunity for the past to be redeemed, but Michael Meade, fearful of disturbing his own precarious purity, indefinitely postpones the duty of helping him and merely repeats the disastrous pattern of their former involvement in his dealings with Toby. The young visitor is innocent and untouched by life, and suggests that single, unambiguous bell-like purity of being which is the community's ideal. Meade imagines himself in love once more, simply and joyfully, as if at the beginning of a long and profound responsibility, but after impulsively kissing the boy, he is plunged back into the guilty torments of old. This kiss acts as the proverbial pebble dropped into the pool, its ramifications spreading out like ripples in surrounding relationships. Far from being corrupted by the gesture, Toby is given an edifying proof of life's 'rebarbative' quality (to borrow his favourite word), and his introduction to the murky adult realm of mixed motive is suitably expressed after he explores the muddy depths of the lake, discovers there the bell of the legend and, being newly anxious to prove his manhood, conspires with Dora in an elaborate practical joke to substitute the old bell for the new one which is to be installed in the convent.

Michael Meade's paralysis of will over the question of Nick Fawley is only exacerbated by the revelation which Toby accidentally procures for him. His guilt where Toby is concerned is matched by jealous fears that Nick will have seen what happened and believe himself to have been replaced in Michael's affections. This proof of his continuing love for Nick renders him powerless; if formerly he kept his distance from fears of jeopardising his new-found security, now he feels his motives for helping Nick would be impure. Like Wilson's character, Bernard Sands, Meade thinks of himself as, 'too tarnished an instrument to do the work that needed doing' (p. 235). Left prey to an accumulating bitterness, Nick's own plot of revenge overtakes that of Toby and Dora and, in a farcical scene, the legend repeats itself. Although Catherine attempts the role of the suicidal nun, Nick is the one who succeeds in killing himself. But having completed his revenge by forcing Toby to confess to the headmasterly James Pace, and thereby ruining Meade for a second time, tragedy is commuted to sober recognition of irony since the pattern of events is altogether too neat. As Michael Meade reflects on Nick:

> His revenge could not have been more perfect. To have seduced Toby would have been crude. Instead, Nick had forced Toby to play exactly the part which Nick himself had played thirteen years earlier.
>
> (p. 296)

Iris Murdoch treats homosexual love in an ironic, unsensational manner, crediting it with equal power to damn or to save. If in this instance it has a destructive effect, this is because its dual possibilities have been separated between the two characters of Michael Meade and Nick Fawley; the former can only theorise on the redeeming power of a pure love, the latter can only act out the curse of a despairing one; each abstracts himself from the realm of ambiguity and mixed motive to live out a fixed idea. But the authenticity of these two men is to some extent sacrificed to the elegant symmetry of the novel's plotted contrasts and confrontations. This is particularly true of Nick, whose character seems dictated by the mechanics of plot and whose melodramatic homosexual guilt is never convincingly explained. That he appears to be conceived with the same false simplicity that the author satirises in her characters is emphasised by the contrasting success in the presentation of his fellow plotter, Dora, whose feelings are shown in greater detail and whose scheming arises plausibly out of her complex—and confused—reactions to the rigid values of Imber. Her individuality endears her to us, but Nick is an abstraction and his suicide has no emotional impact whatsoever.

In *Hemlock and After*, as in *The Bell*, the homosexuality of the hero is more of an intellectual construction, an ironic test devised for pompous idealists, than a deeply felt and integral aspect of character. Bernard Sands and Michael Meade are presented in a detached manner which both amuses and interests, but leaves us emotionally uninvolved with their fate. It is instructive to see how these two authors have, in more recent novels, created homosexual characters whose comic clowning actually lends to their struggles an individual human dignity which does arouse our deeper sympathies. Hamo Langmuir in Angus Wilson's *As if By Magic* (1973) and Simon Foster in Iris Murdoch's *A Fairly Honourable Defeat* (1970) are portrayed more realistically as homosexuals. Their sexuality is an educative force in their lives, finding expression in the ordinary humanity with which they resist the absurd plots and extraordinary patterns of events which would seem designed to reduce them to risible, puppet-like dimensions.

Hamo Langmuir is a plant geneticist whose 'Magic'—a new strain of high yield rice—is revolutionising the agronomic structures of developing countries. 'Magic', in the shape of a fulfilling love affair with Leslie, a working class youth encountered at university, has transformed his personal life, too. However, just as a world tour of inspection reveals unforeseen difficulties with his brainchild, so too, the law of diminishing returns operates in his sexual life. As Leslie grows older and distinctly middle class, Hamo, because of his obsession for youth (working class youth, in particular) chooses to leave him to seek out his 'magic' (chest 30″, hips 35″, preferably aged 20) elsewhere.

His world tour involves him in a journey of self-discovery which is juxtaposed with that of his god-daughter, Alexandra; his scientific, rationalist approach to life is contrasted with her subjectivity and vaporous mysticism. A pretentious creature, Alexandra lives with her two lovers, Ned and Rodrigo, in a literary cloud-cuckoo land, the 'awfulness' of which faces severe competition from that of her 'Look Back in Anger from N.W.3' parents. She merely exchanges the pseudo-reality of their world (her father's novel, evidently castigating his own rich wife for snipping off his working class balls, is acclaimed for its portrait of a marriage which symbolises the 'fruitlessness of the sixties'), for one of pseudo-magic, travelling with her lovers and their mime troupe to hippy colonies in Morocco and eventually to Goa. Whereas Alexandra once rejected Hamo as an 'enemy of magic', by the time their paths cross in Goa she is a level-headed Forsterian heroine with a baby to provide for (a stream of consciousness phase having swept her into one of Lawrentian fecundity), and a determination to confront the practical energies of the outer world which she now identifies in Hamo.

The novel's juxtaposition of real people and fakes is not calculated to present the moral superiority of the one to the other. In fact, our ability to distinguish between the two categories is progressively undermined as all the characters are caught up within the overall theme of a barrenness in modern life which is attributed to the broken connection between those who are bound by empiricism and material realities, and those in whom the allegiance to an inner realm of art and personal relationships has regressed to a mere dabbling in counterfeit magic and mysticism. Thus there is also a law of diminishing returns where Alexandra's much vaunted fecundity is concerned; she is as empty in her literary plenitude as is Hamo in his guise of man of science and 'sterile mutant'. Wilson treats the traditional metaphor of homosexual sterility as ironically as he treats the contrasting one of heterosexual fruitfulness. Hamo has demonstrated his creativity on a world-wide scale —indeed, rice is the very symbol of marriage and fertility, as the author often reminds us. Hamo's problem is to effect personal change, to rediscover fulfilment in homosexual terms, whereas his god-daughter's problem is to halt her dizzying metamorphoses of being and to discover a centre of gravity by contact with the outside world. Appropriately, the meeting in Goa of god-father and god-daughter is one of two comic deities, presented in terms of the 'cross fertilisation' of the practical world of economics and social problems with an inner world of mystical visions and magic.

Its manner of exposing fakes is one of the novel's delights. There is hilarious comedy in the portrayal of Alexandra's parents and the heterosexual domain of The Family, to which Hamo is a spell-bound outsider. Perry, who prides himself on being a 'real man' whose working class origins are a bulwark against his B.B.C. job and bourgeois household, is a particular target for malicious wit. His hopelessly inaccurate picture of the breakdown of the relationship between Leslie and Hamo typifies his mind:

> He could clout Leslie for not marrying Hamo. That was how life treated one. Broadminded as hell about having a queer brother. Trying to get him settled. And Zoe, to do her justice, being wonderfully helpful about it. And then Leslie ups and offs with this ghastly rag-trade queen. Sold himself for money, for that was what the little bastard had done, and into just that sort of impossible screaming world that was too much to stomach, leaving poor old presentable Hamo probably too frightened to have even the odd wank.[7]

But the satirical effects are not always so successful, for too frequently they overreach themselves and compound a fraudulence in the attempted exposure. Whilst camp does mock the predictable, the clichéd and the vulgar, Wilson's contrivances are themselves merely embarrassing at times. Alexandra is ridiculed for the dense fog of magical interconnectedness in which she envelops herself, yet the novel as a whole, with its self-conscious, modish allusiveness (A Passage to India and 'The Magic Roundabout'), indulges in some of the very practices that it mocks. The theme of barrenness would seem to be in danger of rebounding upon the author himself as his own determinedly fertile 'connections' are overworked. The counterpointing of Hamo's partiality for 'chicken' (homosexual slang for an adolescent youth, and a taunt Leslie employs in despair over his lover's failure to respond to him), with the absurd mime of battery chickens that is solemnly performed by Alexandra and her university friends, starts off as a prankish conceit that makes us wince even as we laugh. But the humour begins to flag when the device is extended into the characterisation of Hamo's own 'battery system'—the recharging of his erectile potency through a series of young prostitutes. The artificiality of these transactions is shown in Hamo's failure with Brian, whose emergence as a real person has destroyed the illusion of the standardised model, with the result that Hamo can achieve an erection only by conjuring up scenes from the past. The purpose of the episode is to demonstrate Hamo's inability to relate to the *reality* of another person, but when Brian speaks he does so in 'Wilsonese'. Noting Hamo's belated erection, he remarks,

> So the old magic can still work. Do you want to see the picture through a second time then? . . . For old time's sake with your laughing lad.
>
> (p. 21)

There is little to convince us of Brian's reality, he seems merely an inanimate mouthpiece for the author's laboured correspondences, and as the novel progresses, the endless repetition of the word 'magic' becomes irritating and counter-productive.

Nevertheless, Hamo Langmuir is a successful comic creation. The suffering in which his sexual frustration involves him does impart a certain dignity to his character even in situations that seem designed to make him look ridiculous, as when he reviews his agonising failure to sustain the relationship with Leslie—from his favourite perch on a lavatory seat. His 'distinguished scientist' persona is enlivened by little trace of personality; certainly there is nothing camp about him, and this, in Wilson's analysis, is central to his problems. His fixed sexual tastes seem to make a mockery of his life, as if fate had played a joke on him for which he overcompensates with a stiff, formal manner. Whereas other characters have too much of the histrionic temperament, Hamo has too little. Typically, the author organises his characters around ideas of clumsiness and grace, both physical and spiritual, and accordingly, Hamo is brought to live up to the connotations of his name, foregoing his rigid, puppet-like, hamstrung self and one kind of clumsiness, to enact inner fantasies in 'ham' fashion, to seek fulfilment (the inevitable pun occurs) as 'Homo', and to lay claim to the status of 'hero'. Wilson values in his characters the willingness to look ridiculous in the cause of self-expression and it is this capacity that Hamo's journey releases in him, to lend to his actions, however ludicrous, an inner grace that is more real than the façade of social decorum.

Langmuir's homosexuality is the anarchic element that breaks down fixed patterns in his life, just as it demolishes the carefully contrived scenarios with which his hosts present him on his world tour. Although his professional and his private life have in the past been strictly segregated, now they combine with farcical results. The Ideal Youths whom he pursues turn out to be those whose lives have been dislocated by the social effects that his new rice strain has produced in certain areas. What is more, his attempts to rescue these youths from their plight and thereby procure sexual rewards for himself achieve neither end; he succeeds only in outraging his hosts and in causing additional misery to the objects of his lust. The comedy of sexual frustration is at its wildest in the episode where Hamo is taken to an international gathering of pederasts, agro-business men who pose as 'Uncles' to well-bred oriental 'Nephews', and who explain to their guest that they are reaping the benefits of the prosperity sown by his 'Magic'. Their schoolboy pranks and vulgar rituals horrify Hamo, who is at his coldest and most dignified. But the satire is a two-way process; whilst they are crude exploiters in every sense, they also provide a grotesque pantomime of Hamo's own rigid sexual objectification of people, one which is to haunt him. His distaste for the extreme youth of their protégés is matched by the universal offence given by his interest in an older servant youth, and Hamo's wooden posture on the periphery of life is set in relief by the exuberance and impish vitality of their lust.

Significantly, it is only by involving himself in play-acting that Hamo begins to break free of his repressions. The ability to plot and to shape events is seen as a necessary quality for survival in the world of charlatans and confidence-tricksters that the novel uncovers. But if Hamo's inept schemes disrupt the staged settings of his official tour, so his own sexual fixations are simultaneously broken down as, in scenes of slapstick humour, he falls over himself to perform quixotic deeds, invariably with disastrous consequences. Repeatedly, the Ideal Youth proves to be a chimera, a trick of the imagination; the reality is at once more complicated and more comic. Hamo's conscience weakens the resolve of his lust; the 'hardness' that he finds erotic in these youths is dispelled when they are revealed to be the helpless victims of the economic and social system which he has partly created.

Wilson skilfully correlates Hamo's professional and private dilemma, the solution to which is made to depend on the hero's ability to integrate his homosexuality into his personality and outlook on life. Just as Hamo's objective assessment of social realities qualifies his simplistic sexual idealism, so too, before death cuts short the promise of a new synthesis in his character, his scientific detachment is qualified by his homosexual romanticism. Whereas he had formerly identified with the strong, making sexual mastery his personal goal, increasingly he transfers his allegiances to the weak and rejects the mentality of the sexual colonialist which had marred his chances of happiness in the past. Nonetheless, the attempt to dissociate himself from the bullies without turning other people into scroungers is equally problematic. Hamo's short-sightedness is demonstrated when, moved by the plight of one starved-looking youth who had importuned him, he presents him with the 'magic glasses' (binoculars) given to him by Alexandra, and feels cleansed by the act of giving which expects no reward. But token 'magic' is no good, even as a palliative to the liberal conscience, for as Hamo subsequently learns, the gift succeeded only in bringing about the youth's death. Similarly, Hamo's own absurd death shows that intellect alone is just as impotent; he tries to reason with peasants who are rioting because of the disappearance of their 'rice god'—Hamo himself—only to be murdered by the very people whom he seeks to save. The stage is set for Alexandra to redeem his sacrifice: the 'divine idiocy' of his character combines in her with the talent for plotting which he lacked; his professional legacy, in the shape of a report reconciling rationalism with his new found romantic vision of helping 'weak strains', provides a blueprint for her own life of philanthropy and his legacy of money gives her the means to carry it out. At last, she play-acts 'for real'—battling on the 'home front', pulling down office blocks and replacing them with houses.

In Iris Murdoch's novel, the outcome of the action is also brought to hinge on the interplay between a private world of homosexual romanticism and the everyday one of social responsibility. A *Fairly Honourable Defeat* presents us with a small group of characters who are involved in diagrammatically interlocking relationships which contrast different kinds of love. As in the work of Angus Wilson, the characters have a peculiarly predictable flavour, so much so that an air of self-parody and camp hangs over them. But if Wilson's characters sometimes seem too obviously like favourite puppets, those of Iris Murdoch are allowed a greater illusion of freedom. This is often effected by the 'delegation' of authorial functions to one of the characters. In this novel, Julius King is dealt the part of the malevolent joker, provided with the human materials on which to test out his cynical view of love as a confidence-trick, and the liberty to play puppet-master to characters in his 'novel'. The author, on the other hand, is the shaping spirit of rival moves, seeking to defeat that part of herself which takes malicious delight in 'playing' with people, to test out a contrasting belief in the power of love, of freedom, and of moral choice.

The drama evolves around a 'stagey' setting which is appropriate to the novel's irreverent combination of the serious and the frivolous. A rose garden at the house of Rupert and Hilda Foster is the centre piece; French windows open on to it from the drawing-room; it features a small rectangular swimming pool. The scene promises the plotted entrances and exits of the farce; the pool invites its victim. The scene also reflects the Fosters' thesis that happiness requires order and design, that marriage, for rational, civilised beings, can be the proverbial rose garden. At the same time, there is something too cosy and contrived about the setting, corresponding to the self-satisfied shaping of ideas in the philosophical treatise on weighty matters of life and love that Rupert is able to write in his leisure hours, or in the epigrams with which he sprinkles his conversation.

On the occasion of their twentieth wedding anniversary Rupert and Hilda feel justified in reviewing the comparative weaknesses of friends and relatives, none of whom are able to match their achievement. Their sense of order is frustrated by the emotional entanglements and odd alliances that have developed amongst this group: Morgan, Hilda's sister, has left her husband, Tallis, and whilst in America has had a stormy affair with Julius King, an old friend of Rupert's; both are expected back in London, Morgan having thrown up her studies and Julius his career as a biochemist; Peter, their son, has 'dropped out' of university, their life and schemes for his future, and is living in a squalid room at Tallis's house; Rupert's younger brother, Simon, has turned out to be homosexual, as has Rupert's old friend and Civil Service colleague, Axel Nilsson, with whom for the past three years Simon has been precariously 'married'. Life's stubborn refusal to fall into the shapes they would devise for it is comically suggested in these developments and long before Julius King intrudes into their bower of bliss, we sense the hollowness of their generalisations and vaunted strengths.

Rupert is a paragon of civilised manhood, and yet the very

176

cultivation of his virtues is said to have deprived him of the 'direct language of love'.[8] Simon, on the other hand, chatters away endlessly in this language, but seems as frivolous as his brother is serious. At first, he appears to have been cast in the stereotype of the effeminate homosexual; he is artistic, scatter-brained, softhearted and camp. Whereas Rupert and Hilda pride themselves on the coherence and inner harmony of their union, Simon tries desperately to manipulate the surfaces of life. Their rose garden is an extra, but Simon throws himself wholly into prettification, flower-arranging and interior design in the house that he and Axel have purchased, as if to contain and domesticate the fearful unpredictable creature that is their love. They seem like a parody of the 'normal' couple: Axel is a gloomier version of Rupert, and equally fond of enunciating the truths upon which any relationship should be based; Simon is a giddy version of Hilda, dissipating his energies and dreaming of cassoulets, worshipping his god-like man. 'Love should be without fear' (p. 31), Axel *warns* Simon, and accordingly they each live in terror of losing the other's affections. The serene confidence and stability of the heterosexual couple seems calculated to frame the inevitable insecurity and ludicrous picture of the homosexual 'marriage'.

The effeminate male arouses fears that are traditionally discharged through ridicule, yet Simon Foster is presented in a manner which eventually mocks the stereotype itself. He is a comic character of a different order, and the author establishes the fragility of his world from within his quirky individual consciousness without any trace of a sneer. If the other characters are satirised for their complacency and pseudo-sophistication, Simon is made fun of for the comic scale of his paranoia, his flights of fantasy, and his impressionable nature. This is seen when he works himself into a frenzy over the poor contrast he feels he will make with Axel's old friend, Julius King, and his line of reasoning is imagined with ironic humour:

> Axel would suddenly see how flimsy Simon was, how unsophisticated, how lacking in cleverness and wit, how hopelessly ignorant about things such as Mozart and truth functions and the balance of payments.
>
> (p. 77)

Simon seems the easiest and the most vulnerable target for anyone with a streak of malice; indeed, he is ostensibly selected as

Julius's victim when the latter, exasperated by Morgan's hysterical devotion to him, promises to demonstrate to her his thesis that people are basically fools, toys that can be wound up and propelled in any direction. Julius detests self-deception and is utterly cynical where the spectacle of love is concerned. He plays devil to the gods before which the other characters prostrate themselves; he is the profaner of the temple of love, the 'invisible worm that flies in the night' of the rose garden. Not content with testing the strength of Simon's affections, he selects Morgan and Rupert as the 'donkeys' in his 'midsummer enchantment', persuading each that the other has developed an overwhelming passion for him or her by fashioning plausible love letters from those he steals from Hilda and those he already possesses from the time of his affair with Morgan. Julius cunningly rigs his plot in such a way that its development depends upon the character of each of his principals as well as upon his own fraudulent artistry. They are 'free' to determine the course of events. Hence there is malevolent humour in the fact that Morgan and Rupert are carried along not only by vanity but also by their determination to act in a decent, adult fashion, both seeing an occasion to practise their theories of responsible love. Simon is tricked into witnessing a farcical love scene between these two and thereafter is constrained by threats to a strict silence. But the apparent weakness of character that allows him to be Julius's plaything is equally a measure of the strength of his love for Axel. As Julius's unwilling confidant, he has in theory the power to make or break the spell, but in practice he is paralysed by his fear of losing Axel. Having once appeared to compromise himself by complying with Julius's mysterious request for him to go to his flat (where he finds Morgan dressed only in a dish cloth and where he himself is later found wearing nothing but a brocade curtain), all those imagined insecurities in his life take on a sombre reality. Knowing the premium Axel places on truthfulness and on dignity, Simon seeks to protect himself by an initial falsehood, whereupon he is drawn further and further into a vicious circle of deception.

Julius weaves his black magic around what had seemed a highly sophisticated group of people, reducing them in the process to little children unwittingly playing out the more sinister connotations of 'ring-a-ring-a-roses'. But in one sense, he merely picks out a design which had always been implicit. The novel is organised

178

around attempts to fake and stylise reality, to shrink love to child-like, cosy dimensions. Hilda's roses are called Little White Pet, but when Simon fashions an elaborate crown out of them, it is their sharp thorns that make themselves felt. The pool is toy-like and decorative, and yet it claims its sacrificial victim. Hilda, fear-ful for the safety of the hedgehog which she has made her pet, wonders whether animals have any sense of self-preservation. But in her own world, the attempt to turn love into a 'pet' has ren-dered adults as vulnerable and defenceless as children; they remind us irreverently of nursery book characters; Axel, with his touchy dignity and gloom, plays Eeyore to the dizzy panics of Simon's Piglet; Rupert, as his name suggests, is like an animated Teddy Bear, tottering helplessly towards his doom.

The counter-attack on Julius's cynical equation of love with self-deception is effected belatedly through Tallis and Simon, the two characters who seemed initially the most child-like and who, as 'men', were something of a joke in the eyes of other people. Yet both draw strength from the fact that their private world is one where love is inextricably bound up with fear and suffering, there-by preventing their life from falling in a fixed pattern; indeed, both exist in a state of emotional flux and perpetual confusion. Tallis's embittered father is dying of cancer; his wife mocks him; yet he combines within himself hope and despair, unlike the other char-acters who veer disastrously from one to the other. Simon's genu-inely child-like nature has corresponding strengths, too; he is given to spontaneous, impulsive actions that reveal an instinctive morality. When he witnesses a brutal attack on a coloured man in a Chinese restaurant, he overcomes his fear and intervenes; when Julius traps him in the swimming pool at the celebration party for Rupert's book, goading and taunting him cruelly, Simon finally rebels against the puppet-master and pushes him into the pool. As in The Bell, characters are typified by their relation to water, the formless element. Simon is at home in it, the only person to enjoy the pool; Julius cannot swim and is terrified of water; Rupert, in answer to Hilda's speculation on self-preservation, follows the example of a bumblebee and the hedgehog by drowning in it.

But if Simon is the only character to step outside his designated role, he is still 'fairly honourably defeated' by his homosexuality. The 'ordinary' response he finally makes to Julius releases Simon from the web of words within which everyone else is snared, and yet his ability to defeat his opponent is fatefully compromised by the insular outlook attributed to the nature of his relationship with Axel. Whereas Hilda and Rupert felt protective and kindly towards Axel and Simon, it is in fact the latter couple who have the power to avert the catastrophe that overtakes the other. Simon is willing to brave Axel's cold fury and to risk making a complete fool of himself by confessing all, but he is so thankful to recover his lover's affections that he wants to retreat completely into their private world. Although Axel prides himself on being 'ordinary' and apart from the 'camp world' that Simon formerly frequented, his ordinariness is another contrived illusion since he conceals his homosexuality out of a secret, obsessive fear of appearing ridiculous. But the premium he places on dignity and discretion interferes with his ordinary humanity *and* his happiness as a homosexual, which are shown to be mutually dependent. Instead of acting on Simon's explanations and unmasking Julius, he remarks:

> One doesn't want to be indiscreet and raise a false alarm. If there's no muddle then all's well. If there is a muddle we aren't likely to be able to understand it anyway and our helpful revelations might just make things worse.
>
> (p. 393)

His retreat from the complications of love in the lives of other people echoes the failings of his own relationship and reinforces Simon's preference for the esoteric, separate realm of homosexual romance.

Nonetheless, their relationship survives where the other fails, as a result of what seemed its very vulnerability. The stress of living in a state of insecurity develops in them a resilience and an instinct for self-preservation that is lacking in the other couple. But if Hilda and Rupert had too little fear, Simon and Axel have too much. Their problems are clarified in the process of coming to terms with Rupert's death. Axel concludes that they have lived too much inside themselves, fearing to communicate with one another just as they feared full involvement with the surrounding social world. If they are to be ordinary people *as* homosexuals, then Axel needs to acquire his partner's self-acceptance and some of his expressive, camp qualities, whilst Simon needs to value himself more highly. Just as the novel's discourse on love marries serious and comic elements, philosophy and farce, so the pattern of opposites in the 'marriage' of Simon and Axel needs to be brought into creative synthesis.

This is, however, one of the few English novels where two men in a long-term relationship are portrayed sympathetically and, despite the schematic and stylised mode of characterisation, as credible, vividly imagined individuals. Neither Angus Wilson nor Iris Murdoch treats homosexual men as easy targets for dismissive laughter. On the basis of equality with other characters and types of love, their homosexuals are dealt the criticisms of comedy for common human weaknesses which prevent them fulfilling themselves *in terms of their own sexuality*. These characters contribute positively to a general enquiry into the factors that determine successful relationships and, for both authors, matters of gender are seen to make little difference to the interplay between love and self-deception which is an abiding theme of their work.

NOTES

1. Angus Wilson, *Anglo-Saxon Attitudes* (1956). (London: Penguin, 1974), p. 204. Subsequent page references are to this edition.
2. Angus Wilson, *Late Call* (1964). (London: Penguin, 1968), p. 288. Subsequent page references are to this edition.
3. K. W. Gransden, *Angus Wilson* (Writers and their Work No. 208, 1969), p. 11.
4. Walter Allen, *Tradition and Dream* (1964), p. 292.
5. Angus Wilson interviewed in *Gay News* No. 92, p. 17.
6. Iris Murdoch, *The Bell* (1958). (London: Panther, 1976), p. 99. Subsequent page references are to this edition.
7. Angus Wilson, *As If By Magic* (1973). (London: Penguin, 1977), p. 41. Subsequent page references are to this edition.
8. Iris Murdoch, *A Fairly Honourable Defeat* (1970). (London: Penguin, 1972), p. 26. Subsequent page references are to this edition.

8
Jean Genet

The philosophical and aesthetic complexities of Genet's work afford rich material for analysis, sometimes to the neglect of its homosexual significance. Of course, the sexual content can scarcely be ignored, but what is most frequently stressed is the 'miracle' of its transcendence. The precedent is set in Jean Paul Sartre's massive study, *Saint Genet, Actor and Martyr* (1952), where he describes *Our Lady of the Flowers* (1943) simplistically as an epic of masturbation, the work of a man who has regressed 'toward the childish narcissism of the onanist'—yet proceeds to credit its author with existential profundities which merit elucidation by the master himself. Those who address themselves to Genet's metaphysics are rivalled by those who stress his poetic genius, the brilliance and arresting qualities of his imagery, whilst others see his works as spiritual autobiography or as a case history fascinating to the psychologist or sociologist. From each of these various standpoints his work may be shown to contain myriad features which 'redeem' and render palatable its sexual subject matter. But to what extent do Genet's homosexuals defy the determination of his admirers to 'return' him to the human fold? One wonders how many of those who consider it a mark of their own sophistication to identify with Genet the moral nihilist, poet of evil, and enemy of the bourgeoisie, would in practice dissociate themselves from Genet-as-Divine, the outrageous drag queen of *Our Lady of the Flowers*?

Consideration of Genet's treatment of homosexuality may also be complicated by the fact that his work has been caught up in the post-war debate on obscenity and artistic freedom. It is important to distinguish between the reputation conferred on his works because of their part in the breakdown of cultural taboos, and the reputation earned by their qualitative rendering of homosexual themes. Genet remains foremost among contemporary writers of homosexual fiction for the sheer intensity, lyricism and explicitness of his eroticism, but the question of whether there is much that is of moral interest or that is intrinsically liberating in his presentation of it is a more controversial one. This is evident from the conflicting estimates of those who comment on the relation of his work to gay politics. In his interview with Genet, Hubert Fichte states: 'Although this is exaggerating, I would say that there are no homosexuals in the world today who have not been directly or indirectly influenced by your work';[1] whereas Seymour Kleinberg maintains, 'the sexual politics of Genet's vision is too nightmarish and too offensive to most gays'.[2] Nor is there any consensus of opinion among critics who relate his work to heterosexual values; whilst Kate Millett finds in Genet an ally to the feminist cause, Philip Thody takes exception to his reputation for radicalism and develops the thesis that although his novels seem to illustrate and to defend homosexuality, on closer inspection, the author's treatment is one that paradoxically reinforces the most reactionary of prejudices. Mr Thody is proof of his own thesis: noting the apparent unhappiness, treachery, selfishness and criminality of Genet's homosexuals, together with their feminising effect upon virile men, he claims:

> There are certain activities which, even if society were to condone them, would still be self-defeating because of the emotional contradictions which they inevitably contain. Genet's homosexuals are unfaithful to one another because homosexuality is, of itself, a disappointing form of sexual activity.[3]

It is ludicrous, however, to suppose that Genet, whose experience is as extraordinary as his vision is idiosyncratic, speaks for homosexuals in general. His refusal to enter into any of the traditional arguments in defence of homosexuality is only to be expected when it is precisely its forbidden character in which he revels. Genet's own pretence of speaking for *the* homosexual needs to be understood in terms of particular motives. When he boasts in *Our Lady of the Flowers* that 'Fags are the great immoralists'[4] this is part of a deliberate strategy to present the homosexual as a complete outsider from the conventional world. Genet adopts wholesale the shame and attendant vices attributed to homosexuality, that they may serve as materials in constructing his own 'heroes', rather as Divine retaliates against the omnipresent red, white and blue flags on July Fourteenth and, 'dresses up in all the other colors, out of consideration for them, because they are disdained' (p. 103). Genet wishes neither for any change in the status of the homosexual nor for his acceptance into society, an attitude which was endorsed by his refusal to meet André Gide since he considered him to be a person of 'doubtful morality' owing to the latter's attempt—in *Corydon*—to negotiate with the 'enemy'. Genet makes his own position clear when he states: 'I would like the world not to change so that I can be against the world'.[5] Accordingly, his treatment of sexual stereotypes differs sharply from that of other writers dealt with so far and, in order to examine these differences, it is proposed to focus on the two opposing extremes in his portrayal of the male homosexual: that of effeminate passivity as represented by Divine in his first work, *Our Lady of the Flowers* (1943) and that of active virility as represented by the hero of his last prose work, *Querelle of Brest* (1953).

Images of rigidity and puppetry are commonly used to convey both homosexual repression and the dissolution of self associated with promiscuity. Captain Penderton in *Reflections in a Golden Eye* is as doll-like and inhuman as the 'fags' the narrator of *Junky* likens to yapping puppets on invisible strings. But in *Our Lady of the Flowers,* to lose oneself and to be 'taken over' by homosexuality is curiously translated into a virtue. Although there is astonishing individuality in the overall act of self-definition that has created a legend out of Genet's life, his characters aspire to an archetypal as opposed to an individual identity. To be dehumanised takes on a perverse nobility, a process exemplified by Divine's struggle to be a queen among queens. The stereotype of the queen is as potent in its effects upon the homosexual as upon the heterosexual imagination, and one might argue that the reaction against the tyrannous image of effeminacy has caused some homosexuals to purchase liberation at the expense of others by equating self-respect with manliness. The name, Divine, carries some of the ironic meanings attached to the English slang for an effeminate male, 'queen', which are not so obvious in *'tante'*, the equivalent French word. To be a queen is in fact to be on the lowest echelon of homosexual rank; in a world where 'butch' is beautiful, it is to reproduce in miniature the position of the homosexual within the hierarchy of manhood. In the case of the 'drag queen', it implies an identification with the female role that amounts to a compensation for not being able to pass as a man;

yet it also implies delusions of grandeur and sovereignty that cause outrage by claiming the symbols, rituals and mannerisms of a different system of values; it calls for denunciation of the imposter, of the thief, in order to restore the *status quo* and reaffirm the miscreant's lowliness. Genet draws on these associations in his characterisation of Divine; the queen's theft of what in other contexts is sacred and taboo is paralleled in his literary technique when he appropriates and converts to his own sacrilegious purpose the 'jewels' and 'rich garments' of the language which condemns him.

Divine could well have been the creature who terrifies David, the reluctant homosexual hero of *Giovanni's Room*, whose fears of losing himself in a debased underworld seem personified in the figure that materialises out of the shadows of Guillaume's bar:

> it looked like a mummy or a zombie . . . it walked on its toes, the flat hips moved with a dead, horrifying lasciviousness . . . the thin, black hair was violent with oil, combed forward, hanging in bangs; the eyelids gleamed with mascara, the mouth raged with lipstick. (p. 33)

For Baldwin, as for his hero, the flamboyantly effeminate male is a horrifying warning of the dehumanising effect of the promiscuous underworld, whereas for Genet to be such an object is in itself a miracle. This is the effect Divine creates in the minds of the clientele at Graff's café when she makes her début in the Parisian night world. What scandalises the customers is her composure, her gracious refusal to register their estimate of her, the audacity with which she wears her gaudy attire, and her belief in herself. There is a comic contrast between the delicate bird-like gestures with which she sips her tea and the sheer vulgarity of the gawping onlookers whose eyes belie 'what the contemptuous, spiteful, sorrowful, wilting mouths were saying' (p. 73). Nonetheless, Genet's intentions are not so much to venerate Divine's stubborn individuality as those almost supernatural powers which derive from an obliteration of self, for her moment of triumph is imagined when,

> The café disappeared, and Divine was metamorphosed into one of those monsters that are painted on walls—chimeras or griffins for a customer, in spite of himself, murmured a magic word as he thought of her: 'Homoseckshual'. (p. 74)

The 'magic word' is her verbal bouquet, a tribute to her status as a creature of legend, enabling her to depart with the aplomb of a star, 'wriggling in a spray of flowers and strewing swishes and spangles' (p. 75). This process of glorifying in contempt and of converting malicious stereotype into an idealised state of being is what obviously poses problems of interpretation in Genet's work, especially for the reader who happens to be homosexual.

Certainly, the sexual politics of Genet's vision may seem offensive to those who wish to assert the sheer ordinariness of homosexuality or to refute the very notion that 'homosexual' designates an individual rather than an act. But if Divine would scarcely grace that campaign, neither can 'she' be regarded simply as a symbol of Genet's masochistic self-contempt. Although there is a danger in attributing to the author a political consciousness which would have been alien to him at the time when this novel was written, it is still possible to relate Divine's progress towards saintliness to concepts which have emerged in the gay liberation movement. The transformation of shame to pride, and vulnerability to strength, summed up in the idea of 'coming out', is anticipated —and taken to strange extremes—in the metamorphosis of Louis Culafroy, a sensitive, lonely country boy, into Divine, the 'Quite Giddy'. But if 'coming out' implies taking on one's full individuality as well as affirming group solidarity, the process is reversed with Genet. The fact that Divine is mocked by other queens and abused by her lovers is essential to the sainthood her author bestows on her. Nevertheless, Genet could well be regarded as 'elder statesmen' to those in the gay movement who have no wish to beg for admission at society's door and who adopt in a spirit of retaliatory pride terms that were formerly pejorative. Thus, to proclaim oneself a 'faggot' becomes accusatory, a reminder of past persecution when sexual heretics were burned to death; to wear a pink triangle is to commemorate those countless homosexuals singled out for Hitler's concentration camps; to 'steal' and put to different (and ironic) usage the word 'gay' echoes the aesthetic thefts Genet performs on a spectacular scale, organising through poetry his own 'forbidden universe', embroidering abjection with the language of beauty, religion and nobility.

Divine's story describes a process akin to the 'negrification'— persistence to the point of madness in what they are condemned to be—urged upon his fellows by one of the Negroes in *The Blacks*.

Her life is presented as a spiritual trial, with the result that she takes on a complexity quite beyond her role as Genet's surrogate self imagined in cohabitation with the pimps and hoodlums of his sexual fantasy. That she illustrates other aspects of her author's destiny is suggested by the account Genet gives in *The Thief's Journal* of how he took his identity from the shame and hatred directed at him by the other inmates of the Mettray reformatory: 'I owned to being the coward, traitor, thief and fairy they saw in me'.[6] But this acquiescence was undertaken as a form of 'training' and of 'spiritual exercises' which developed in him an absolute control over his innate sensitivity. The annihilation of self to which experience similarly leads Divine is embodied in the form of the novel which opens with her funeral ceremonies, interweaves in funereal tribute fragments of her Parisian life and of the country existence of Louis Culafroy, her former self, and closes with her actual death. Our recurrent image of Divine is of her gazing out of her garret at the intertwining ghosts in the cemetery below.

Cast out by other children in the village, hated by his mother, singled out by fate for mysterious suffering, Louis Culafroy is described as one of the 'Elect' (and is perhaps kin to that other 'dead child' with 'festering spiritual wounds', Audrey, Burroughs' character in *The Wild Boys*). Even the solace he finds in friendship with Alberto, another 'untouchable', is mixed with torment; the latter is a 'snake-fisher' and in the cause of their love, Louis must inure himself to contact with the creatures he loathes. Joy and despair are equally inseparable in Divine's relations with pimps and hoodlums such as Darling, Our Lady and Seck. Yet she is stripped even of this measure of happiness as her author, playing God to his own creation, jolts, squeezes and shatters her, in order to track down her 'essence' and make of her a saint. Thus Darling suddenly abandons her; Seck and Our Lady turn to one another; Divine ages, loses her hair, her bottom, her customers; she is jeered at on the streets and continually arrested. However, degradation confers a paradoxical nobility on her as she humiliates herself in the face of likely derision: 'Calling herself an old whorish whore, Divine simply forestalled mockery and insults' (p. 130). When her pearl crown tumbles to the floor before a crowd of pimps and queens, she is inspired to snatch her dental bridge from her mouth, place it on her head, and so reclaim her sovereignty; but we are told, her gesture was a slight thing compared to the grandeur of soul required for the other: taking the bridge from her head, putting it back in her mouth, and fastening it on.

(p. 182)

However, it is Divine's sexual life rather than the set-pieces of her public humiliation which subjects her to prolonged emotional battering. Through her, Genet explores the dilemma of his own erotic fixation upon the type of man who is precisely the one most liable to scorn his love. In *The Thief's Journal*, he tells us,

Toward what is known as evil, I lovingly pursued an adventure which led me to prison. Though they may not always be handsome, men doomed to evil possess the manly virtues.

(p. 5)

Yet if homosexuality is a standard feature of prison life, so too is sexual hypocrisy, and as an effeminate homosexual, Genet is as much of an outcast within the world of evil with which he identifies as he is in society at large. Deprived of social definitions of manhood, prison and the criminal underworld that feeds it become for Genet a realm where masculinity is stripped to its essence and its archetypal gestures. But as an outsider to these 'manly virtues', he is acutely sensitive to their theatricality and his erotic vision is simultaneously one which is highly critical. He treats the murderers and hoodlums of his masturbatory fantasy— the offspring of the 'family' of pin-ups that adorns his cell wall— like private dolls, like those hollow lead soldiers that he and a Negro cell-mate decorated and arranged in lascivious couplings. He dismantles and reassembles his idols, delighting in his power over them, exorcising the tyranny by examining its component parts —the gold chain over the bulging fly, the brutal gesture, the slang —yet having once de-mystified the super-male, he chooses to love the 'man' within the 'god', in keeping with his determination to cherish what is base.

Like their author, Culafroy and Divine are obliged to love what they also fear and loathe, for this renunciation of their inborn delicacy is what leads them to 'sainthood'. The process of self-sacrifice has its intermediate stage in Divine's abject submission to the cruelty of the pimps who live like parasites on her, supported by her earnings as a prostitute. The pimp's strength seems absolute: when Darling makes an appearance at Divine's funeral, he passes through the assembled queens,

188

Indifferent and bright as a slaughterhouse knife . . . cleaving them all into two slices which came noiselessly together again, though emitting a slight scent of hopelessness.

(p. 63)

Similarly, the queen's weakness seems absolute, and Divine's life is one of grovelling, despairing worship. However, for self-sacrifice to reap spiritual benefits, it must become a deliberate choice. Just as Culafroy finds miraculous the very absence of any miracle when he desecrates a church, so Divine brings herself to marvel at the discovered hollowness of her male Gods. The intensity of her worshipping uncovers continual proofs of treachery, hypocrisy, and an unsuspected vulnerability. Whilst Darling and Our Lady allow her to take liberties with them in the privacy of the garret, they react with brutality if she compromises their virile image in public. With her perception of their utter selfishness is born a profound 'intellectual scepticism' that finally defeats her instinctive 'emotional consent' to domination. But ironically, this in turn leads her to redouble her imposture; whereas submission had been 'natural', now she must sham that response by a conscious effort of will. She intercepts and punishes in herself any act of meanness towards the pimps, who are merely perplexed when she suddenly humiliates herself in their presence. With characteristic perversity, she renounces her intelligence, forcing herself to conceal her secret scorn and to love her oppressors for their revealed weaknesses.

When Genet hymns masturbation as the 'Pleasures of the solitary, gesture of solitude that makes you self-sufficient unto yourself, possessing intimately others who serve your pleasure without their suspecting it' (p. 124), he also touches on the paradox of Divine's passivity. Her submissive worship composes an endless gesture of solitude before her indifferent gods, but at the same time these 'spiritual exercises' develop inner strength and a subtle transference and theft of power takes place. The gushing admiration that her lovers ward off with feigned apathy to protect themselves from the slur of homosexuality has the effect, however, of secreting the poison of another consciousness into their lives, rather as Divine slyly introduces her own urine into the food she prepares for Gabriel, the soldier, in order to teach him a 'dog's attachment'. This process is especially evident in Darling, who begins to strut and swagger, who becomes in effect a male impersonator,

189

a camp figure, and is increasingly dependent upon Divine to bolster up his illusions of grandeur. As the roles of 'master' and 'slave' are insidiously reversed, so he becomes the sexual object he imagines that he exploits in Divine. This is rendered into grotesque comedy as she festoons his penis with flowers, talking to it as her pet, and thinking of the individual to which it is attached as some lesser extension of the instrument in her service.

Through Divine, Genet takes his own 'slaughterhouse knife' to these male idols. She invades their very hollowness until even the façade of virility begins to crumble. Since Darling is destined for prison, there is something poignant, flower-like and ephemeral about the self-assured posturing that precedes his humiliation. He tells himself that a man who buggers another is thereby a 'double male', but his boast is contradicted as certain of Divine's mannerisms begin to escape him and, with his arrest, he is brought to experience fully her role of being acted upon. Similarly, the young murderer, Adrien Baillon, lives out the prophecy of his nickname when he goes in drag to a gay bar with Divine, believing his manly credit in the eyes of his fellow hoodlums to be such that they will appreciate the joke. But he becomes 'Our Lady of the Flowers' in reality when, on return to the garret, his flirtation with Seck culminates in eager submission to penetration. Divine's influence is also at work in the circumstances that lead to his confession of murder after his arrest on the lesser charge of dealing in cocaine. We are told that because of Divine, 'the minds of Darling, Our Lady, and their cronies bristle with ridiculous gestures' (p. 244), and she is indirectly responsible for the presence of the dismembered wax dummy in the apartment where Our Lady is arrested, which puts the idea of murder into the minds of the police. The object neatly symbolises the effect that Divine ('soul sister' to Myra Breckinridge) has had on the wax dummies of men she collects around her.

Although the pimps with whom she lives 'blossom' under her attentions, Divine herself is shorn of her petals. When she and the other queens appear in court at Our Lady's trial they are, in contrast with his apotheosis, bereft of the symbolic magic of their names—'like the paper flower that the dancer holds at his fingertips and which, when the ballet is over is a mere wire stem' (p. 260). Just as Divine turns sexual passivity into an active force so, as age deprives her of objects to love, she conspires in her own misery. She abandons herself voluptuously to suffering, and as her own 'ballet' draws to its close, engages in the wildest of gestures; she renounces her body's search for pleasure, even to the extent of shaving off her eyebrows to make herself the more repulsive; she renounces her kindness and, determined not to be a saint on God's terms, engineers the death of a child. To bestow sainthood upon Divine is, of course, precisely calculated to outrage conventional attitudes and to make of her a moral transvestite, too. Genet applies religious concepts to his characters in the manner of finely-rehearsed insults, as when he takes the idea that God works in mysterious ways to enter the individual soul, and wonders whether,

> For the gigolo who cruises the tearooms, perhaps He has a way that theology has not yet catalogued, perhaps He chooses to be a tearoom.
>
> (p. 112)

And in the case of Divine, humiliation is equated with beatitude, degradation with nobility, and moral solitude—purchased ultimately by the death of a child—with grandeur of soul.

In so far as homosexuality symbolises evil in the conventional mind, then Genet chooses to cultivate evil, but defiantly to fashion it into 'flowers'. However, his association of homosexuality with degradation, self-destruction, infidelity, immorality, and crime can hardly be taken at face value. Although some critics have seized on these associations to remark upon Genet's 'depressing realism', it must be asserted that his portrayal of homosexuality is highly subjective, stylised and shaped to particular ends. When Darling rams home his giant penis, 'So hardly and calmly that anuses and vaginas slip onto his member like rings on a finger . . . that his virility, observed by the heavens, has the penetrating force of the battalions of blond warriors who on June 14th, buggered us soberly and seriously' (pp. 103–4), the homosexual fantasy is subordinated to the delights of revenge as Genet 'slips onto' the phallic totem other images which are determined by his contempt for French society. When Our Lady kills a defenceless old man and is described as, 'a beribboned wedding feast skipping . . . down a sunken April road' (p. 114), or when sainthood is bestowed on Divine, Genet is engaged in a deadly form of self-propaganda, for such is the violent incongruity between the person or act described and the value judgment imposed by the imagery that we are forced

to inquire into the hatreds the author nurtures. Just as he celebrates the 'glories' of murder in language which is deliberately
offensive, so he seeks to maximise the shock of his homosexual
idolatry, as when Divine prostating herself before Darling, coos
and clucks over his penis, baptising it with pet names like 'Jesus
in His Manger'. Genet would like us to believe that homosexuality
is inherently evil, for this allows him his revolt in a world in
which heterosexuality has a monopoly on goodness and permits
him to invest with the poetry of grandeur that which is commonly
held to be sordid and immoral.

Few would disagree with the equation of murder with evil, but
homosexuality does not carry the same charge of a moral absolute.
Consequently, Genet is obliged to enforce its opprobrium by devising 'incriminating' circumstances which preserve the impact of his
defiant, self-damning preference for the solitude of the outcast.
For although his novels, written in the 1940s, reflect the more
rigid attitudes of the pre-war period, homosexuality remains the
weak link in his chain of evil and threatens the consistency of his
moral nihilism. His poetry relies on our perception of its incongruity if it is to convey his angry stance of choosing to love what
he simultaneously affirms to be 'base', but there are often occasions
when his lyrical, tender eroticism uncovers *intrinsic* beauty in a
relationship—as is seen in Culafroy's love for Alberto, and in
Divine's brief idyll with the soldier, Gabriel. What is more paradoxical is that whilst Genet sets out to 'blacken' the homosexual
and so outrage the bourgeoisie he despises, at the same time his
novel delivers its own embittered attack on the very forces that
bring about the degradation in the relationships it parades. Divine
is not so much a martyr to society's persecution as to the cult of
virility which has its extreme form in the pimps, hoodlums and
murderers whom she choose to love. It is the tyranny of a heterosexual image of manhood and not the homosexual impulse which
is both revealed and criticised as a source of evil in the novel's
own world. What is so often referred to as the author's *méchan-
ceté pédérastique* is, from another point of view, the expression
of justifiable homosexual anger at the hypocritical heterosexual
pose of his virile heroes. Genet exposes the relativity of what seem
the absolutes of 'masculinity' and 'femininity'—which convert
the possibility of love between men into the gestures of a brutal
power play and which are themselves responsible for the lack of

reciprocity in the relationships described. That homosexuality threatens to become a moral positive is seen above all in the character of Divine, by the side of whom the nominal hero, Our Lady, is an insipid shadow. Divine is portrayed sympathetically and often humorously as an effeminate male, and is the only character to display—albeit unconventionally—a kind of heroism. She is the vehicle of those sensitive, delicate qualities that Genet fails so completely to destroy in himself, and until her author determines —by her gesture of killing a child—that she should join the 'Elect' of murderers, she subverts the equation of homosexuality with evil as surely as she undermines the domination of her 'masters'. If her idols are revealed to be poseurs, then the possibility of homosexual reciprocity arises; but this runs contrary to the goal of absolute moral solitude Genet imposes upon Divine, and it is only by an act of 'will' that she is destined to be a saint and not a homosexual hero. He makes the revealing comment that,

> Darling is merely a fraud ('an adorable fraud,' Divine calls him), and he must remain one in order I preserve my tale. It is only on this condition that I can like him. I say of him, as of all my lovers, against whom I butt and crumble: 'Let him be steeped in indifference, let him be petrified with blind indifference.'
>
> (p. 113)

Thus, in the interests of revenge, Genet must freeze his picture of the relativity of 'masculine' and 'feminine' qualities within men and sacrifice any idea of homosexual fulfilment to that of sainthood.

If in *Our Lady of the Flowers* Genet pays homage to the inner nobility that informs Divine's gestures of solitude, in *Querelle of Brest* the attraction of moral isolation is weighed against that of homosexual brotherhood. Whereas Divine's life narrows to one of utter aloneness, *Querelle of Brest* begins from a point where its hero has seemingly achieved this ideal. Querelle is 'Divine': remote, self-sufficient and solitary. His supremacy is achieved, however, through the cultivation of a god-like virility; like the warship, *Le Vengeur*, in which he arrives home to the port of Brest, he bristles with armaments, he prides himself on having no rival amongst men. Nevertheless, Querelle must do battle with the ordinary world to which—as the title suggests—he is linked. His task is intimated when Genet ponders the significance of the name,

'Brest', connecting it with the verb *se brester*, meaning 'to breast oneself for a course of action', and with its root form, *bretteur*, meaning 'one who squares up to his opposite number' or 'one who picks a quarrel'. But in this novel opposite qualities are usually revealed to be aspects of one another, and so it is that the opposite number to which Querelle must square up on his return to Brest is his brother, Robert, his twin self and a symbol of that bond with other men that he denies. When the two men do in fact fight physically—because Robert, the personification of his brother's heterosexual pride, feels insulted by Querelle's homosexual activities—it seems to onlookers that Querelle is fighting himself, as if neither brother wished to end the struggle which was at one and the same time a means of uniting them and, 'merely the vulgar projection visible to men's eyes' of, 'a struggle to remain single individuals'.[7] Although Querelle aspires to a singleness of identity, even his name implies dissension within himself as well as with those around him, and perhaps—with its twin components of male and female, *queue*, the slang for penis being sounded in conjunction with *elle*—it also implies the nature of that battle.

Querelle's return to his home port, then, entails a confrontation with that duality and ambiguity from which he would extricate himself. Genet evokes the spirit of the place with images which maintain a continuing sense of duality: solitude and brotherhood, hardness and softness, masculinity and femininity. Physically, the town is hard and forbidding, and because of its concentration of itinerant workers—dockers, stone masons, sailors—is predominantly male in atmosphere. It is an exuberantly phallic landscape, but one in which images of verticality and solitariness—the upright cannons, posts, masts, bollards, towers and ramparts—are opposed by horizontal, connecting images—the chains, ropes and dockside paraphernalia that are said to 'anchor' the sailors even when they are at the other side of the world. The granite walls, defences and solid buildings give the town the air of a citadel. The men are imbued with these same qualities; the masons trudge home powdered with dust like animated statues; individuals are described variously as 'rocks', 'fortresses', 'towers' or 'walls' of strength. But again, images of insularity and fortification are contrasted with others which stress the bonds between men. In addition to the universal code of masculinity, comradeship develops among particular bands of workers and group identity is reinforced by the 'uniform' common to the work in question; individuals blur into composite images, and are subordinated to the democratic anonymity of some manly archetype—the mason, the docker, the policeman, or the sailor. Just as the convicts who once sailed from the port were chained together in pairs, so these larger fraternities contain 'couples', like Mario and a fellow police-man who are 'united by a singular friendship' (p. 18). Individuals also form pairs by stepping outside group loyalties: Mario is closely involved with a petty crook, Dédé, who informs on his criminal brothers; Gil, a young stone mason, is drawn to a young-ster from the town, Roger, to the intense jealousy of Theo, an older mason, who longs for Gil.

The sharp, hard lines of the landscape are blurred and softened by the fog which lays siege to the town. It creates an atmosphere of mystery and mysticism, rendering ambiguous all that it touches; it is the magnificent symbol of Genet's eroticism, curling out ten-drils of desire around the objects it treasures. The fog sculpts, surrounds and caresses the men of the town; it is a tactile, palpable element, into which one need only stretch out a hand to brush against,

> the naked, warm, unwrapped-from-shirt-folds and ready for action, strong pulsating penis of a stevedore or matelot who, burning hot yet ice-cold, transparently erect, is waiting to spurt a jet of spunk into the blanket of fog.
>
> (p. 96)

It links and binds, a conductor of emotion, cover for crime and 'unnatural love', an infinitely sensitive web that registers all that happens within its compass: 'No matter where the blow fell, the fog would be wounded and spattered with blood' (p. 96). Like the sea from which it rises, it is a tender, poeticising element, sending wave upon wave of emotion against the 'Querelle Rocks'. In curi-ous ways, the fog is also an instrument of narrative form. The angle of vision is one which dissolves the fixed outlines of character and scene; the solidity and singleness of individuals gives way to an impression of merging identities. Figures loom out of and recede back into the narrative 'fog', our sense of their reality being further disturbed as the author instructs us to regard them as the emana-tions of our own subconscious or as those of Lieutenant Seblon, Querelle's superior officer, a character who is said to be 'outside' the book. There are sudden shifts in perspective; sometimes the focus contracts to a microscopic, dreamy contemplation of an object or a person, at other times it expands to a panoramic vista of the town, or even of the whole coastline—'festooned' by the navy, which 'knots' and 'bunches' in the ports along the Atlantic. Similarly, linear progression in events is replaced by an ordering that is web-like and fluid, until the cliché 'the plot thickens' takes on a comic dimension as threads of false and genuine evidence shuttle between the two quite separate murders that take place in Brest, to weave them into one.

Genet creates Querelle from the qualities he finds erotic in men, but at the same time he presents through his hero the hypothesis that the cult of virility brings about its own destruction. By turning himself into an abstraction, by severing his bonds with other people, by projecting his own share of 'feminine' characteristics on to others, Querelle is forever fighting a losing battle—for the human ambiguities he seeks to defeat are merely the manifestations of an enemy within. From the age of fifteen he is singled out from his brother and from other men by the 'vivid smile' he directs not so much at other people as at his 'mystic star', as if in recognition of an extraordinary destiny. He perfects the gestures of aggressive manhood; he consorts with thieves; he further separates himself from his brother by going to sea, becoming an isolate even among other sailors who admire and yet hate him for his superiority. Inevitably, Querelle is represented by images of insularity and verticality: as a youngster he had arrogantly taken the tower at the entrance to La Rochelle harbour as the symbol of his own virility; he 'lays out' his victims, to become in murder solitary and statuesque; he invests hard objects—jewels or even his own testicles—with magic powers; his killings form a 'charmed hedge' around him; he has immured himself in the strangest of 'ivory towers'; he spins out of himself his own foggy shroud of mystery, 'the opaque envelope which, he liked to believe, hid him from view' (p. 51). Nonetheless, his pursuit of strength in solitude is profoundly disturbed when he is faced with evidence of intense, exclusive relationships between men. Wandering into a bistro, he is secretly fascinated by the almost 'visible thread' that unites the glances of Gil, the young mason, and Roger. Similarly, when he goes to see the owner of La Feria brothel in connection with the smuggling of opium, he is unnerved by the conjunction of Norbert's massive bulk with the masculine beauty of Mario, the police officer; they seem to merge into one united wall of strength, causing him to inwardly swoon and almost betray the 'delicate nature' to which he could never admit. Afterwards, he must consciously reconstruct and bolster up his defences by drawing on all the symbolic force of The Navy. These psychological manœuvres are submitted to a slow motion analysis which is humorous in its exaggerated solemnity; by invoking and magnifying all the archetypal gestures of the sailor,

> His body was fitted with guns, iron-clad, armed with torpedoes. . . . He was now LE QUERELLE, a huge destroyer, a greyhound of the ocean, a vast, intelligent, thrusting mass of metal.
> (p. 44)

Cleaving the fog and using his voice like a siren, he takes out his annoyance on a passer-by, who is accused of trying to 'capsize' him.

By taking ruthless self-assertion to its very limits in murder, Querelle cultivates a masculine 'essence' which lifts him into the sphere of absolutes, of Platonic form. But the virile 'purity' he seeks is itself rendered ambiguous since the hard, durable objects into which his friends and accomplices are 'transmogrified' are jewels, bracelets and necklaces—symbols of feminine adornment that he stores up for himself. Querelle's realm of absolutes contains the very qualities from which he had determined to cut himself free. He cannot dispell from himself the aspiration to love and be loved, for this too is presented as a Platonic 'essence' deep within him. Just as La Feria brothel is the 'Cave of Harmony' at the heart of the granite town, so beneath the quarrelsome surface of his dealings with his brother, 'lay a region far removed where their astonishing resemblances were united as in wedlock' (p. 169). Furthermore, it is specifically the idea of homosexual brotherhood that exerts an unconscious hold on Querelle. This is illustrated when he struggles to disentangle his thoughts from those of his brother by devising a 'whole scheme of single-handed deeds' (p. 25), only to find himself drifting into an erotic reverie of a partnership with a fellow sailor, Vic, from which he surfaces to discover that his hand has been closed around his penis—the irony being that in masturbation as in crime he cannot bring off a deed 'single-handed'. Querelle's subconscious mind reproduces those swirling mists

197

within which opportunities for crime are rivalled by opportunities for sex. That homosexual temptation is the opponent of his virile self is further suggested by the counterpointing of his reveries with the flirtation of Gil and Roger—the two men who so fascinated him in the bistro.

Gil is also tormented by ambiguity and when he strolls with Roger into the thick fog around the ramparts, his view of himself dissolves. His attempt to persuade himself that it is Roger's sister to whom he is attracted is thwarted by their maddening resemblance and by the sexual excitement this provokes in him. He presses against the youth 'with a vengeance', whilst the latter's attempt to control his love for the young mason 'drains' the strength from his body. The scene is both highly erotic and comic in its minute exposition of a posturing which exhausts the two men, causing them to lean on one another to be 'shored up' against the emotional battering which is, in effect, only intensified by this further proximity. Gil wonders whether,

> To tear aside the fog, to rid himself of it by a brisk and brutal gesture, by a ferocious look, would perhaps be sufficient to re-affirm his virility.

> (p. 31)

But the outward projection of the threat posed by his own homosexual awakening leads him to reaffirm his virility by the murder of Theo—the older mason who persuaded their workmates to join in his mockery of Gil's 'unmanliness' after the latter had rejected Theo's own obsessive love yet proceeded to involve himself with Roger. Despite the fact that neither Theo nor Gil has any effeminate characteristics, such is the fixed idea of the homosexual that the other masons come to supply the police with fantastic proofs that Gil was a 'nancy-boy'. The episodes decribing Gil's relationship with his fellow masons present in vivid detail the pernicious effects that the fear of homosexuality may have within a working class context where prestige is narrowed to manliness. In fact, it is the apparent contradiction between Theo's aggressive bulk and the gentleness that overflows from his eyes which frightens Gil most of all.

Querelle seeks to avenge himself in a more insidious manner for the homosexual temptation which other people arouse in him. His scorn for tenderness, passivity and effeminacy are traced to

198

his first encounter with a 'queer', in Beirut. In the 'downy' atmosphere of the Armenian's room, Querelle feels that he has met his opposite: 'something so provocatively and precisely exaggerated in its fragility that it must inevitably invite death' (p. 306). And yet the other man's gentle words and airy gestures have a hypnotic effect upon Querelle, stirring reciprocal feelings of peace and calm in him and causing him to drop his guard—until, to his dismay, he reveals his true name. Having endangered himself in this manner, it is not so much an external vision of male fragility that Querelle smashes in the Armenian as an image of his own vulnerability. Similarly, his murder of Vic is not just a ruthless means of insuring against any possible betrayal of their joint opium smuggling venture, nor simply a device to secure all the profits to himself. The very idea of a bond with another man is an affront to Querelle's demented sense of supremacy; the success of their operation depended upon the use of a cord to draw the packet over the harbour wall, yet Querelle symbolically severs that link when he cuts through Vic's jugular vein. It is noticeable, however, that his decision is triggered off by the calculated rejection of an erotic contact; at the precise moment when the stiff material of Vic's coat rubs against his own, the idea of murder arises:

> rather like the mounting of amorous emotion, and almost, it would seem, through the same channel, or rather through *the negative of that channel*.
>
> (p. 73)

But with poetic justice, Querelle is brought to expiate his deed through that same 'channel'. To be a 'joyous moral suicide' is simultaneously to be unbearably alone, so it is only by condemning himself that Querelle can resist the temptation to confess his crime, and thus the punishment he prescribes himself is for Norbert to bugger him.

The tortuous logic by which Querelle arrives at the decision to submit to the very act denied him by his cult of virility, further emphasises his essential ambiguity. Under the guise of a deliberate choice, he balances his convoluted metaphysical equation of crime and punishment, thinking to ensure his freedom by sacrificing what is most precious to him. But this 'single-minded' action is simultaneously a means of yielding to his most secret desires. When Querelle hears the gruff voice of Norbert commanding him to bend over, he feels that his own strength and vitality are speaking through the 'executioner'. Nor can he conceal the pleasure he derives from his punishment; according to his partner, he shows none of the 'natural' male's sexual shame; he hopes for a kiss; he ejaculates at the moment when in imagination he grafts the handsome face of Mario on to the muscular frame of the brothel keeper. Not content with an 'expiation' that becomes a regular practice, Querelle subsequently has sex with Mario and with Gil; these three relationships mark stages in the expression of his duality and in the gradual release of the 'feminine' qualities that he had locked deep within himself.

The portrayal of sex between these men is coloured by the duality of the author's own motives. Although he states that his novel is addressed to 'inverts', the invitation to vicarious pleasure also extends a sly challenge to the 'conventional' reader to experience an outlawed sexuality. The accounts of sex are not framed in a manner which suggests the indulgence of any exclusive audience of 'inverts'. If Genet delights in breaking the taboos which traditionally inhibit descriptions of male nakedness, he also delights in betraying those qualities we think of as male. This is illustrated in the mock solemnity with which he meditates on Querelle's shapely buttocks and invites us to inspect every feature —in particular, the voluptuous feminine curves and the soft downy texture—so that we might understand the 'monstrousness' of male love affairs. But just as homosexual titillation is slanted aggressively towards a wider audience, so Genet's personal erotic fantasies incline to satire. There *is* something 'monstrous' in the denial of all tenderness between these coupling deities and the brutal detail of their encounter composes a ridiculous charade. The determinedly he-man conversations that take place after sex are comic in the elaborate subterfuges which they employ to deny any idea of a bond between them. Each man is reconciled to his behaviour by telling himself that he is merely using the other as an instrument of his own pleasure; each professes amazement, however, when the other has been forced to a sheepish admission of having enjoyed his part in the proceedings. Although Norbert scorns 'homosexuals' and congratulates himself on the absence of any sentimental feeling towards the sailor, he cannot prevent himself from admiring the latter's body and grudgingly acknowledging his own attraction to it. In the same way, Querelle dis-

misses his own actions as a 'skylark' whilst growing increasingly
dependent on these 'unlooked-for' pleasures.

In the novel's world of rigid role-playing, to admit desire for
another man is to betray one's vulnerability to superior strength.
Thus the rituals of the ensuing courtship between Querelle and
Mario take the shape of an extended power struggle. Beneath a
superficial show of aggression, they conspire to evolve some formula
which will allow them to satisfy their lust without either having
to compromise his masculine pride. Mario's allusion to Querelle's
submissive practices obliges the latter to re-establish his honour in
a fight, but once this has put the two men back on an equal footing, they can proceed—albeit warily—towards their mutually
desired goal. Under the safe cover of the fog, they can joke about
sex and, with exaggerated displays of innocence, tease and excite
one another. Although Querelle protests to the last that he has no
interest in the sizeable erection his companion *dares* him to touch,
the fateful progress of the policeman's penis towards the sailor's
mouth is elevated to the level of ceremonious initiation by humorous comparison with a train's passage into a tunnel: 'It was
speeding towards the serene, peaceful, and terrestial unknown, to
something so long denied the matelot' (p. 251). The details of
their love-making form a grotesque comedy of gestures which seek
both to express and to repress feeling. Querelle reconciles himself
to his first kiss with a man by thinking of it as an act of 'cul-
pable' love and therefore consistent with his pursuit of evil. Nonetheless,

> They kept their mouths soldered together with tongues either
> crushed or the tips of them in sharp contact, neither daring to
> place them on the rough cheeks where a kiss would have been
> a sign of tenderness.
>
> (p. 251)

The love of one man for another is conveyed elsewhere with a
lyricism that provides a satirical measure of Querelle's arid coupling with Norbert and his hypocritical play-acting with Mario. In
Lieutenant Seblon, the only character to be described as 'homosexual', is concentrated all the tenderness Querelle seeks to exclude from life. Yet Seblon is a tragic figure; like Querelle, he is
the victim of a set picture of manhood, sacrificing himself in its
cause. The officer compartmentalises his life in terms of the 'mas-

culine' and 'feminine' components of his psyche, allowing his homosexuality full expression only in a secret journàl where he weaves a lush prose poem around the object of his love. Seblon cultivates a brusque manner in keeping with his rank and profession, but however fiercely he represses his sensitive qualities they usurp the very channels by which he seeks to express his masculinity; thus he affects a clipped, curt way of speaking but takes it to an extreme where it becomes imbued with a tell-tale preciosity. Although Querelle exults in his power and flaunts his body in studied poses before the officer, Seblon's ill-disguised adoration has ambivalent effects: on the one hand, it reinforces the sailor's homosexual narcissism until he becomes increasingly dependent on such confirmation of his power; but on the other hand, it exacerbates his sense of aloneness and the unconscious drive to destroy this in sexual friendship. By the time their ship is ready to sail again, exhausted by the burden of his solitude Querelle has come to long for the comfort—as opposed to the sadistic pleasures of the past—that he might obtain from Seblon, from 'the deep, tender, generous friendship which a homosexual alone can offer' (p. 332).

One of the most extraordinary scenes in the novel is where the barrenness brought about by manly repression of feeling is contrasted with a hoped-for flowering of love in the relationship between Mario and Dédé. With a microscopic analysis of symbolic gesture, Mario is described as barricading himself within the stony fortress of his body to brood on secret fears. Dédé's intuitive knowledge of what troubles the policeman fills him with tenderness for the vulnerability of his god. But instead of drawing comfort from the affection Dédé shows, Mario withdraws even more deeply into himself, expending fanatical energy on controlling the outward posture of his body, since he feels that to admit to fear or to give way to his own desire for the youth would be to give Dédé a hold over him. Nonetheless, he is made to suffer, for his very immobility delivers him up to Dédé's imagination; he covers the impassive, rock-like head with tiny kisses, whistling and twittering around him like a flock of birds:

> Dédé hoped against hope that a smile might make the head burst open and imprison the birds; the rock refused to smile, to burgeon into flower, to cover itself with nests.

(p. 64)

202

But for Dédé, the liberation of feeling is not equated with weakness, on the contrary, it becomes an active force, holding to ransom the terrified male within the statuesque figure of the policeman, and the youth's initial shame at his outburst is replaced by a new sense of strength and an exhilarating awareness of his freedom of action.

The question of whether or not the Querelle 'rock' will flower becomes the centre of suspense in the novel's mystical psychodrama. Even though Querelle professes not to believe in the possibility of love between men and considers himself forever set apart from his fellows, he is seen by other characters as the very symbol of brotherhood. Longings are focused on him from every quarter: apart from Seblon's adoration and the compulsive attraction towards him experienced by Norbert and Mario, he is idolised by the two youths, Roger and Dédé, who, like Madame Lysiane, are obsessed by the double-headed deity of the two brothers. Far from being the independent, solitary figure he sees himself as, Querelle becomes the very agent of connection in the shifting, symbiotic relationships that bind together these characters—as omnipresent and as elusive as the fog itself. The course Querelle fixes to take himself away from the image of fraternal love in his twin only brings him face to face with another double: Gil, his fellow murderer, whom he discovers to be hiding out in the old convict prison. As if to meet this challenge of fate, the sailor determines to plant a 'Querelle seed' in the young mason—that is to say, to recreate him in his own image as a 'real' murderer and a 'real' man. But ironically, the 'Querelle' that burgeons from this seed is too much a reflection of the sailor's hidden self. Each man draws forth in the other the homosexual longings he had sought to repudiate in murder. For the first time in his life Querelle finds himself devoting his energies to the deliberate seduction of another man, finally to act out not only desire but tenderness and love as well.

In betrayal, Querelle takes a last stand against the homosexual brotherhood to which he is inexorably drawn. The freedom he hopes to purchase by arranging for Gil's arrest is not so much immunity from police investigation as immunity from sexual ambivalence. That it is his masculine 'honour' which is in greatest peril is further suggested by the chosen manner of his vengeance for his brother's insults: Madame Lysiane, formerly the mistress of Robert, is destined to solve the problem of how to tell the two men apart, for Querelle's penis is found to be decidedly larger—and far less susceptible to her feminine charms. In fact, Querelle can purchase his freedom only by a continual betrayal of himself. As he admits, those he sacrifices in the cause of virile 'purity' are, 'the leaves, as it were, at the extremity of my branches' (p. 308). But like branches, his desires continue to put forth new leaves. And so, our last image of him is not one of triumphant self-sufficiency, but of him clinging drunkenly to Lieutenant Seblon, telling the officer that he is 'the only one', and smiling 'at being so very near to the brink of shame from which no escape was possible, and in which he might well discover lasting peace' (p. 346), before kissing him tenderly. Nonetheless, Querelle is cheated of the very friendship he has taken for granted. Ever since Gil (acting under Querelle's instructions) ambushed and robbed him, Seblon has experienced his own metamorphosis, his masochistic fantasies having been fulfilled by the beauty and violence of his assailant to such an extent that he now seeks to take full responsibility for the crime. Once liberated, his feelings become a new strength; he becomes Gil's 'protector' just as he becomes Querelle's 'protector' when he rescues him from an angry mob and is rewarded by a kiss. But Seblon is the instrument of Genet's own revenge upon his brutal hero, for the Lieutenant is arrested on the day *Le Vengeur* sets sail, thereby attaining the martyr's victory, whilst Querelle is summarily dispatched into lonely oblivion.

Querelle of Brest weaves a valediction around the solitary figure of the moral suicide, acknowledging its aesthetic beauties yet setting these against the more compelling attractions discovered in the idea of brotherhood. If in *Our Lady of the Flowers*, Genet arranges a forcible marriage of 'evil' between the criminal and the homosexual, in *Querelle of Brest*, the partners to this alliance are in perpetual quarrel. Homosexuality becomes the opposite number to which the practitioner of evil must square up. Murder is depicted as the ultimate assertion of virility, as a calculated rejection of the homosexual impulse and of the emotional bond between men. This last novel insists upon duality and sexual ambivalence, upon the beauty and the irrepressible power of erotic feeling; it shows both the sadistic murderer and the masochistic homosexual to be self-defeating abstractions from the ambiguous reality of male comradeship. Just as Divine cannot ultimately sacrifice the 'man' within 'her' except by becoming party to a fraud, so too Querelle has a 'femininity' which is indestructible. Despite his avowed moral nihilism, Genet rages against the system of values that polarises human characteristics into 'male' and 'female', 'heterosexual' and 'homosexual' and which sets the one above the other. Although his characters are removed from the moral complexities of involvement in society, they are still rigidly bound by the symbolic gestures of sexual identity which it inculcates. The ritualism of behaviour that is traditionally male is isolated and subjected to microscopic scrutiny in Genet's work and, in common with other writers dealt with in this study, he confirms that the exploration and the assertion of homosexual identity necessarily involves a criticism of our overall definitions of manhood and sexual role. And although his work may stand as a symbol of the victory of self-expression, at the same time it underlines starkly how the literature of the post-war period that treats homosexuality—however positively or defiantly—is engaged not so much in a celebration of love between men as in an exposure of the continuing obstacles to self-fulfilment and of the comedy and tragedy of the still unrealised potential of that love.

NOTES

1. Jean Genet interviewed by Hubert Fichte (December 1975), reprinted in *Gay Sunshine Interviews Volume 1* (San Francisco, 1978), p. 73.
2. Seymour Kleinberg, Introduction to *The Other Persuasion* (New York, 1977), p. xvi.
3. Philip Thody, 'Jean Genet and the indefensibility of sexual deviation', *20th Century Studies* No. 2 (November 1969), p. 71.
4. Jean Genet, *Our Lady of the Flowers* (1943). Translated from the French by Bernard Frechtman (London, 1964). (London: Panther, 1966), p. 107. Subsequent page references are to this edition.
5. Jean Genet interviewed by Hubert Fichte (December 1975), reprinted in *Gay Sunshine Interviews Volume 1* (*op. cit.*), p. 79.
6. Jean Genet, *The Thief's Journal* (1949). Translated from the French by Bernard Frechtman (London, 1965). (London: Penguin, 1967), p. 145. Subsequent page references are to this edition.
7. Jean Genet, *Querelle of Brest* (1953). Translated from the French by Gregory Streatham (London, 1966). (London: Panther, 1969), p. 150. Subsequent page references are to this edition.

Index

206